James Madison
AND THE FUTURE OF
Limited Government

James Madison
AND THE FUTURE OF
Limited Government

EDITED BY JOHN SAMPLES

CATO
INSTITUTE
Washington, D.C.

Library of Congress Cataloging-in-Publication Data

James Madison and the future of limited government / edited by
John Samples.
    p. cm.
    Includes bibliographical references and index.
    ISBN 1-930865-22-8 (paper : alk. paper) -- ISBN 1-930865-23-6
    (cloth : alk. paper)
    1. Madison, James, 1751–1836--Contributions in political science.
I. Samples, John Curtis, 1956–

JC211.M35 J36 2002
321.8'092--dc21

                                                                2002071636

Cover design by Amanda Elliott.
Cover Illustration by © Bettmann/CORBIS.

Printed in the United States of America.

CATO INSTITUTE
1000 Massachusetts Ave., N.W.
Washington, D.C. 20001
www.cato.org

Contents

Introduction

John Samples

James Madison advanced the cause of liberty before, during, and after the Constitutional Convention of 1789. His constitutional vision of limited government has enabled Americans to enjoy liberty and its material and spiritual rewards. As we begin what may be the next American century, the 250th anniversary of Madison's birth offers a chance to reflect on the future of his legacy. The essays in this volume, first presented at a conference at the Cato Institute in March 2001, explore the relevance of Madison's ideas for the future of the United States and the world. Madison, it turns out, may offer as much to coming generations as he has to the living.

Reviving Limited Government

In the *Federalist Papers*, Madison noted that the Framers tried to create a government strong enough to control the governed and yet somehow able to control itself. The Framers saw the Constitution as a social contract that delegated power from the people to advance the goals cited in the Preamble. That delegation was both limited to the powers enumerated in the Constitution and constrained by the Bill of Rights.

Judge Alex Kozinski and co-author Stephen Engel as well as Roger Pilon point out in their contributions to this volume that the original Constitution did not grant Congress a general power to spend. It did grant the authority to raise money to pay national debts as well as to provide for the common defense and the general welfare. Madison denied that the "general welfare" clause gave Congress unlimited authority to tax and spend. The clause granted authority to spend only in pursuit of the powers enumerated in Article 1, Section 8, of the Constitution.

Contemporary American government has slipped free from these constitutional constraints. Kozinski and Engel document how the general welfare clause of the Constitution became an excuse for unlimited congressional spending and a spur to a burgeoning federal Leviathan. Roger Pilon expertly traces the downfall of Madison's idea of enumerated powers, first in the ideas of the Progressives and later in the political acts of the New Deal. Madison would be shocked by a federal government that consumes one-fifth of national wealth and regulates most economic activity. He would be less shocked that the federal government is largely in the business of redistributing wealth. *Federalist* No. 10 argued that redistribution arose from a flawed human nature and tended to destroy republican liberty.

Congress has not fulfilled Madison's high expectations for representative democracy. He conjectured that delegating power from the voters to their representatives would "refine and enlarge the public views, by passing them through the medium of a chosen body of citizens, whose wisdom may best discern the true interest of their country, and whose patriotism and love of justice, will be least likely to sacrifice it to temporary or partial considerations."[1] Today most members of Congress spend most of their time either pushing for pork for their districts or acting as ombudsmen for constituents who have problems with federal programs. Members of Congress have little time or incentive to look beyond local concerns toward the national interest.[2] Far from "refining and enlarging" public opinion, members of Congress seem to have become parochial servants of special interests. As James Buchanan notes, this struggle to redistribute income and wealth feeds on itself, leading both to a strong federal government that endangers liberty and to citizens seeking wealth through political activity, rather than individual effort.

Madison's friend Thomas Jefferson offered a clear solution for constitutional failure. In the Declaration of Independence, Jefferson argued that government existed to secure the rights of life, liberty, and the pursuit of happiness. When a government failed to secure those rights, "it is the Right of the People to alter or to abolish it, and to institute new Government...." Roger Pilon shows in his contribution that American government currently lacks legitimacy as defined by consent to a constitutional order. He recommends amending the Constitution to accommodate the welfare state or else rolling back the expansive government built up over seven decades. Jefferson reminds us that a third alternative always exists: the right of a people to institute a new government.

Madison was not as keen as Jefferson was on abolishing and instituting governments. As Robert McDonald shows, Madison hoped prejudice and settled habits would support the new constitution. Yet he was not just a defender of tradition. Joyce Malcolm's essay indicates that Madison thought government could be reformed through reasoned action. In that spirit, some contributors to this volume suggest paths for restoring limited government for the United States.

Professor Malcolm shows that Madison did not support judicial review in theory or practice. Yet the Supreme Court offers hope in the endless battle to restrain the state. A majority of the Court has partially revived federalism in recent years. Kozinski and Engel, and Pilon, analyze this trend in Supreme Court jurisprudence and insist that reviving federalism requires judicial limits on what Congress can regulate. Matters that should be left to the states (i.e., producing most public goods) should be legally off limits to Congress.

My own essay examines the citizen initiative as a way to protect liberty and constrain government. Madison had his doubts about direct democracy, a skepticism that perhaps led him to exaggerate the promise of representative democracy. His skepticism was not mere prejudice; the history he read in the months before the constitutional convention told terrible stories of majority tyranny in direct democracies. Looking at more recent evidence, I conclude that the initiative as practiced in 23 states has by and large advanced the cause of liberty. That conclusion does not refute Madison's skepticism about direct democracy for the nation as a whole. Lacking experience with a national initiative, I believe we can only speculate about its effects on liberty or any other political value. If the United States in the future takes up the question of a national initiative, Madison's doubts about pure democracy should be the starting point for our deliberations. But it need not be our final judgment.

Factions and the Future

Madison believed both that all political power came originally from the people and that voters would be the best guardians of the Constitution. He also saw the need for "auxiliary precautions" to uphold the Constitution. As Joyce Malcolm notes, these precautions often resulted in divided sovereignty. The division of power between national and state governments created a healthy competition that might restrain the overly ambitious. As Madison saw it, the three branches of the national government would be jealous defenders of their turf and thus effective checks against unrestricted power in the capital.

Madison feared that abuses of power might grow out of a majority faction's possessing unrestrained political power. He believed differences over the distribution of property or over religious doctrine divided citizens, and that when passions ran high, such divisions fostered factions that might strive to oppress the wealthy or unorthodox minorities. Indeed, political passions, coupled with the human tendency toward factionalism, might even lead to civil war. How might factions be tamed and controlled? Palmer, Levy, and Hayes are among the contributors to this volume who address the question of factions in contemporary American politics.

Multiculturalism

The political philosopher Chandran Kukathas explicates how contemporary multiculturalism challenges liberal societies:

> In modern societies, particularly the societies of the liberal democratic West, cultural diversity poses a challenge not only to the makers of government policy, but also to the philosopher looking to understand how it might be possible—in principle—for people of different ways to live together. The challenge is posed because society's institutions have been challenged, as the members of different groups have demanded "recognition." They have demanded not simply recognition of their claims to a (just) share of the social pie but, more important, recognition of their distinct identities as members of particular cultural communities within society.[3]

Tom G. Palmer and Jacob Levy take up this challenge within a Madisonian framework. They address in different ways the question of whether factions founded on cultural differences endanger the American republic.

Palmer denies the received wisdom that classical liberals believe politics can never rise above particular interests to attain a common good. According to Palmer, Madison believed Americans share a limited though real common good defined by liberty and a regime of rights. Madison's liberal republic has no place for group-specific rights or the subordination of citizenship to group identity. Madison would not, Palmer avers, endorse notions like "racially authentic" representatives and group reparations.

Levy takes a different tack. He recounts Madison's overlooked political activity and reflection related to American Indians. Madison comes off well in Levy's account; he recognized that the Cherokees in particular had justice on their side in their claims against the United States. Levy concludes that Madison believed some groups threatened by a majority—like the American Indians—might require special group protections.

Religion

Madison thought religious commitments could sometimes lead to the oppression of a minority by a majority. His famous *Memorial and Remonstrance against Religious Assessments* excludes religious faith from the ambit of political power. Walter Berns provides a provocative explication and critique of Madison's thinking on religion and politics. Berns argues that Madison rejected the view common to his time and to much of American history that government should support religion as a way of improving public morality and instilling the virtues needed in a self-governing republic. Berns challenges Madison's view that republics should be completely secular, while Michael Hayes suggests that Madison's separation of religion and politics comports well with both Christianity and conservatism. The true vocation of the Christian, Hayes concludes, lies in the private sphere of persuasion and ministry.

Majorities

Madison worried that majority factions would endanger the new American republic. My contribution to this volume argues that the historical record of direct democracy in states with the initiative provides little evidence of majority tyranny. Moreover, contemporary Americans should be at least as concerned about minority factions. The economist Mancur Olson has demonstrated that the costs and benefits of political activity give intense minorities ample opportunity to exploit rationally apathetic majorities, especially through congressional policymaking. As a result, government grows larger than a majority wishes. Minority factions bent on plunder are the most harmful ill of the contemporary American body politic.

Madison and the World

Some see Madison as more Virginian than American, and certainly as more American than a citizen of the world. Yet that impression is a mistake. To prepare for the constitutional convention, Madison importuned Thomas Jefferson, then living in Paris, to buy for him all the leading European books on constitutions and the history of republics. Madison was a citizen of the world and a student of all of human history. Both James Dorn and John Tomasi believe that Madison's legacy should inform the future of humanity.

James Dorn argues that Madison would counsel emerging democracies to avoid simple majoritarianism in favor of a constitutional republic that protects liberty and property rights. Dorn marshals data showing that limited, constitutional government offers developing countries both freedom and prosperity. After decades of statism, poverty, and restrictions on freedom, the leaders of developing nations may be ready to consider Madison's realistic reflections on the limits of politics and government.

John Tomasi draws upon Madison to imagine what an international government might look like in the era now upon us. To quote Jefferson again, the United States began with the belief that all men are created equal and endowed with certain rights. That universality has been subject to much doubt, not least from postmodern theorists. Tomasi renews Jeffersonian universality through Madisonian means. His essay should provoke (and delight) the friends of liberty.

A liberal might say that a "United States of the World" may be the destiny of coming generations; if so, we should hope that Madison's skepticism about political power informs the making of any global constitution. Madisonian worries about a world government are germane. In *Federalist* No. 10, Madison notes that property is the most important source of factions that pose the danger of civil war. Creating an international polity might well threaten property if the "South" had working majorities in the new government and decided to expropriate the wealth of the "North." Seeking peace through world government might instead bring war and even greater restrictions on human freedom.

Conclusion

Joyce Malcolm recalls that Madison once asked:

> Is there no virtue among us? If there be not, we are in a wretched situation. No theoretical checks—no form of government can render us secure. To suppose that any form of

> government will secure liberty or happiness without any
> virtue in the people is a chimerical idea.[4]

Many of the contributions to this volume explicitly or implicitly
address Madison's tough question anew. Do Americans possess
enough virtue to maintain a limited government? The historian
H. W. Brands suggests that Americans have long possessed the
prime virtue needed for a classical liberal society, skepticism about
government:

> From before they had become a nation, and continuing until
> almost the middle of the 20th century, Americans registered
> chronic skepticism regarding a more active role for the fed-
> eral government in their lives. Every generation harbored
> its advocates of skepticism, but every generation comprised
> a larger collection of skeptics.[5]

James Buchanan is less optimistic. He sees the conduct of individuals
as part of a society where everyone seeks to take wealth from someone else. Roger Pilon indicates how far the American people have
moved away from the personal attitudes necessary for limited government. As government grows, individuals focus on gaining favors
from the state. In an older language of politics, unlimited government corrupts its citizens and undermines the virtues needed to
support a republican form of government. Buchanan recommends
"investments" in ethics, especially in restoring the old puritan constraints on individual conduct, constraints that pushed people
toward self-reliance rather than political rent-seeking.

Difficult questions about human nature complicate all speculation
about the future. Should we be pessimistic about freedom and limited government? In the end Madison believed humans were neither
angels nor devils:

> As there is a degree of depravity in mankind that requires
> a certain degree of circumspection and distrust: So there
> are other qualities in human nature, which justify a certain
> portion of esteem and confidence. Republican government
> presupposes the existence of these qualities in a higher degree
> than any other form.[6]

Like Madison we may hope that the republican qualities of human
nature as nurtured and constrained by constitutions triumph over

the traditional enemies of freedom. The essays in this collection offer due honor to the architect of the American Constitution and a hopeful start toward that victory. James Madison matters now more than ever.

Notes

1. *The Federalist* No. 10 (James Madison).

2. Dennis C. Mueller, *Constitutional Democracy* (New York: Oxford University Press, 1996), chap. 1.

3. Chandran Kukathas, "Liberalism and Multiculturalism: The Politics of Indifference," *Political Theory* 26 (October 1998): 686.

4. James Madison, "Speech in the Virginia Ratifying Convention" June 20, 1788, *Papers of James Madison*, vol. 11, p. 163.

5. H. W. Brands, *The Strange Death of American Liberalism* (New Haven: Yale University Press, 2001), p. 1.

6. *The Federalist* No. 55 (James Madison).

1. Madison's Angels

James M. Buchanan

> But what is government itself, but the greatest of all reflections on human nature. If men were angels, no government would be necessary. If angels were to govern men, neither external nor internal controls on government would be necessary. In forming a government which is to be administered by men over men, the great difficulty lies in this: you must first enable government to control the governed; and in the next place oblige it to control itself.
>
> James Madison, *The Federalist* No. 51

I could scarcely go wrong by starting with this most familiar passage from James Madison's justly acclaimed *The Federalist*, No. 51. Here Madison succinctly provides a justification for government itself and, at the same time, offers the reason for constitutional constraints on political authority. I shall not challenge Madison's statement here. Indeed, Madison retains an honored place in my personal pantheon.

What I propose to do, instead, is to examine Madison's statement more carefully. But, at the outset, let me say that my initial project was to examine what must have been Madison's counterfactual image of a society without governance, a society of angels. Just what sort of behavior would such angels exhibit, and what would the social interaction among the separate angels look like? I soon found myself in difficulty. As my old professor Frank Knight always said, it remains nearly impossible to describe what heaven would be like. Nonetheless, it does seem to me that Madison must have had some such image in mind when he wrote that statement.

We may begin to unravel some of his thinking.

Consider Madison's use of the word "angels" twice in the passage cited. I suggest that Madison did not intend to refer to the beings called angels in modern dictionaries. There, angels are defined as beings that possess suprahuman attributes or qualities. Such a definition, in Madison's construction, would rob the passage of much of its meaning. By "angel" I think that Madison referred to a being recognizable as human but who does indeed treat others in a fashion that, if generalized to all persons, would eliminate the need for governance. All of us can, I think, imagine such persons to exist, as ideals toward which we might strive but not as divinities of unattainable perfection. The most imaginative element in Christianity is surely the attribution of humanity to Jesus.

This interpretation of Madison allows us to place ethics alongside politics as alternative and complementary means to move beyond the ever-threatening Hobbesian jungle.

We may note, in particular, that Madison remained unclear about the particulars of the behavioral requirement. He did not say that government would be unnecessary if only all persons behaved like angels all of the time. He did not assume that all persons could be identical. But some persons, some of the time, surely behave toward each other in such fashion as to make explicit governance of those persons unnecessary. And, Madison did not imply that no persons were ever angels. Recognizing that individuals are different in relevant behavioral dimensions allows us to construct an ethical spectrum that may be used to describe societies potentially, ranging from one extreme defined by "all persons behave as angels all of the time" to the other extreme defined by "no person behaves as an angel any of the time."

Madison does not directly address the subsidiary question that such a spectrum prompts: Does the need for, and the range and scope of, government vary as societies find themselves differently located along an ethical scalar? Can and does ethics serve as a substitute for politics, and in what degree and in what manner? Can we make government less necessary by making more persons more like angels more of the time?

It seems clear that there are externalities between ethics and politics considered as instruments to keep our behavioral proclivities within acceptable limits. The libertarian ideal of ordered anarchy comes closer to realization if and when more persons more of the time behave like Madison's angels. On the other hand, and conversely, an increase in the politicization of our society almost necessarily reduces the proclivities of persons to behave like angels. In a paper written a quarter century ago entitled "Markets, States, and the Extent of Morals," I suggested that, if we politicize activities that extend beyond our moral capacities, we necessarily generate increased exploitation. To put this argument in Madisonian terms, if we put too much reliance on politics, we may stifle even those behavioral motivations that might qualify as near-angelic. This conclusion becomes especially relevant as and if we allow our political units to become too large, in both membership and territorial extension. A returned James Madison would surely stand aghast at the behemoth that is the United States federal government.

How can we act like angels, even in limited aspects of our behavior, when we are thrown, willy-nilly, into the gladiatorial pit of present-day political reality? Madison was not suggesting that we are necessarily gladiatorial, always out to destroy one another, facing a fate from which only politics can save us. Such interpretation would distort the meaning of the message. Madison would say that now, as in 1788, we need laws to control our behavior. But he would surely also say that now the political realm has gone far beyond his imagined constitutionally ordered limited governance.

We create and maintain institutions of governance to preserve social order in light of the proclivities that we, as members of the community, exhibit in our behavior, one toward another. The attainability as well as the desirability of this order remain critically intertwined with those proclivities, as measured along our imaginary ethical scalar. We must move well beyond Madison and realize that justification of marginal extensions of government must be grounded on something other than the universal human attribute of ethical fallibility. At the margin, the positive benefit-cost ratio from investment in ethics may be much larger than those from investment in politicization, which may indeed be negative. We may be logically libertarian in our opposition to all efforts to enlarge the range and scope of governance while, at the same time, we may be persuasively puritan in our discourse on behavioral attributes.

Finally, we should never forget what was surely James Madison's starting point, namely, his presumption that the ideal society is one in which all persons are indeed angels and in which governance has no place.

2. Recapturing Madison's Constitution: Federalism without the Blank Check

Alex Kozinski and Steven A. Engel

James Madison spent the last six years of his life troubled by a national debate over federalism. On the one side stood the "nullifiers," who claimed that the Tariff of 1828 was unconstitutional and that the states, as sovereign entities, retained the right to ignore it, or even secede from the Union. On the other side were the nationalists, who argued that sovereignty resided only in the federal government and that the states had no authority to question its dictates. Madison feared the nullifiers much more than the nationalists, but the old man was convinced that both camps misunderstood the government that his generation had established. The nation must not forget, he warned, that the Constitution had set in motion a regime "so unexampled in its origin, and so complex in its structure" that the traditional "political vocabulary" of sovereignty could not apply.[1] The Founders had divided sovereignty between two governments, leaving the federal and state governments each supreme in their respective spheres.

The one thing Madison refused to do during his last days was to release his notes on the Constitutional Convention, which he had tirelessly recorded more than forty years before. The Convention had deliberated in secret; so to many Americans of his time, Madison's notes were a buried treasure of constitutional wisdom. Madison refused requests that he release them during the nullification crisis, fearing that the public might then read them with partisan eyes. Instead, he repeated his desire to postpone their publication until after his death, when no one could malign his motives for publishing them. Madison hoped that the notes would be regarded as a gift to the people of the United States.

Well, not exactly a gift. Madison was also convinced, like some contemporary public figures, that private publishers would pay big money for his memoirs. Madison expected that his wife, Dolly, and his family might live for some time off the proceeds. He instructed Dolly on the fine points of extracting a good deal from the publishers in New York.

It turns out that Madison had mistaken the commercial value of this national treasure. Dolly Madison wrote to Congress that the reputable publishers were not sure the debates would be a best seller, and so they would not publish them unless the widow paid some of the production costs. She might therefore lose money if the notes failed to sell as well as Madison expected. Mrs. Madison asked whether the government might be willing to buy the manuscript. After some haggling, she agreed to accept $30,000 (the equivalent of $467,470 in the year 2000)[2], so long as she retained the foreign copyright.

But there was a problem. A number of members believed that Congress had no authority to purchase the copyright. John Calhoun, the arch-proponent of state's rights, expressed his admiration for the manuscript, but he asked Madison's supporters what part of the Constitution gave Congress the power to purchase a copyright and publish a book. Madison himself, Calhoun recalled, had argued that Congress's power to raise money for the "general welfare" did not permit spending beyond the constitutionally enumerated powers of the federal government. Fortunately for Madison's family, Madison's vision of a limited spending power did not carry that day.

With the publication of Madison's account of the Constitutional Convention, his position as the "Father of the Constitution" seemed assured. But as the debate over purchasing his manuscript reveals, not all of Madison's constitutional views survived him. In considering Madison's legacy today, we might ask whether this Founding Father would even recognize the federal government we have today.

So why do we honor Madison as our constitutional father? As his description of the debates reveals, the Constitution was the work of many men. Madison was one of the most vocal advocates of the system that emerged from the Convention, but he was hardly the only one. Nor was he the sole architect of the great compromises that made the adoption possible. Madison shared the writing of the *Federalist Papers* with Alexander Hamilton and John Jay, and by the time Madison appeared at the Virginia Ratifying Convention, six other states had already ratified.[3] Although no one did more than Madison to ensure the ratification of the Constitution, he is not the father of the Constitution in the sense that Thomas Jefferson is the father of the Declaration of Independence.

We honor Madison as the Father of the Constitution because of his contribution on the plane of ideas. Madison was the political philosopher of the Constitution, the one who articulated the grand theory on which the text was based.[4] As the national government descended into crisis in the 1780s, Madison researched in painstaking detail the fate of confederacies and republics in the past. He concluded that republics that grew too large inevitably collapsed into tyranny. On the other hand, confederacies inevitably were undone by rivalries among their constituent republics. As Madison pored through the books that his friend Thomas Jefferson sent him from France, he sketched out a new political system, which he believed might rescue the Union from its weakened state and from the mistakes of the past.[5]

The name of this political theory was federalism. Its secret was a form of dual sovereignty that had never been tried before. Madison posited that state and federal governments might coexist as sovereigns over the same space, representing and acting on behalf of the people of the United States, the ultimate source of authority. The national government would enjoy a limited set of powers, which Madison described as "few and defined," enabling it to deal with those matters that concerned the states collectively, such as national defense and interstate commerce. At the same time, the states would retain everything else—powers that were "numerous and indefinite, extend[ing] to all objects which, in the ordinary course of affairs, concern the lives, liberties, and properties of the people, and the internal order, improvement, and prosperity of the State."[6]

The states would retain all the attributes of sovereign nations, "form[ing] distinct and independent portions of the supremacy, no more subject, within their respective spheres, to the general authority than the general authority is subject to them within its own sphere."[7] But the Constitution would limit the states in two ways. They could neither regulate in ways that frustrated national policies on matters of national concern nor violate any of the explicit limitations in the Constitution, which in Madison's day were few in number but have grown considerably since the adoption of the Fourteenth Amendment.

Madison understood that this federal system had the potential to be superior to any historical alternative. By creating a system of dual sovereignty, the Constitution established a central government with the authority to secure national goals while, at the same time, maintaining the local autonomy necessary for good republican government. The smaller republics would provide their citizens with a greater chance to participate in the democratic process and their representatives would more closely reflect their interests. Rather than imposing a uniform solution to local problems, the state governments would enact laws suited to the character and interests of their citizens.

While a consolidated government might obtain some of those benefits by delegating power to local governments, divided sovereignty fundamentally changed the business of government by introducing competition into that oldest of monopolies. Federalism aimed at producing many of the benefits one would expect from open competition. The most important benefit, Madison recognized, was that each government would stand watch over the other, to prevent its rival from abusing the liberty of the citizens and to provide instruments of judicial redress.[8]

The multiplication of governments would also improve the quality of institutions. As each state government chooses its own way, there will be a greater diversity of choices. Some may be bad choices, but others will not. The good ones may be followed, replicated, and improved upon. Competition among governments also gives the states an incentive to innovate as they compete for taxpayers and encourages them to improve their infrastructure and laws in order to attract a mobile citizenry. Many bad ideas are also avoided, because states know that businesses and citizens may vote with their feet.

Madison well understood the virtues of this "compound republic." But while we may praise this system on a theoretical level, we should consider whether it really reflects our present system of government. Madison described a limited federal government, whose powers were few and defined, limited to regulating only national objects. Contrast that vision to the federal government of today. By the mid-1980s, the federal government had effectively set a national speed limit, minimum wage, and drinking age. It is a federal crime to grow marijuana on your land or to shoot a wolf menacing your cattle. Many Americans turn to the federal government to provide them with health care, disability and unemployment insurance, and a social security pension. And in return, Americans give more than a third of their income to the federal government. We may talk about a federal government of limited powers, but for much of the past century it would be difficult to discern any limits on that power.

At some point in the recent past, the Supreme Court began to remember that the Constitution contemplated a federal government of limited authority. In several decisions, the Court took small steps to recapture the Madisonian Constitution, often citing Madison himself. The Court barred Congress from requiring state officers and state legislatures to carry out federal policies;[9] it imposed upon Congress clear statement rules to ensure that decisions altering the federal balance are not made lightly;[10] and it revived the Eleventh Amendment as a protection of the states' sovereignty.[11]

These decisions reflect a desire to recapture the system of dual sovereignty that Madison envisioned. When the federal government regulates every aspect of our society, we lose the benefits of energetic state governments. State politicians have proven unwilling to resist, because it always seems better to have someone else pay the bills, and many state politicians run for election with the ambition of someday ascending to federal office. Thus, if the Supreme Court neglected to enforce the constitutional limitations on federal power, few state or local politicians would mourn the demise of federalism.

Through recent decisions, the Court has attempted principally to protect state sovereignty by constraining the *means* through which the federal government might regulate state actions. But protecting federalism by limiting the choice of means at the national government's disposal is an incomplete solution. Congress must have broad discretion in choosing how to exercise its powers, and in any event, if Congress is determined to regulate an area, it may always choose alternative means to achieve the same goal. So long as the end result is constitutional, the legislature will find a way to reach it.

In two recent instances, though, the Court has taken the more significant step of striking down laws it regarded as beyond the *ends* permitted by the Constitution. Although there was nothing particularly objectionable about the means used in either case, the Court concluded that the *object* of the legislation was a matter of local, not federal, concern. In the first of those decisions, *United States v. Lopez,* the Court held that Congress could not make a federal crime out of possessing a gun near a high school.[12] The Court began by quoting what it called "first principles," which, not surprisingly, turned out to be James Madison's words: "The powers delegated by the proposed Constitution to the federal government are few and defined. Those which are to remain in the State governments are numerous and indefinite."[13]

The Court reached the unremarkable conclusion that prohibiting gun possession in schools, though no doubt a good idea, fell outside Congress's power to regulate interstate commerce. When Alfonso Lopez, a Texas high school senior, packed his .38-caliber handgun and went to school, few ordinary people would assume he was engaging in commercial activity, much less commercial activity with implications in Oklahoma, Arkansas, or Louisiana. But, in deference to Congress, the Court had concluded 50 years earlier that pretty much anything could affect interstate commerce if enough people were doing it.[14] *Lopez* reflected the judgment that, at least in the most obvious instances, the Court was once again willing to place some things outside Congress's reach.

The Court reiterated this conclusion in 2000 in *United States v. Morrison,* when it struck down a civil remedy provided by the Violence Against Women Act.[15] The Court concluded that Congress lacked the power to create a remedy for violence against women, not because the end was unimportant, but because under our constitutional scheme, what is federal is not coextensive with what is important. We entrust the states with the authority to protect citizens against crime. If the states refuse to protect certain citizens, the federal government might intervene, as it did during the civil rights era. But absent evidence that the states were hostile to women, the area lay beyond the concern of the national government.

For those convinced of Madison's wisdom, the *Lopez* and *Morrison* decisions represent necessary steps in restoring the balance of powers between state and federal governments. If we are to enjoy the benefits of dual sovereignty, we must allow the states to solve the local problems within their competence. They should not be reduced to clients of the federal government, allowed to regulate only those matters that the national government chooses to leave in their hands.

Although these recent decisions may help restore the federal balance, they will never be more than pennyweights so long as the Supreme Court neglects one critical part of Madison's Constitution.

While the Court has recognized that Congress may not regulate fields beyond its enumerated powers, it has granted Congress the power to spend without limit. The days where Congress debated the constitutionality of purchasing Madison's copyright are long gone. Instead, we see debates over whether Congress should bribe the states into passing stricter drunk-driving laws. Madison recognized in his own time that an unlimited federal spending power could not coexist with a truly federal government. So long as the Supreme Court ignores Madison's warning, true federalism will remain a thing of the past.

The Constitution lacks a spending clause, but the first enumerated power grants Congress the authority to levy taxes and otherwise raise money "to pay the Debts and provide for the common Defence and general Welfare of the United States."[16] The first thing to note about this clause is that it does not speak of spending at all. Instead, it qualifies Congress's power to raise money by noting that it must be for the purpose of paying the nation's debts and of providing for national defense and the general welfare. The meaning of that last phrase, the acknowledgment that Congress may provide for the "general welfare," has been a source of controversy since the nation's founding.

The Constitution's critics feared that clause granted Congress the power not simply to spend money but to adopt any measure that would in effect provide for the general welfare. Not so, Madison wrote in *The Federalist*. That clause refers only to the purposes for which Congress may raise money. It does not authorize Congress to spend money for any purpose whatsoever. The General Welfare Clause precedes Congress's other enumerated powers and, as Madison wrote, "Nothing is more natural nor common than first to use a general phrase, and then to explain and qualify it by a recital of particulars."[17] In short, it would make no sense to list a series of particular purposes, which would all be rendered unnecessary by an all-encompassing general phrase. Thus, the General Welfare Clause does not permit spending for all purposes. The clause permits spending only in the exercise of those powers enumerated in Article 1, section 8, of the Constitution.

Madison offered a second justification for such a reading of the General Welfare Clause. The phrase "common defense or general welfare" was lifted right out of the restrictive Articles of Confederation. The Articles provided that "[a]ll charges of war, and all other

19

expenses that shall be incurred for the *common defense or general welfare"* should be paid by requisitions from the states.[18] The drafters of the Constitution copied this clause, but added the power to levy taxes directly, rather than forcing the government to rely exclusively on state contributions. Nothing indicated an intention to broaden Congress's power to spend, and Madison argued that the General Welfare Clause could not in any way be construed as expanding Congress's powers beyond the enumerated objects of the Constitution.

But that's precisely how Alexander Hamilton chose to read the clause broadly during his tenure as Secretary of the Treasury. The great nationalist of the Federalist era, Hamilton advocated a reading that would enable Congress to spend for any purpose that served the "general welfare," whether that purpose lay within its enumerated powers or not. Ignoring the clause's origin in the Articles of Confederation, Hamilton argued that the General Welfare Clause was a catchall, allowing Congress to deal with the numerous incidents that would otherwise be left without provision. The only limit, said Hamilton, was that "the object to which an appropriation of money is to be made [must] be General and not local; its operation extending in fact, or by possibility, throughout the Union and not being confined to a particular spot."[19] This constraint would allow Congress to devote money to national causes, but it would prevent the federal government from spending for local matters, such as the projects that are the pork of modern politics.

Madison sharply criticized the Hamiltonian view, because he recognized that there was no "power of any magnitude which, in its exercise does not involve, or admit, an application of money."[20] The tendency of Hamilton's construction, Madison argued, would be to destroy the meaning and effect of the principle of enumerated powers. If Congress were found to be able to spend money on any national purpose, then the federal government would soon find itself involved in regulating spheres of activity reserved to the states.

History left the question to the future, since for a while Congress lacked both the will and the resources to intervene too heavily in local affairs. But the enactment of the Sixteenth Amendment in 1913, giving Congress the power to tax income, created a revenue machine that would fuel a growing appetite for national power. When the New Deal Congress asserted hitherto unknown federal authority, the Supreme Court confronted head-on whether Hamilton or Madison's view of the Spending Clause would prevail. In 1936, in *United States v. Butler*, the Court considered whether Congress could authorize the Secretary of Agriculture to pay farmers not to grow crops in order to artificially raise the market price.[21] This was a classic case of Congress spending money to regulate a field not otherwise within the domain of congressional power, at least as Congress's authority under the Commerce Clause was then understood.

The Supreme Court concluded that Hamilton's was the better reading of the spending power. Without elaborating on its reasons, the Court held that the General Welfare Clause gave Congress the power to spend for any general purpose. Although *Butler* invoked another reason to strike down the statute, the damage was done, and the next year, the Court relied on it to hold that Congress might set up a national system of unemployment insurance.[22] These days, the Court would justify such spending under Congress's power to regulate interstate commerce, but back then, the Court concluded that simply because unemployment was a problem of national concern, Congress could address it through its power of the purse.

Given the green light by the Supreme Court, Congress put federal money into all areas of the national life over the ensuing decades. Congress not only spent money but conditioned spending in order to regulate states and citizens. The state legislatures readily accepted the federal money, concluding there was more to gain from accepting the funding than from asserting their independence. In 1984 Congress enacted a law that directed the Secretary of Transportation to penalize states where the legal drinking age was under 21, by reducing the federal highway funds granted to the state each year. South Dakota filed suit claiming that the condition on highway funds was unlawful because it regulated an area reserved to the states. Although in the 1980s Congress could regulate just about anything under the Commerce Clause, the amendment repealing Prohibition had expressly given the power to regulate alcohol consumption to the states. Thus, South Dakota would seem to have had a pretty good argument that Congress was trying to regulate a matter beyond the scope of federal power.

In those early days of the Rehnquist Court, many hoped it might back South Dakota and constrain the spending power. But the Court did not see things that way; it affirmed once more that Congress's power to spend for the "general welfare" could go beyond its enumerated powers.[23] The Court suggested there might be a limit on

21

how far Congress could condition the receipt of spending: The spending must be reasonably related to the purpose of the federal grant. But the Court applied this test in a way that was not much of a limit at all. It concluded that a state's drinking age was related to highway funds, because a higher drinking age would reduce teenage drinking, which would reduce the number of drunk teenagers on the highways, which would lead to safer highways.

That's an awfully attenuated way of ensuring that the states do not misuse highway funds. In fact, it does not have much more to do with the highways than guns at school have to do with interstate commerce. What really happened is that Congress decided a 21-year-old drinking age was a good idea, and it pressured the states to follow suit. But the drinking age is exactly the kind of local issue that the Constitution leaves to the states to regulate. Maybe some states want no drinking age; others prefer an 18-year-old drinking age; and some want to ban alcohol altogether. But whatever policy a state chooses, our federalism understands it as a decision for the people of the state who must live under it. By placing a rider in a funding bill, Congress constrains state prerogatives by imposing a national standard on a quintessential local issue.

If Congress may regulate alcohol consumption through federal highway funds, then there really are no areas that Congress cannot touch. Federal education grants may be used to develop a national curriculum, and federal welfare funds may be used to rewrite state family law. Employee Retirement Income Security Act benefits can be used to replace the state law of trusts and estates, and federal crime aid might require states to establish life tenure for judges. And, of course, federal funds may be used to require states to pass those laws struck down in *Lopez* and *Morrison*, making a mockery of the notion that the states remain supreme in their own spheres of activity.

For those of us who believe in Madison's Constitution, this is not a trivial problem, and it cannot be resolved by saying that the states are free to refuse to accept federal money. Over the course of the 20th century, federal funds have become the lifeblood of the state government budgets. In 2001, for example, the federal government gave states $273 billion in grants for federal programs and another $40 billion for specific projects. Virginia, for instance, received 20 percent of its annual revenues directly from the federal government;

Maryland received 22 percent; and my home state, California, received 29 percent of its annual revenue in federal funds.[24]

Most of this government spending falls within the broad powers that the federal government enjoys over interstate commerce. But so long as the federal government is free to use its spending powers to regulate areas beyond its enumerated powers, there will never really be areas free from federal control. If we are serious about recovering Madison's Constitution, then the Supreme Court must turn its attention to this lever of federal power. We must recognize, as Madison did, that the competition, democracy, and heterogeneity at the heart of our federalism require state sovereignty in fact as well as in theory.

Notes

1. Drew McCoy, *The Last of the Fathers* (New York: Cambridge University Press, 1989), p. 150.

2. This sum was calculated by The Inflation Calculator at www.westegg.com.

3. See Robert Allen Rutland, *James Madison: The Founding Father* (New York: McMillan, 1987), p. 34.

4. See Stanley Elkins and Eric McKitrick, *The Age of Federalism* (New York: Oxford University Press, 1993), p. 83.

5. See Rutland, pp. 12–13.

6. *The Federalist* No. 45 (James Madison).

7. *The Federalist* No. 39 (James Madison).

8. See *The Federalist* No. 51 (James Madison).

9. *Printz v. United States*, 521 U.S. 898 (1997); *New York v. United States*, 505 U.S. 144 (1992).

10. See *Solid Waste Agency v. United States Army Corps of Eng'rs*, 121 S. Ct. 675, 684 (2001); *Gregory v. Ashcroft*, 501 U.S. 452 (1991).

11. *Alden v. Maine*, 119 S. Ct. 2240 (1999); *Seminole Tribe of Fla. v. Florida*, 517 U.S. 44 (1996).

12. 514 U.S. 549 (1995).

13. *Lopez*, 514 U.S. at 552 (quoting *The Federalist* No. 45).

14. See *Wickard v. Fillburn*, 317 U.S. 111 (1942).

15. 120 S. Ct. 1740 (2000).

16. U.S. Constitution, art. I, § 8, cl. 1.

17. *The Federalist* No. 41 (James Madison).

18. Articles of Confederation, art. VII (1781) (emphasis added).

19. Alexander Hamilton, "Report on Manufactures" (Dec. 5, 1791), in *The Papers of Alexander Hamilton*, ed. Harold C. Syrett, vol. 10 (New York: Columbia University Press, 1961–79), p. 302.

20. James Madison, "Report on the Virginia Resolution (1800)," in *The Debates in the Several State Conventions on the Adoption of the Federal Constitution*, ed. Jonathan Elliot, vol. 4 (Charlottesville, Va.: Michie, 1941).

21. 297 U.S. 1 (1936).

22. See *Helvering v. Davis*, 301 U.S. 619 (1937).

23. See *South Dakota v. Dole*, 483 U.S. 203, 207 (1987).

24. For the 2000–2002 biennium, Virginia took in $43.7 billion in revenue, of which $8.7 billion was in federal funds. See "Frequently Asked Questions about Virginia's Budget," www.dpb.state.va.us/budget/faq/faq.htm; "Maryland Budget Priorities FY 2001," www.dbm.state.md.us/html/budgetpri.html; "California Department of Finance, State Budget Highlights, 2000–2001," www.dof.ca.gov.

3. Madison's Constitutional Vision: The Legacy of Enumerated Powers

Roger Pilon

In reflecting on James Madison and the future of limited government, the first challenge is to understand Madison's constitutional vision. That would be easier to do had modern political sensibilities not strayed so far from it—had we not become so accustomed to effectively unlimited government and indifferent, largely, to constitutional restraints on the size and scope of government. The second challenge is to understand how and why the limited government Madison sought to secure became the vast Leviathan we know today. Indeed, given the current reach of federal power, Madison's promise in *Federalist* No. 45 that the powers of the new government would be "few and defined" strikes the modern ear as not a little quaint. At the outset, therefore, we have to grant that Madison's legacy is less than certain, even as we draw from it to speculate about the future of limited government.

To say that Madison's legacy is uncertain is not to say, of course, that he left us nothing. Quite the contrary, although the federal government today is far larger than he imagined it would be, Madison's constitutional vision has doubtless spared us the kind of oppressive and even tyrannical government we've seen so often around the world since his plan was first unveiled. In fact, more than 200 years after it was first erected, most of Madison's structure is still standing. Looking over the events of that period, that is no small accomplishment. On balance, therefore, one would have to say that the legacy of Madison's vision has been relatively stable government, even if more government than Madison would have wanted.

To learn from that mixed legacy, it will be useful to begin with a brief overview of Madison's vision, focusing in particular on his constitutional doctrine of enumerated powers. Our main concern in that will be with Madison's conception of political legitimacy, especially as it contrasts with our own. Having sketched that vision, we will then trace its history to the present. That story has two main parts, with the Progressive Era marking the divide; the New Deal, which is usually taken to have ended Madison's limited government, simply institutionalized the ideas of the progressives. Finally, to speculate about the future, we will look briefly at the recent turn the Supreme Court has taken in its federalism jurisprudence, which it has couched in the language of "first principles." Madison would have been pleased with that turn, but he would have noticed, too, how much more is needed if limited constitutional government is to be restored.

Madison's Vision

Students of Madison often begin by noting the central role he played in bringing the Constitution about—so central that he is ordinarily thought to be the father of the document. They proceed then to describe the structure of government he helped to craft, focusing on federalism, the separation of powers, and other such devices. Prior to such structural devices, however, are Madison's principles of government, grounded in morality and prudence. And prior to those is his basic moral vision, from which the political principles and the constitutional structure ultimately flow.

At the outset, therefore, we need to examine Madison's moral vision and recognize, in particular, that he was very much a product of the nation's founding in 1776, even if he was not present at the founding. Thus, like others at the constitutional convention of 1787, he took his inspiration, and his moral vision, from the principles set forth first in the Declaration of Independence. We need to begin, therefore, with those principles, not least because they illuminate the document that followed some 11 years later.[1]

The Declaration's Moral Vision

In the Declaration the Founders outlined their philosophy of government in the course of explaining, and justifying, their decision to dissolve the political bands that had tied them to England. The importance of their concern with justification—with laying down the principles of legitimate government—cannot be overstated, for it set our course ever after. America truly is different from other nations: from the start, we have taken justification, and political legitimacy, seriously.

26

And what are those principles? Drawing on the Lockean natural rights tradition[2] and the better parts of the common law, both grounded in reason,[3] the Founders spoke first of the moral order. Only then, after they had outlined the moral order, did they turn to the political and legal order their moral vision entailed. Thus, unlike in the ancient world, or even in the *ancien régime*, they began with morality, not with government.[4] And they began, in particular, with a premise of moral equality: we're all created equal, as defined by our natural rights to life, liberty, and the pursuit of happiness. Note that those rights—rights, essentially, to be free—preexist government. We don't get our rights from government; on the contrary, whatever rights or powers government has come from us. That crucial point is made clear when government is introduced at last. Government's purpose, the Declaration says, is to secure our rights, its *just* powers *derived from the consent of the governed.* Thus, legitimate government is twice limited—by its ends, to secure our rights, and by its means, which must be consented to.[5]

Clearly, that is a libertarian vision. We're born with the right to plan and live our lives as we see fit, and with every other right that basic right entails. Government exists not to plan our lives for us but simply to secure the rights we already have and those we create over time. Thus, Madison envisioned a limited government: most human affairs were to take place not through government but in what we call today the private sector. We enter that sector with our property rights—broadly understood as lives, liberties, and estates, as Locke put it.[6] Once there we create new rights and obligations and alienate current ones through the mechanisms of promise or contract, on one hand, or tort or crime, on the other.[7] The purpose of government in that scenario is not to create those rights and obligations but simply to recognize and enforce them, through powers we have given it. That was the concept of legitimacy that Madison brought with him when he went to Philadelphia in 1787. It is a far cry from the modern conception of government as providing goods and services through all manner of statutorily created redistributive and regulatory schemes, their "legitimacy" grounded in majoritarian politics.[8]

Among countless statements by Madison illustrating that vision, one of his clearest, pertaining to the commercial world that is the subject of so much regulation today, was made in the very first Congress:

> I own myself the friend to a very free system of commerce,
> and hold it as a truth, that commercial shackles are generally
> unjust, oppressive and impolitic—it is also a truth, that if
> industry and labour are left to take their own course, they
> will generally be directed to those objects which are the most
> productive, and this in a more certain and direct manner
> than the wisdom of the most enlightened legislature could
> point out.[9]

Long before 20th century economists like Ludwig von Mises and
Friedrich Hayek were explaining systematically the folly of social
planning, there with the essential insight was Madison. Yet modern
progressives still cling to the idea that enlightened legislatures, better
than the parties themselves, can regulate commerce in everything
from agriculture to education, manufacturing, medicine, and more.
That uncritical faith in government is endemic today, so much so that
it leaves little room for any concern about legitimacy. For Madison,
however, legitimacy is the first concern: he begins his remarks by
speaking of "shackles," saying that commercial shackles are generally "unjust and oppressive" because they interfere with a "free
system of commerce"—the natural order. If that simple point about
illegitimate interference with individual liberty is now foreign to
the modern mind—unthinkingly accustomed as it is to paternal
government—how far more distant must Madison's theory of *constitutional* legitimacy be?

The Constitution's Theory of Legitimacy

We come, then, to that theory. Madison was driven not simply
by the idea that excessive governmental interference with liberty is
illegitimate because inconsistent with the moral principle that each
individual has a right to live his own life, free from such interference.
To be sure, that principle grounded the rest. But it was secured,
practically, through a quite different theory of *political* or *constitutional* legitimacy, aimed at showing how government and governmental powers might arise legitimately, and how other powers might
be shown to be illegitimate. Known as the doctrine of enumerated
powers, that theory truly is the centerpiece of the Constitution and
the foundation of Madison's conception of constitutional legitimacy.

To appreciate it, however, it is useful to notice first that the practical problem the Framers faced when they got to Philadelphia was
how to create a government at once strong enough to do what

government is mainly created to do—secure our rights—yet not so powerful or extensive as to violate rights in the process. In tackling that problem, Madison was well aware, as he showed in his famous "if men were angels" discussion in *Federalist* No. 51, that we have to start with people as they are, then try to both empower and restrain them by creating institutional arrangements that pit power against power and ambition against ambition. That explains the Constitution's many checks and balances, from the division of powers (federalism) to the separation of powers, to the provision for judicial review, to periodic elections, and much more.

The most basic limit on power, however, could not have been simpler in its conception. In fact, it can be reduced to a short admonition: if you want to limit power, don't give it in the first place. Notice, however, that that is not simply an instruction for limiting government. More important, it is a principle of legitimacy. In fact, it draws from the Declaration's claim that government's *just* powers are derived from the consent of the governed. In a word, powers are legitimate if and only if they have been delegated by the people and enumerated in the document through which the people constitute themselves as a political entity, their constitution. Thus, the doctrine of enumerated powers.

We find that doctrine implicit in the Constitution's very first words, the Preamble: "We the people . . . do ordain and establish this Constitution." At the outset, all power rests with the people; no power rests with government, there being none yet in existence. And in the very next sentence, the first sentence of Article I, we find the doctrine again, a bit more explicitly: "All legislative Powers *herein granted* shall be vested in a Congress. . . ." (Emphasis added.) Thus, the people grant some of their power to the government that comes into being after ratification. But by implication, again, not all powers were "herein granted." We discover which powers were granted by reading the rest of the document—primarily Article I, section 8, in the case of Congress. Finally, in the Tenth Amendment, the final documentary evidence of the Framers' plan, we discover the doctrine of enumerated powers in its most explicit formulation: "The powers not delegated to the United States by the Constitution, nor prohibited by it to the States, are reserved to the States respectively, or to the people." That final statement makes it clear beyond doubt that power is divided: some has been delegated to the federal government, as enumerated in the Constitution; the rest is reserved to the states—or to the people, never having been delegated to either level of government. In sum, the federal Constitution creates a government of delegated, enumerated, and thus limited powers.

To the modern mind, accustomed to thinking that government exists to solve such personal problems as how to pay for education, daycare, or prescription drugs, the ideas just articulated are utterly foreign. Yet on numerous occasions and subjects, Madison was quite clear about the limits imposed by the doctrine of enumerated powers. In his *Report of 1800*, for example, he wrote that

> in all the co-temporary discussions and comments, which the Constitution underwent, it was constantly justified and recommended on the ground, that the powers not given to the government, were withheld from it; and that if any doubt could have existed on this subject, under the original text of the Constitution, it is removed as far as words could remove it, by the 12th amendment, now a part of the Constitution, which expressly declares. . . .[10]

(Madison was referring to the present Tenth Amendment, which was originally the final of 12 amendments Congress submitted to the states for ratification in 1789. Two failed ratification.)

And in his actions, too, Madison took the doctrine of enumerated powers to be the bedrock limit on federal power. Thus, in 1794, when faced with a bill appropriating some $15,000 for relief of French refugees who had fled to Baltimore and Philadelphia from an insurrection in San Domingo, Madison rose on the floor of the House to object that he could not "undertake to lay [his] finger on that article of the Federal Constitution which granted a right to Congress of expending, on objects of benevolence, the money of their constituents."[11]

Years later, as president, Madison would continue to insist on constitutional fidelity. Thus, in 1817 he vetoed a comprehensive plan for internal improvements that Congress had passed, saying that "the legislative powers vested in Congress are specified and enumerated in the eighth section of the first article of the Constitution, and it does not appear that the power proposed to be exercised by the bill is among the enumerated powers. . . ."[12] Noteworthy in that veto message, moreover, were his comments on the role of the judiciary:

> Such a view of the Constitution [as the bill contemplated]
> would have the effect of excluding the judicial authority
> of the United States from its participation in guarding the
> boundary between the legislative powers of the General and
> the State Governments, inasmuch as questions relating to
> the general welfare, being questions of policy and expedi-
> ency, are unsusceptible of judicial cognizance and decision.[13]

Madison's concern was not, as in the modern view, to have the judiciary defer to the political branches as those branches decide wide-ranging questions of policy. Rather, quite the opposite, it was to uphold the power of the judiciary to say that Congress had no power to decide questions of policy if doing so would take it beyond the boundaries of its enumerated powers. He was saying, in short, that it fell ultimately to the judiciary to police the doctrine of enumerated powers, not as a matter of policy but as a matter of principle. It fell to the judiciary to tell Congress, simply, "You haven't the power you purport to have. You are acting without constitutional authority."

Thus, the doctrine of enumerated powers speaks explicitly to powers, only implicitly to rights, which helps to explain why it is so foreign to the modern ear. Madison understood that if you want to protect rights from government abuse, you would be wise not to give government the power in the first place that can then be used to abuse rights. That is a lesson we have forgotten. As we have asked government to do more and more for us, we have forgotten that a government big enough to give us everything we want will be powerful enough to take everything we have.

The Demise of Enumerated Powers

The history of the demise of Madison's plan is long and tortured, but it falls into two main periods, with the Progressive Era marking the intellectual divide, as noted earlier, and the New Deal marking the institutional divide.[14] Expansive government had its friends from the outset, of course. Perhaps the earliest example was Alexander Hamilton's 1790 *Report on Manufactures*, calling for a kind of national "industrial policy."[15] Congress voted the report down, but that hardly brought an end to efforts to expand the federal government's role in our lives. For the most part, however, those efforts died in

Congress. And when they survived there, they were often vetoed by the executive or, eventually, found unconstitutional by the courts.[16]

A fine example of presidential respect for constitutional limits occurred in 1887, 100 years after the Constitution was written, when President Grover Cleveland vetoed a bill appropriating some $10,000 to buy seeds for Texas farmers suffering from a drought. Cleveland's veto message is instructive on the old way of thinking:

> I can find no warrant for such an appropriation in the Constitution; and I do not believe that the power and duty of the General Government ought to be extended to the relief of individual suffering which is in no manner properly related to the public service or benefit. A prevalent tendency to disregard the limited mission of this power and duty should, I think, be steadfastly resisted, to the end that the lesson should be constantly enforced that, though the people support the Government, the Government should not support the people.[17]

Stern words, but the climate of ideas was changing even then. The "prevalent tendency" to disregard limits that Cleveland noted would gather intellectual steam over the next 50 years, reaching a crescendo in 1937 when President Franklin Roosevelt's notorious Court-packing scheme would lead to a fundamental rewriting of the Constitution—without benefit of constitutional amendment.

The Progressive Era

The Progressive Era that spurred on that change drew from many sources. In philosophy the classical theory of natural rights had long been under attack. British utilitarianism, looking not to rights but to future goods—in particular, to the greatest good for the greatest number—was now the norm,[18] together with its cousin, American pragmatism.[19] Both enjoyed an easy affinity with democratic theory, which had been gaining ground for some time in politics. Among the new social sciences, German ideas about good government and the virtues of social planning were all the rage. Practitioners of those sciences, imbued often with moral zeal and a hubris all but unbounded, sought to better the human condition much as the hard sciences were doing. Thus, at century's end we could find the *Encyclopedia of Social Sciences* stating confidently that "almost all social thinkers are now agreed that the social evils of the day arise in large part from social wrongs."[20] And by 1920 the president of the National Conference of Social Work could call upon social engineers to impose "a divine order on earth as it is in heaven."[21] This activism, just to be clear, was to be carried out not by private institutions but by government. Indeed, in 1922, Frank Dekker Watson, director of the Pennsylvania School for Social Service, commended the ongoing "crowding out" of private by public charity, for only thus would "public funds ever be wholly adequate for the legitimate demands made upon them."[22]

What such activism among the intellectual vanguard most reflected, of course, was a fundamental shift in our conception of government. Whereas the founding generation had seen government as a necessary evil, to be guarded against at every turn, modern thinkers saw government as an engine of good, an instrument through which to solve all manner of "social" problems, the kinds of problems that had arisen with industrialization and urbanization following the Civil War. Looming before the moderns, however, was the Constitution, standing starkly athwart their agenda. And the courts, for the most part, were upholding the Constitution, nowhere more clearly than in the famous *Lochner* decision of 1905,[23] in which the Supreme Court held New York State's maximum hours statute for bakers to be unconstitutional because it violated the freedom of contract.

Things came to a head during the New Deal when the activism shifted from the state to the federal level. Watching one program after another go down in constitutional flames, Roosevelt in 1937 threatened to pack the Supreme Court with six new members.[24] Not even Congress would go along with that. Nevertheless, a cowed Court got the message. There followed the famous "switch in time that saved nine," with the Court essentially rewriting the Constitution.

Rewriting the Constitution

The Court did its rewrite in two main steps. In 1937 it effectively eviscerated the doctrine of enumerated powers. Then in 1938 it bifurcated the Bill of Rights, creating a two-tiered theory of judicial review in the process. The 1937 rewrite involved the General Welfare and Commerce Clauses, both of which were meant to be shields against overweening government. When the Court was through they had become swords for promoting government. The 1938 changes effectively removed the Court from reviewing most of the programs that followed from the 1937 changes.

Madison spoke and wrote often about the General Welfare Clause because it was a source of congressional mischief from the start. Indeed, Hamilton was of the view that the clause granted Congress an independent power to spend for the general welfare, provided only that the spending was general and not particular or local.[25] That was not the dominant view, however. In fact, Madison, Jefferson, and many others were at pains to point out that if that reading were correct, then enumerating Congress's other powers would have been pointless, since anytime Congress wanted to do something it was not authorized to do it could say simply that it was spending for the general welfare. Given the prominence of the doctrine of enumerated powers in the minds of the Framers—indeed, many thought it obviated the need for a bill of rights[26]—it is difficult to believe that many Framers thought they were giving Congress so unbounded a power—much less that ratification would have succeeded under such an understanding.

Here, for example, is Madison on the point, writing to Edmund Pendleton in 1792: "If Congress can do whatever in their *discretion* can be *done by money*, and will promote the *general welfare*, the Government is no longer a limited one possessing enumerated powers, but an indefinite one subject to particular exceptions."[27] And in his *Report of 1800* Madison wrote:

> Money cannot be applied to the General Welfare, otherwise than by an application of it to some *particular* measure conducive to the General Welfare. Whenever, therefore, money has been raised by the general Authority, and is to be applied to a particular measure, a question arises whether the particular measure be within the enumerated authorities vested in Congress. If it be, the money requisite for it may be applied to it; if it be not, no such application can be made.[28]

Far from being an independent grant of power, therefore, the General Welfare Clause, if anything, limited Congress's spending *on enumerated ends or powers* to those that served the *general* welfare as opposed to any particular or sectional welfare.[29]

In the *Butler* decision of 1936,[30] however, the Court came down, albeit in dicta, on Hamilton's side. Then a year later, in the *Helvering* decision,[31] the Court elevated its dicta to the holding of the case. With Congress now free to spend for "the general welfare," it was only a matter of time before the modern redistributive state emerged, with Congress spending on all manner of programs not remotely authorized by the Constitution.

A similar fate awaited the Commerce Clause. As the history surrounding the adoption of that clause makes clear, Congress was given power to regulate commerce among the states as a defense against the kinds of protectionist measures that had arisen in the states under the Articles of Confederation, measures that were leading to a breakdown in interstate commerce. In fact, it was to address that problem, in significant part, that a new constitution was called for. Under it, Congress would be given the power to "regulate" interstate commerce—to make it "regular." The idea was to ensure an open, national market, to ensure that goods and services would flow freely among the states. It was not to enable Congress to regulate anything it wanted for any purpose it wanted.

In his 1817 message to Congress vetoing the Bonus bill, among other places, we find Madison's view of the scope of the commerce power.

> "The power to regulate commerce among the several States" can not include a power to construct roads and canals, and to improve the navigation of water courses in order to facilitate, promote, and secure such a commerce without a latitude of construction departing from the ordinary import of the terms strengthened by the known inconveniences which doubtless led to the grant of this remedial power to Congress.[32]

It was that "remedial power" that the Court invoked in 1824 in its first great Commerce Clause case, *Gibbons v. Ogden*.[33] In that decision the Court found that a New York statute granting a monopoly to ferry the waters between New York and New Jersey conflicted with the power of Congress to regulate the trade, which it had already done by statute. In his concurrence, Justice Johnson stated the larger matter plainly: "If there was any one object riding over every other in the adoption of the constitution, it was to keep the commercial intercourse among the States free from all invidious and partial restraints."[34] Thus, the function of the Commerce Clause.

In its *Jones & Laughlin* decision of 1937,[35] however, the Court found that Congress had power under the Commerce Clause to regulate anything that "affected" interstate commerce, and for any reason. Plainly, there is virtually nothing that does not, at some level, affect interstate commerce, which means that Congress today can regulate anything and everything. Over the years, it has moved far in that direction, giving us the modern regulatory state in the process.

But the Court was not through rewriting the Constitution, for the Bill of Rights was still standing. After 1937, claims that Congress was acting beyond its authority were rendered, in effect, without merit. One could still invoke one's rights, however. To address that impediment to expansive government, the Court in 1938, in the notorious *Carolene Products* decision,[36] bifurcated the Bill of Rights, distinguishing two kinds of rights and two levels of judicial review. If a law implicated "fundamental" rights like the right to vote or speak, the Court would give it "strict scrutiny" and probably find it unconstitutional. By contrast, if a law implicated "nonfundamental" rights like those of property or contract—rights pertaining to "ordinary commercial transactions"—the Court would give it minimal scrutiny, meaning it would probably pass constitutional muster. That scheme was nowhere to be found in the Constitution, of course. It was written from whole cloth to make the world safe for the programs of the New Deal. In effect, the Constitution was democratized. A constitution for limited government was converted, to a significant degree, into one for parliamentary majoritarianism.

The Future of Limited Government

After some 65 years of this, we should hardly be surprised that many Americans think of the Constitution as having instituted a majoritarian democracy, not a limited republic. Indeed, they will be forgiven, after listening to the Castro-length State of the Union addresses that came from our last administration, for thinking that there is no problem too trivial or too personal for federal attention. But that view afflicts both major parties and both political branches, state and local officials, and many of our judges. In a word, government has become a service industry, striving to satisfy the demands of its customers.

It is instructive, in this connection, to cite remarks Madison gave in 1792 in opposition to a bill aimed at encouraging cod fisheries. In defense of the doctrine of enumerated powers, Madison rose on the floor of the House to say:

> There are consequences, sir, still more extensive. . . . If Congress can apply money indefinitely to the general welfare, and are the sole and supreme judges of the general welfare,

they may take the care of religion into their own hands; they may establish teachers in every state, county, and parish, and pay them out of the public treasury; they may take into their own hands the education of children, establishing in like manner schools throughout the union; they may assume the provision for the poor; they may undertake the regulation of all roads other than post roads; in short, every thing, from the highest object of state legislation, down to the most minute object of police, would be thrown under the power of Congress; for every object I have mentioned would admit the application of money, and might be called, if Congress pleased, provisions for the general welfare.[37]

How prescient.

In 1995 the Supreme Court heard a case coming out of Texas that challenged the constitutionality of the Gun-Free School Zones Act of 1990 on the by-then novel theory that Congress had no authority to enact such a statute.[38] Conventional wisdom was puzzled that such a claim would be made. More surprising still, the claim had been upheld below. The smart money said, therefore, that the Supreme Court took the case so that it could reverse the mistake of the court below—nine to nothing, it was predicted. Well, as is often the case, conventional wisdom was wrong. By a vote of five to four the Court upheld the court below. The Commerce Clause, the Court said, does not authorize Congress to regulate anything and everything. More important still, Chief Justice William Rehnquist began his opinion with a ringing statement: "We start with first principles. The Constitution establishes a government of enumerated powers."[39] For nearly 60 years, no such statement had come from the Court. Official Washington was awakened from its dogmatic slumbers.[40]

The Court's opinion in the case was a breath of fresh air, but it went only so far, as Justice Clarence Thomas made clear in his concurring opinion. Still, it was a start, and it has been followed by a number of other such opinions, all pointing to something of a revival of Madison's doctrine of enumerated powers. That the Court has circumscribed its opinions should probably not surprise us. After all, were it to give us a true reading of the General Welfare and Commerce Clauses, the whole edifice of the modern welfare state, in all its illegitimacy, would come tumbling down, and the country is not ready for that.

We come, then, to the future of limited government, about which one can only speculate. That our present arrangements are constitutionally illegitimate is increasingly said by critics of those arrangements.[41] But proponents, too, have often said as much.[42] If constitutional legitimacy is important—and it should be in a nation purporting to be governed by the rule of law—then we have essentially two choices. We can either amend the Constitution so that it authorizes all the government we now have. Or we can carefully roll back those programs and policies that Mr. Madison's Constitution, as amended, does not authorize. Those of us who cherish the right to be free, the right to plan and live our own lives, will prefer the latter course, to be sure. If that course is to be pursued, however, it cannot be done through the courts alone. In addition, it will be necessary to rekindle among the people that love of liberty that so animated and inspired the founding generation, especially Mr. Madison. Perhaps this volume will begin that process.

Notes

1. I have discussed the issues that follow more fully in Roger Pilon, "The Purpose and Limits of Government," ch. 2 in *Limiting Leviathan*, Donald P. Racheter and Richard E. Wagner, ed. (Cheltenham, U.K. and Northampton, Mass.: Edward Elgar Publishing, Inc., 1999); reprinted as *Cato's Letter No. 13* (Washington: Cato Institute, 1999).

2. John Locke, "Second Treatise of Government," in *Two Treatises of Government*, Peter Laslett, ed. (New York: Mentor, 1965).

3. "The notion that the common law embodied right reason furnished from the fourteenth century its chief claim to be regarded as higher law," Edward S. Corwin, *The "Higher Law" Background of American Constitutional Law* (Ithaca and London: Cornell University Press, 1955), p. 26. Not all of the common law could be justified, of course. In fact, Madison took a somewhat jaundiced view of parts of it and was concerned in particular that it not be frozen by being constitutionalized: "If it be understood that the common law is established by the constitution, it follows that no part of the law can be altered by the legislature ... and the whole code with all its incongruities, barbarisms, and bloody maxims would be inviolably saddled on the good people of the United States." James Madison, *The Report of 1800*, Jan. 7, 1800, cited in *James Madison's "Advice to My Country,"* David B. Mattern, ed. (Charlottesville and London: University Press of Virginia, 1997), pp. 21–22.

4. In the tradition of Enlightenment state-of-nature theory, one starts one's argument with the individual, not with government, asking first what rights individuals have against each other. That helps avoid begging any questions about the rights or powers of government, which must be derived from the rights individuals first have and hence have to yield up to government when they create that institution through a constitution. See, for example, Robert Nozick, *Anarchy, State, and Utopia* (New York: Basic Books, 1974), p. 6.

5. See Carl L. Becker, *The Declaration of Independence: A Study in the History of Political Ideas* (New York: Vintage, 1958); Bernard Bailyn, *The Ideological Origins of the American Revolution* (Cambridge, Mass.: Belknap, 1967); Morton White, *The Philosophy of the American Revolution* (Oxford, Oxford University Press, 1978).

6. "Lives, Liberties and Estates, which I call by the general Name, *Property.*" Locke, ibid., para. 123 (*original* emphasis).

7. I have developed the theory of rights more fully in Roger Pilon, *A Theory of Rights: Toward Limited Government* (Chicago: unpublished Ph.D. dissertation, University of Chicago, 1979).

8. For some of the justificatory problems of majoritarian democracy, see Robert Paul Wolff, *In Defense of Anarchism* (New York: Harper & Row, 1970); Roger Pilon, "On the First Principles of Constitutionalism: Liberty, Then Democracy," *The American University Journal of International Law and Policy,* vol. 8 (1992–93), p. 531.

9. James Madison, Speech in Congress, Apr. 9, 1789, cited in *Advice*, note 3, p. 21.

10. James Madison, *Report of 1800*, in *The Papers of James Madison*, vol. 17, David B. Mattern et al., ed. (Charlottesville and London: University Press of Virginia, 1977), p. 308.

11. 4 *Annals of Congress* 179 (1794).

12. James Madison, *Veto Message*, March 3, 1817, cited in *The Mind of the Founder*, Marvin Meyers, ed. (Hanover and London: University Press of New England, 1981), p. 308.

13. Ibid.

14. I have discussed the issues that follow more fully in Roger Pilon, "Freedom, Responsibility, and the Constitution: On Recovering Our Founding Principles," *Notre Dame Law Review*, vol. 68 (1993), p. 507.

15. See *Industrial and Commercial Correspondence of Alexander Hamilton*, Arthur Harrison Cole, ed. (Chicago: A. W. Shaw Company, 1968).

16. I do not mean to overstate the restraint that prevailed for our first 150 years, for that period did witness genuine inroads on the doctrine of enumerated powers. In comparison to what followed from the New Deal, however, those inroads were limited and did not amount to anything like the fundamental rewriting of the Constitution that occurred in 1937–38. For an excellent discussion of those inroads, published in 1932, see Charles Warren, *Congress as Santa Claus* (Charlottesville: The Mitchie Company, 1932).

17. 18 *Congressional Record* 1875 (1887).

18. Thus, Jeremy Bentham, the father of British utilitarianism, wrote in 1791 that talk of natural rights was "simple nonsense: natural imprescriptible rights, rhetorical nonsense,—nonsense upon stilts." "Anarchical Fallacies," in *Works of Jeremy Bentham*, vol. 2, Richard Doyne, ed. (Edinburgh: W. Tait, 1843), p. 501.

19. For pragmatism in law, see Robert S. Summers, "Pragmatic Instrumentalism: America's Leading Theory of Law," *Cornell Law Forum*, vol. 5 (1978): 15.

20. *Encyclopedia of Social Reform*, p. 270, William D. P. Bliss, ed. (New York: Funk and Wagnalls Company, 1897), p. 15.

21. Owen R. Lovejoy, "The Faith of the Social Worker," vol. 44 *Survey*, p. 209, May 8, 1920.

22. Frank Dekker Watson, *The Charity Organization Movement in the United States: A Study in American Philanthropy* (New York: Macmillan Company, 1922), p. 332.

23. *Lochner v. New York*, 198 U.S. 45 (1905).

24. See Merlo J. Pusey, *The Supreme Court Crisis of 1937* (New York: DaCapo Press, 1973).

25. See Hamilton's *Report*, ibid., note 15, p. 293: "It is, therefore, of necessity, left to the discretion of the National Legislature to pronounce upon the objects which concern the general welfare, and for which, under the description, an appropriation of money is requisite and proper. And there seems to be no room for doubt, that whatever concerns the general interests of learning, of agriculture, of manufactures, and of commerce, are within the sphere of the national councils, as far as regards an application of money. The only qualification of the generality of the phrase in question, which seems to be admissible, is this: That the object, to which an appropriation of money is to be made, be general, and not local; its operation extending, in fact, or by possibility throughout the Union, and not being confined to a particular spot."

26. In fact, Hamilton himself made that point in *Federalist* No. 84: "Why declare that things shall not be done which there is no power to do? Why, for instance, should it be said that the liberty of the press shall not be restrained, when no power is given by which restrictions may be imposed?"

27. James Madison, "Letter to Edmund Pendleton," Jan. 21, 1792, in *The Papers of James Madison*, vol. 14, Robert A. Rutland et al., ed. (Charlottesville: University Press of Virginia, 1984) (original emphasis).

28. James Madison, *Report of 1800*, in *The Papers of James Madison*, vol. 17 (Charlottesville and London), p. 315 (original emphasis).

29. See Hamilton's comments, Note 25 above.

30. *United States v. Butler*, 297 U.S. 1, 65–66 (1936).

31. *Helvering v. Davis*, 301 U.S. 619, 640 (1937).

32. James Madison, *Veto Message*, Note 12 above, p. 308.

33. 22 U.S. 1 (1824).

34. 22 U.S. 1, 231 (1824).

35. *NLRB v. Jones & Laughlin Steel Corp.*, 301 U.S. 1 (1937).

36. *United States v. Carolene Products*, 304 U.S. 144 (1938). For a devastating critique of the case, and the facts behind it, see Geoffrey P. Miller, "The True Story of Carolene Products," 1987 *Supreme Court Review*, p. 397.

37. James Madison, "Bounty Payments on Cod Fisheries," February 6, 1792, in *The Papers of James Madison*, 14.

38. *United States v. Lopez*, 514 U.S. 549 (1995).

39. Ibid., at 552.

40. See Roger Pilon, "It's Not about Guns," *Washington Post*, May 21, 1995, p. C5.

41. See, for example, Gary Lawson, "The Rise and Rise of the Administrative State," *Harvard Law Review* 107 (1994): 1231. "The post-New Deal administrative state is unconstitutional, and its validation by the legal system amounts to nothing less than a bloodless constitutional revolution"; Richard A. Epstein, "The Proper Scope of the Commerce Power," *Virginia Law Review* 73 (1987): 1388. "I think that the expansive construction of the [commerce] clause accepted by the New Deal Supreme Court is wrong, and clearly so. . . ."

42. See, for example, Laurence H. Tribe, *American Constitutional Law* (New York: Foundation Press, 2000), p. 816: "The Court's application of its substantial effect and aggregation principles in the period between 1937 and 1995, combined with its deference to congressional findings, placed it in the increasingly untenable position of claiming the power to strike down invocations of the Commerce Clause, while at the same time applying a set of doctrines that made it virtually impossible actually

to exercise this power." The tortured "principles" and "doctrines" the Court has invented over the past 60 some years to try to square the circle were all but predicted by one of the principal architects of the New Deal, Rexford G. Tugwell, offering his reflections some 30 years after the tortured reasoning first took place: "To the extent that these [New Deal policies] developed, they were tortured interpretations of a document intended to prevent them." Clearly, they knew what they were doing. "Rewriting the Constitution: A Center Report," *Center Magazine*, March 1968, p. 18.

4. The Novelty of James Madison's Constitutionalism

Joyce Lee Malcolm

On May 4, 1789, barely a month after the first session of the First Congress began work, James Madison called upon his colleagues to amend the untried new constitution. He was fulfilling a campaign pledge to add a bill of rights, but one that bespoke a genuine philosophical conversion. He had gradually come to agree with Thomas Jefferson that a bill of rights was, as Jefferson put it, what "the people are entitled to against every government on earth . . . and what no just government should refuse, or rest on inference."[1]

Four months later, as the final draft of that list of rights neared completion, their weary patron wrote Edmund Pendleton: "The difficulty of uniting the minds of men accustomed to think and act differently can only be conceived by those who have witnessed it."[2] Madison had witnessed it and his success in negotiating the process is the key to his greatness. Madison was, to use a seeming oxymoron, a realistic visionary, a quality refined through arduous experience.

When it came to uniting the minds of men on the broad issues Madison was a master. He had succeeded brilliantly in Philadelphia in 1787 and again in that first session of Congress. On both occasions he got what he wanted, a strong federal government and an assertion of essential liberties without debilitating amendments. But it is important to remind ourselves that to accomplish his chief goals, he was forced to yield time after time, often on significant points. Both the Constitution, of which he has been dubbed the father, and the Bill of Rights, which he clearly fathered, differed from his original proposals, the former quite markedly. His was a triumph of tenacity, political energy, and a readiness to continue even when his proposals were defeated. When certain his colleagues were misguided, Madison never retreated from first principles.

Although Madison's constitutional legacy does not include the Constitution in all its particulars, there is a unique Madisonian constitutional legacy. As an historian of English political and legal thought I have an unusual vantage point from which to assess this contribution, one perhaps more akin to that of Madison's contemporaries than to that of most modern Americans. And so with 18th-century Anglo-American eyes, peering through 21st-century glasses, I hope to add a somewhat different perspective to our consideration of this most persistent, patient, and ultimately successful architect of our government.

The Legacy of the English Constitution

Students of American government have tended to downplay the legacy the English constitution bequeathed to the American Framers. Yet in its essence and in numerous, more specific ways the new American government took its spirit, basic form, and system of checks from the mother country. To understand the original aspects of the Madisonian legacy it is necessary to acknowledge what was not original. Patrick Henry can help us here. With typical rhetorical flourish, he reminded the Virginia ratifying convention of their debt to England:

> We are descended from a people whose government was founded on liberty: our glorious forefathers of Great Britain made liberty the foundation of every thing. That country is become a great, mighty, and splendid nation; not because their government is strong and energetic, but, sir, because liberty is its direct end and foundation. We drew the spirit of liberty from our British ancestors.[3]

Indeed, he found the British system more sound in important respects than the proposed constitution:

> In the British government there are real balances and checks: in this system there are only ideal balances. . . . The President and senators have nothing to lose. They have not that interest in the preservation of the government that the king and lords have in England. They will, therefore, be regardless of the interests of the people. . . . when the commons of England, in the manly language which became freemen, said to their king, *You are our servant*, then the temple of liberty was complete. . . . And I am free to own that, if you cannot love

a republican government, you may love the British monarchy; for, although the king is not sufficiently responsible, the responsibility of his agents, and the efficient checks interposed by the British Constitution, render it less dangerous than other monarchies, or oppressive tyrannical aristocracies.[4]

Henry's praise of the English government can serve to highlight four important departures of Madison's constitutionalism from English political ideology:

- Madison espoused a made-to-measure government rather than the English fidelity to an ancient foundation;
- Madison endorsed a republic as opposed to a limited monarchy;
- Madison wanted a sharper division of powers within the central government;
- Madison placed sovereignty in the people rather than their representatives in Parliament.

I should like to consider each of these in turn.

A Willingness to Innovate

Today "right thinking" people bless innovation in almost any sphere and belittle a preference for the status quo, let alone the past. Yet, the English constitution and common law are rooted in tradition, and proudly so. Political innovations in England were couched in terms of a return to the good old ways, to ancient intent, to nature and reason, to true law. The drafters of the English Bill of Rights of 1689, meeting after James II had fled the realm, insisted King James was the innovator, and that in promulgating a list of thirteen rights they were merely "Vindicating and Asserting their auntient Rights and Liberties" as "their Auncestors in like Case have usually done."[5]

They were taken at their word. Nearly 200 years later the famed British historian Thomas Macaulay rejoiced that "not a single flower of the crown was touched. Not a single new right was given to the people. The whole English law, substantive and adjective, was, in the judgment of all the greatest lawyers . . . almost exactly the same after the Revolution as before it."[6] Macaulay conceded that some controverted points had been decided, albeit "according to the sense of the best jurists," and that there had been "a slight deviation from the ordinary course of succession," but concluded, "This was all:

and this was enough."[7] We now know that nine of the thirteen articles in the Bill of Rights were not "ancient and indubitable."[8]

Why had the Convention Parliament been so anxious to be seen as preservers, not innovators? First, popular opinion held that "all innovation in government is dangerous, for seldom comes a better." More crucially, for practical political reasons Englishmen clung doggedly to the belief that their great rights and their limited government were no one's gift, not King John's at Runnymede, nor any other king's, but had existed "time out of mind."[9] They passionately affirmed an ancient foundation for such limitations on the Crown as regular meetings of Parliament, orderly legal procedures, and an independent judiciary. After all, what a king gave a king could take away, but liberties that no one knew the origin of, that seemed part of nature were, in the language of the American Framers, inalienable. Thus, ancient practice trumped novelty. When government officials became too powerful or kings attempted to intrude upon individual liberties they were wicked innovators, trampling upon the good old ways. And, in fact, the theory of divine-right monarchy and the emergence of absolute rulers *were* novelties of the 17th century.

In contrast to his English predecessors, Madison was ready to innovate. Before preparing a draft plan of government for the Constitutional Convention Madison conducted what he referred to as "researches into the History of the most distinguished Confederacies, particularly those of antiquity."[10] He then set out to devise a system suitable to America's vast geography and 13 separate states. He explained his new design to Washington: "Conceiving that an individual independence of the States is utterly irreconcilable with their aggregate sovereignty; and that a consolidation of the whole into one simple republic would be as inexpedient as it is unattainable, I have sought for some middle ground, which may at once support a due supremacy of the national authority, and not exclude the local authorities wherever they can be subordinately useful."[11] His system, he admitted, was intended to "operate in many essential points without the intervention of the State legislatures" and to give the central government "a negative *in all cases whatsoever* on the legislative acts of the States, as heretofore exercised by the Kingly prerogative."[12] This federalist concept with its tilt toward strong, but limited, central government was Madison's boldest innovation, but one he thought would be compelling. "I am ready to believe," he hastened to assure Washington before the Convention, "that such a change would not be attended with much difficulty."[13]

Perhaps Madison's confidence convinced him to take notes of the proceedings of the Constitutional Convention so later generations could satisfy their curiosity about what he described as "the objects, the opinions, & the reasonings from which the new System of Govt was to receive its peculiar structure & organization."[14] In his notes Madison tells us he was even at pains to include "a compromise on some middle ground, by mutual concessions."[15]

To James Madison government was an object of study, not an ancient blueprint perfected over centuries by numberless generations. He believed a new government designed to cope with a unique situation could best be fashioned through deep research into earlier forms, systematic thought about the advantages and disadvantages of each type of confederation, and the study of political theory. As a man of practical affairs, honed by his frustrations as a member of the Continental Congress, he also appreciated that however elegant the resulting scheme for a new government might be, it still needed to be thrashed out by men of various opinions and talents. This he felt could be accomplished. Madison's constitutionalism embodied a rational, scholarly approach to the design of government. If it was backward looking, it was only to learn from the past, not to perpetuate or restore it.

A New Kind of Republic

Madison departed from the English constitutional legacy by emphasizing particular aspects of the concepts of "republic" and "democracy." In the 18th century a republic was defined as "a state in which power rests on the people and their elected representatives or officers as opposed to one governed by a king or similar ruler; a commonwealth."[16] To the English of Madison's time it was the last part of that definition that mattered: a republic was a country without a king. After all, the first part of the definition of a republic, "a country in which power rests with the people and their elected representatives," actually applied to Great Britain. Power rested on the people and their elected representatives in Parliament, where everyone in the realm was theoretically present in person or by proxy. No statute could be passed, no tax levied, without Parliament's approval.

England's only experience with a republic, a kingless government, followed the execution of Charles I in 1649 and the abolition of monarchy. But the republican regimes of the Rump Parliament and of Oliver Cromwell were both deeply unpopular. During those 11 years the people were never represented at all because no interregnum government dared submit to a general election.

By contrast, the traditional English constitution, with its balance of the one, the few, the many—monarchy, aristocracy, and democracy—arguably represented the population of the realm. Thus Patrick Henry could boast that the "temple of liberty was complete" when "the commons of England, in the manly language which became freemen, said to their king, *You are our servant.*" He could assure his colleagues, "if you cannot love a republican government, you may love the British monarchy."[17] Englishmen believed a republic was simply a government without a king. Power in England already rested with the representatives of the people.

Madison chose not to dwell on the distinction between a monarchy of whatever sort and a republic. Instead he focused on a distinction between a direct democracy and a representative one.[18] In *The Federalist* No. 10 Madison argued that a republic was a government in which "a small number of citizens" was "elected by the rest," thus excluding a direct democracy.[19] Stressing the obvious, Madison explained that his republic could embrace a "greater number of citizens and extent of territory" than a direct democracy. He also denied that Holland, Venice, and Poland, all commonly designated as republics in his time, deserved that label.[20] Not only is Madison's emphasis contrary to the then existing notion of a republic, it is contrary to our present definition.

Nor is that all. Madison's discussion of a republic in *The Federalist* No. 10 also gives a peculiar twist to what his contemporaries understood as "democracy" and what we understand by it. Democracy was, and still is, usually defined as "Government by the people; that form of government in which the sovereign power resides in the people as a whole, and is exercised either directly by them . . . or by officers elected by them." Democracy embraces both direct and indirect representation. Madison dismissed direct democracy as imprudent and treated representative democracy as alone worthy of consideration.

The question is why in *Federalist* No. 10 Madison insisted upon idiosyncratic definitions of both "republic" and "democracy," the two terms most basic to our understanding of American government. His motive seems to have been tactical. Democracy had a bad reputation. Its dangers had been rehearsed ad nauseam by generations of political theorists. Madison himself wrote that pure democracies "have ever been spectacles of turbulence and contention; have ever been found incompatible with personal security, or the rights of property; and have in general been as short in their lives, as they have been violent in their deaths."[21] History was a witness to the truth of that comment. As for republics, all known and successful republics were small countries, even smaller than some American states. Unabashed innovator though he was, Madison knew the experiment of using a republican form to govern a large territory was unique and likely to excite vehement opposition, especially since the great Montesquieu himself had insisted a republican form was suitable only for small territories, preferably mountainous ones or islands like England. So Madison refined both concepts—democracy and republic—to deflect fears about the unprecedented experiment of governing a large country with a republican form and to persuade his colleagues and the American people to turn their back on Montesquieu and embark on a great republican experiment.

The Division of Powers

Madison was prepared to follow Montesquieu, and the English constitution, however, in dividing powers within the central government. Still Patrick Henry preferred the English system which, he argued, had "real balances and checks" while the proposed America Constitution had "only ideal balances."[22] According to English political theorists the English king and House of Lords had a genuine and permanent interest in the preservation of the kingdom. The king's power depended upon the prosperity of the realm, and as an heir and a father he would feel duty-bound to preserve the prerogatives of his office. The lords were large landowners with a stake in the general welfare. Unlike the French nobility, they were subject to taxation and the common law. They saw themselves as holding the balance between the king and the people. Both king and lords, therefore, had an interest beyond a short-lived political career. By contrast, Henry argued that the new president and senators had nothing to lose, for Madison's divisions within the government relied solely upon technical checks and balances that came from shared or distinct functions.

Although many of Madison's checks did copy English forms, some of his original proposals—that the upper house would be chosen by the lower house from candidates picked by the states and that the Congress would choose the president—were rejected by the Convention.[23] And where the three branches of the English government sat together in Parliament, Madison, following Montesquieu, called for greater separation. The president had to approve statutes but never sat in Congress—nor did the federal justices.[24] By contrast the lords themselves were the highest court of appeal in England, while the entire Parliament was, and still is, considered Britain's highest court.

The Sovereign People

Lastly, Madison's determination that sovereignty must reside with the people, not the legislature, provides a distinction between the governments of England and America which has driven the two constitutions in starkly different directions. In the 18th century this was, to a greater extent than is usually appreciated, a distinction without a difference. It is true that by the time Madison was at work, sovereignty in England had come to reside in the Parliament where king and kingdom, lords and commoners, as well as all branches of government were represented. Yet, in practice, both the English and American constitutions placed ultimate power in the hands of the people's representatives. Both relied upon the rule of law to limit government and protect rights, and upon elections and checks and balances within central government to prevent any group or branch of government from becoming tyrannical. Ten years before the American Revolution William Blackstone boasted that "all parts" of the English constitution:

> form a mutual check upon each other. In the legislature, the people are a check upon the nobility, and the nobility a check upon the people; . . . while the king is a check upon both, which preserves the executive power from encroachments. And this very executive power is again checked, and kept within due bounds by the two houses. . . . Like three distinct powers in mechanics, they jointly impel the machine of government in a direction different from what either, enacting by themselves, would have done; but at the same time in a

direction partaking of each, and formed out of all; a direction
which constitutes the true line of the liberty and happiness
of the community.[25]

Yet these internal checks do not check the Parliament as a whole,
because Parliament represents the whole.

Americans of Madison's generation were convinced Parliament
had too much power. In the early 17th century when Sir Edward
Coke argued that Parliament "cannot be confined, either for causes
or persons, within any bounds," actual parliamentary sovereignty
was a long way off.[26] With their eyes on royal pretensions Coke's
generation believed rights were safer with Parliament. But parliamentary sovereignty was no longer a dream in 1765, when Blackstone wrote that Parliament could "change and create afresh even
the constitution of the kingdom and of parliaments themselves."
Parliament could, in his famous phrase, "do every thing that is not
naturally impossible."[27] As a great champion of rights Blackstone
seemed worried that what a parliament could do "no authority
upon earth can undo," and quoted the warnings of a 16th-century
statesman, a 17th-century jurist, and an 18th-century philosopher.
He cited Elizabeth I's great minister, Lord Burleigh, that "England
could never be ruined but by a parliament," and Sir Matthew Hale's
fear that since Parliament was the kingdom's highest court, "if by
any means a misgovernment should any way fall upon it, the subjects
of this kingdom are left without all manner of remedy." Blackstone
added Montesquieu's dark prophesy that "the constitution of
England will in time lose it's [sic] liberty, will perish . . . whenever the
legislative power shall become more corrupt than the executive."[28]

To prevent the tyranny of a branch of government, and the tyranny
of majorities, Madison and his colleagues placed ultimate power in
the people, not the Congress. But that made little practical difference
in the absence of institutional arrangements and favorable circumstances. Those Madison felt he had. The very size of the United
States and its diversity of interests would, he believed, protect minorities, and the federal system would diffuse power. Still he saw a
need for some central power to impose limits on the states. "Without
the royal negative or some equivalent control," he wrote Jefferson,
"the unity of the system would be destroyed. The want of some
such provision seems to have been mortal to the ancient Confederacies, and to be the disease of the Modern."[29] His solution was for

Congress and the central republic to play the role of the King of England with veto power over state laws.[30] Based on personal experience, he worried more about the states infringing upon the federal government than vice versa. To protect the Constitution itself Madison proposed a "council of revision" comprised of the national executive and "a convenient number of the National Judiciary" with authority to veto any act of Congress or of a state legislature. Congress was to have the final word, however. Madison would have enabled Congress to overrule the council by passing a vetoed act again, or again vetoing a state act.[31]

Madison's Convention colleagues endorsed his goals but disliked his means. They made the Constitution and federal laws the supreme law of the land, delimited spheres of power, and specified acts the states could not perform.[32] The delegates seemed less fearful of the power of the states than Madison was.

Contrary to Madison's wishes, they gave the states substantial power in, and over, the central government, with equal representation in the Senate, power to select senators, and the major role in the Electoral College. At the end of the Convention Madison wrote in dismay to Jefferson of the changes he had dutifully recorded but deeply regretted.[33] American sovereignty resided in the people but the strategies meant to keep it there were not Madison's.

Popular sovereignty per se has not protected American liberties. They have been guarded instead by the decision to make the Constitution the supreme law of the land and, following that, John Marshall's conviction that this must mean the federal courts could veto both state and federal acts that contravened that document. This was not Madison's scheme of Congress vetoing federal and state laws.

Indeed Madison had grave doubts about judicial review. While he acknowledged that "[A] law violating a constitution established by the people themselves, would be considered by the Judges as null and void," he felt judicial review was contrary to the principle of majority rule and "makes the Judiciary Department paramount in importance to the Legislature, which was never intended and can never be proper."[34] Alexander Hamilton, by contrast, argued in *Federalist* No. 78 that the Constitution could limit the power of government "in no other way than through the medium of the courts of justice; whose duty it must be to declare all acts contrary to the manifest tenor of the constitution void."[35] "Without this," he added, "all the reservations of particular rights or privileges would amount to nothing."

In 1803 John Marshall found "The question whether an act repugnant to the constitution can become the law of the land deeply interesting to the United States."[36] In his landmark opinion, *Marbury v. Madison*, Marshall wrote:

> The distinction between a government of limited and unlimited powers is abolished if those limits do not confine the persons on whom they are imposed and if acts prohibited and acts allowed are of equal obligation. It is a proposition too plain to be contested, that the constitution controls any act repugnant to it; or, that the legislature may alter the constitution by an ordinary act. Between these alternatives there is no middle ground.
>
> Certainly all those who have framed written constitutions contemplate them as forming the fundamental and paramount law of the land, and consequently the theory of every such government must be that an act of the legislature repugnant to the constitution is void.[37]

Madison was disturbed by Marshall's opinion.[38] As president he vetoed bills he felt were unconstitutional to avoid giving Marshall an opportunity to entrench judicial review. He would be chagrined by the power of today's federal courts. He would have trusted Congress more completely, and probably been disappointed.

Madison's original design for the federal government, with the upper house selected by the lower house and the president chosen by the two, would have resembled the modern English parliament in concentrating power in the lower house. That power has provided the leader of the majority party in the English parliament virtual carte blanche. Lacking judicial review, and notwithstanding regular elections, the 20th-century parliament has time after time altered the traditional constitution and infringed ancient rights "by an ordinary act."[39]

Through a simple majority vote in 1911 the House of Commons curbed the powers of the hereditary House of Lords. In 2000 it abolished the hereditary lords entirely. The English courts have failed to intervene to protect the constitution or individual rights. In 1913 an English court felt it necessary to affirm that the English Bill of Rights "still remains unrepealed, no practice or custom, however prolonged, or however acquiesced in on the part of the subject, can be relied on by the Crown as justifying any infringement of its provisions."[40]

As Sir Matthew Hale foresaw three centuries ago, with Parliament itself the kingdom's highest court, "if by any means a misgovernment should any way fall upon it, the subjects of this kingdom are left without all manner of remedy." There has been no remedy for the people of England when judges, headed by the Law Lords, see their task as merely enforcing statutes passed by the people's representatives in Parliament. A constitution that is the supreme law of the land and judicial review have kept American rights vigorous. Madison's uneasiness was justified, however. Judicial review has given the Supreme Court supreme power. But there seems no workable alternative if limited government is to prevail.

Conclusion

Although the American Constitution departs markedly from the original design of its "father," and the Bill of Rights he championed owes its vitality to judicial review, which he opposed, Madison still contributed greatly to American government and to limited government. In Jefferson's first Inaugural address the new president listed what he deemed the essential principles of the fledgling government, principles Madison's design had incorporated: a federal government which was "the sheet-anchor of our peace at home and safety abroad; a jealous care of the right of election by the people . . . ; absolute acquiescence in the decisions of the majority . . . the supremacy of the civil over the military authority" and key individual rights, principles Jefferson characterized as a "bright constellation."[41]

Madison's contribution to this "bright constellation" and to the future of limited government begins with his confidence that government can be crafted on republican principles for particular peoples and situations and that such a government can be made sufficiently vigorous to keep the peace yet sufficiently limited to ensure individual liberty. His daring federal and republican scheme united, but did not submerge, the independent states that formed it and managed to preserve the sovereignty of the people, despite a large population and extensive geography. The Madisonian balance between the federal government and that of the states has shifted further from the states than Madison probably intended, yet the fabric remains sound.

This tricky equilibrium between power and liberty, between states and central government, majorities and minorities is one modern entities such as the European Union would do well to study. The EU shares many of the problems that faced the newly independent American states but has been more concerned with creating a powerful government than in preserving either democracy or popular sovereignty.

Madison's conviction that a government representing multiple interests, separation of powers, and checks and balances would protect minorities has been less well-founded. The framework he helped establish is crucial, but it has taken a sensitive majority and courts committed to principles of equal justice to ensure its success. Within the federal government the power of the executive has needed constant monitoring to prevent it from upsetting the intended balance. However clever the original design, the preservation of limited government demands unceasing vigilance. Madison realized that.

At the end of the day this father of the Constitution and Bill of Rights did not place his trust wholly in parchment barriers. He understood that however well-planned it may be, a constitutional system ultimately depends for its success upon the people themselves. On June 20, 1788, as the Virginia Ratifying Convention debated the proposed constitution, Madison pleaded with its members to place their confidence in the people:

> I have observed, that gentlemen suppose, that the general legislature will do every mischief they possibly can, and that they will omit to do every thing good, which they are authorised to do. . . . I consider it reasonable to conclude, that they will as readily do their duty, as deviate from it: Nor do I go on the grounds mentioned by gentlemen on the other side—that we are to place unlimited confidence in them, and expect nothing but the most exalted integrity and sublime virtue. But I go on this great republican principle, that the people will have virtue and intelligence to select men of virtue and wisdom. Is there no virtue among us? If there be not, we are in a wretched situation. No theoretical checks—no form of government can render us secure.[42]

Forms can help, but Madison knew the ultimate security was a people committed to limited government and the rule of law.

A century before the American constitutional convention an English Convention Parliament was summoned to re-establish the kingdom's government in the wake of King James's flight. As he considered election to that body, one anonymous Englishman mused, "I . . . always cherisht some Cynical Notions, which made me very much slight and disregard the Honours and Flatulencies of a giddy World: But the thoughts of being one of the Great Planters of a Government which shall last for Ages, and perhaps till Time has run out its last Minutes, is no Ordinary thing."[43] Americans are fortunate that among the "Great Planters" of their government was a visionary young Virginian whose work, and the principles upon which it was founded, can, with vigilance, "last for Ages, and perhaps till Time has run out its last Minutes."

Notes

1. Michael Kammen, ed., *The Origins of the American Constitution: A Documentary History* (New York: Penguin, 1986), pp. 133–34.

2. Madison to Pendleton, 14 September 1789, in Helen Veit, Kenneth Bowling, Charlene Bickford, eds., *Creating the Bill of Rights: The Documentary Record from the First Federal Congress* (Baltimore: Johns Hopkins University Press, 1991), p. 296.

3. Jonathan Elliot, ed., *The Debates in the Several State Conventions on the Adoption of the Federal Constitution*, 5 vols. (Philadelphia: J. B. Lippincott, 1863), 3:53–4.

4. Ibid., pp. 165–6.

5. "The Bill of Rights, 1689" 1 Will. & Mar., Sess. 2, c. 2.

6. Thomas Macaulay, *The History of England from the Accession of James II*, 6 vols., ed. C.H. Firth (London: Ward, Lock & Co., 1913–1915), 3:1308–10.

7. Ibid., p. 1310.

8. See Lois G. Schwoerer, *The Declaration of Rights, 1689* (Baltimore: Johns Hopkins University Press, 1981); Joyce L. Malcolm, "The Creation of a 'True Antient and indubitable' Right: The English Bill of Rights and the Right to Be Armed," *Journal of British Studies* 32 (July 1993), 226–49.

9. For example Edward Coke in the Preface to his 8th Report writes: "I have positively affirmed out of record, that the grounds of our common laws at this day were beyond the memory or register of any beginning, and the same which the Norman conqueror then found within this realm of England." Sir Edward Coke, *The Reports of Sir Edward Coke, Knt.*, 6 vols. (London, 1826), 4:iv–v.

10. James Madison, *Notes of Debates in the Federal Convention of 1787 Reported by James Madison* (Athens, Ohio: Ohio University Press, 1966), Madison's Preface, p. 17.

11. Madison to Washington, 16 April 1787, Philip B. Kurland and Ralph Lerner, eds., *The Founders' Constitution*, 5 vols. (Chicago: University of Chicago Press, 1987), 1:250.

12. Ibid., emphasis in the original.

13. Ibid.

14. Madison, *Notes*, p. 17.

15. Ibid., p. 18.

16. See "republic" in *The Oxford English Dictionary* (Oxford: Oxford University Press, 1977).

17. Elliot, *Debates in the Several States,* 3:165–6.

18. See the discussion in Madison, *Notes,* p. xx. In *The Federalist* No. 30 Madison takes issue with the customary designation of Holland, Venice, and Poland as examples of republics.

19. See *The Federalist* No. 10 (James Madison).

20. *The Federalist* No. 39 (James Madison).

21. *The Federalist* No. 10 (James Madison).

22. Elliot, *Debates in the Several States,* pp. 165–6.

23. The Virginia Plan, 29 May 1787, *Founders' Constitution,* 1:251.

24. The English king did not normally sit in Parliament either, although he could, whenever he wished, preside in the House of Lords.

25. See William Blackstone, *Commentaries on the Laws of England,* 4 vols. (1st ed. 1765–1769; repr. Chicago: University of Chicago Press, 1979), 1:150–51. And see John Murrin, "The British and Colonial Background of American Constitutionalism" in *The Framing and Ratification of the Constitution,* ed. Leonard Levy and Dennis J. Mahoney (New York: Macmillan, 1987), pp. 34–35.

26. Blackstone, *Commentaries,* 1:156.

27. Ibid., 1:156.

28. Ibid., pp. 156–7.

29. Cited by Michael Zuckert, "A System without Precedent: Federalism in the American Constitution," in *The Framing and Ratification of the Constitution,* p. 145.

30. See Zuckert, p. 145. Also see pp. 146–48.

31. Virginia Plan, *Founders' Constitution,* 1:251.

32. Zuckert, p. 144.

33. Ibid., p. 148.

34. Bernard Schwartz, *A History of the Supreme Court* (Oxford: Oxford University Press, 1993), p. 12.

35. Ibid., p. 13.

36. John Marshall, *Marbury v. Madison* (1803).

37. Ibid. Madison was Secretary of State under President Jefferson at the time and was the defendant in this key case.

38. See Kermit Hall, ed., *The Oxford Companion to the Supreme Court of the United States* (Oxford: Oxford University Press, 1992), p. 517.

39. Parliament has limited the right to remain silent, the right to trial by jury, and effectively abolished the right of Englishmen "to have arms for their defence."

40. *Bowles v. Bank of England* (1913).

41. Thomas Jefferson, *First Inaugural Address* (1801), in *Messages and Papers of the Presidents, 1789–1897,* ed. James D. Richardson, 6 vols. (Washington: Published by authority of Congress, 1901), 1:322.

42. Madison, Virginia Ratifying Convention, 20 June 1788, *Founders Constitution,* 1:409–410.

43. A. B. and N. T., "Some Remarks upon Government . . .," (1688/89) in *The Struggle for Sovereignty: Seventeenth-Century English Political Tracts,* ed. Joyce Lee Malcolm, 2 vols. (Indianapolis: Liberty Press, 1999), 2:869.

5. The Madisonian Legacy: A Jeffersonian Perspective

Robert M. S. McDonald

Two stark realities complicate any attempt to formulate a "Jeffersonian" interpretation of James Madison's legacy. The first is that much of what we call Jeffersonian can with equal fairness be termed Madisonian. The second is that many of the most glittering facets of Madison's legacy—state and federal constitutionalism, the Bill of Rights, Virginia's Statute for Religious Freedom, the resistance to Federalist politics in the 1790s, and the Republican administration of government in the decades that followed—to lesser or greater degrees form part of Jefferson's legacy as well.

Together, in a collaboration that spanned half a century, the two Virginians shaped the substance of public life in the United States. From their joint service during the American Revolution in their home state's House of Delegates to their cooperative founding of the University of Virginia, Jefferson and Madison documented their remarkable partnership through a voluminous correspondence that Julian P. Boyd, founding editor of *The Papers of Thomas Jefferson*, described as "the most extended, the most elevated, the most significant exchange of letters between any two men in the whole sweep of American history."[1] It is not, however, the most exciting, for only rarely did Jefferson and Madison disagree. The few times they did are instructive.

The Earth Belongs to the Living

Their most striking differences were external. Jefferson was tall—nearly six-foot-three—while Madison stood five-foot-six. Jefferson dressed comfortably—some said sloppily—and gained renown during his presidency for the bedroom slippers in which he reportedly received foreign diplomats and the trademark red waistcoat so often the subject of Federalist lampoons. Madison, on the other hand, usually dressed in black. Despite periodic migraine headaches, Jefferson took pride in his good health; Madison, conversely, at the age of 18 developed an enduring habit of predicting his imminent demise. Both could be shy in the company of strangers, but each warmed in the presence of close acquaintances. Jefferson's conversations, Senator William Maclay once remarked, were "loose and rambling and yet he scattered information wherever he went, and some even brilliant sentiments sparkled from him." Madison, however, was known for both erudition and oral precision—as well as the occasional ribald joke.[2]

Their subtle differences as men of state reflected these temperamental distinctions. While the scribe of independence was decisive, the father of the Constitution was deliberative. Jefferson, an optimist, generally trusted popular will; Madison, a canny pragmatist, sought to restrain democratic majorities through his system of checks and balances. Jefferson's ideas burst forth like great flashes of light. Madison's thoughts, if somewhat less brilliant, burned like eternal flames. "Jefferson was the more speculative, inventive, and theoretical" of the pair, according to the editor of their correspondence, James Morton Smith: "gifted at coining generalizations and powerful metaphors and writing felicitous prose. Madison was tougher-minded, more analytical, the more persistent student of politics, the harder-headed thinker of the art of the possible."[3]

Consider the most famous of their few disagreements. Writing in 1789 from France, where he served as American minister, hobnobbed with philosophes, and contracted revolutionary fervor, Jefferson asserted that because "the earth ... belongs to the living," one generation must not bind its progeny to its laws or shackle its children with its debts. After calculating the span of a generation, he contended that all acts of government should expire and all loans should be repaid after two decades.

Madison, who had labored long to secure ratification of the Constitution, politely rebuked his friend's proposal. After assuring Jefferson that his idea was "a great one," he warned him that a terminal government likely would be weak and that successor governments might not be equally enlightened in their regard for basic rights. Madison insisted, moreover, that the debts of the old oftentimes helped to fund improvements that benefited the young.[4]

A closer look at their exchange on this point both helps us to recognize the differences between Jeffersonian and Madisonian political theory and shows that an enduring faith in the federal framework and the federal union constitutes one of Madison's most important independent contributions to posterity.

Jefferson began his letter by claiming for himself a good deal of philosophical originality. He believed very few of his pronouncements prior to this point were truly innovative; even his Declaration of Independence, as he would later tell Madison, sought merely to encapsulate the beliefs of "the American mind."[5] But in this instance, as he immodestly told his friend, "the question whether one generation of men has a right to bind another, seems never to have started either on this or on our side" of the ocean. What made this fact so startling is that the question led to so many "consequences as not only to merit decision, but place also, among the fundamental principles of every government."

Jefferson "set out on this ground" with a dictum that he described as self-evident: "*that the earth belongs in usufruct to the living* [and] that the dead have neither powers nor rights over it." It was bad enough that the laws of the living should pass to their descendants, who had no part in making them. Worse yet, "the public debts of one generation devolve on the next." He conceded that in private life anyone who inherits land "is required to pay the debts of his ancestor," but the arrangement was "municipal only, not moral; flowing from the will of the society, which has found it convenient to appropriate lands [made] vacant by the death of their occupant, on the condition of a pa[y]ment of his debts." Even so, he maintained that "between society and society, or generation and generation, there is no municipal obligation, no umpire but the law of nature. We seem not to have perceived that, by the law of nature, one generation is to another as one independent nation to another." Putting this principle into practice, he thought, would do justice to generational sovereignty; in addition, it would limit the ability of a government to unleash "the Dog of war," a beast that costs not only money but also lives and sometimes even the rights of citizens whose leaders compromise liberty in times of emergency.

Jefferson believed that his theory of generational sovereignty also "proved that no society can make a perpetual constitution, or even a perpetual law. The earth," he wrote, "belongs always to the living generation. They may manage it then, and what proceeds from it, as they please"—so long as they remain in the majority. Since "persons and property make the sum of the objects of government," their government was valid only so long as they outnumbered all other enfranchised generations. "Every constitution then, and every law, naturally expires at the end of 19 years," Jefferson asserted. "If it be enforced longer, it is an act of force, and not of right."[6]

In his cordial but pointed response, Madison viewed "the doctrine as not in *all* respects compatible with the course of human affairs." He thought paying all public debts after 19 years was a noble principle; indeed, during Jefferson's presidency, Madison worked with his friend to retire nearly one-third of all that the United States had borrowed. But he recognized that "debts may be incurred for purposes which interest the unborn," such as "repelling a conquest, the evils of which descend through many generations." A generation's debts were just, he wrote, if it gave more than it took.

Should laws expire after 19 years? Madison resisted the idea. "Unless such laws should be kept in force by new acts" passed well in advance of the old ones' expiration, "all the rights depending on positive laws," including "most of the rights of property would become absolutely defunct; and the most violent struggles" would ensue between those who stood to gain by retaining laws and those who stood to gain by replacing them. The uncertainty would also depreciate property values and encourage attempts to delay payment of or default on debts—actions that Jefferson clearly opposed and that Madison believed represented a form of "licentiousness already too powerful."

Perhaps most dangerous in Madison's mind was Jefferson's idea that constitutions, like debts and laws, should also periodically expire. Madison contended, in fact, that the notion raised "some very powerful objections. Would not a government so often revised become too mutable to retain those prejudices in its favor which antiquity inspires, and which are perhaps a salutary aid to the most rational government in the most enlightened age?" Veneration of constitutional tradition, he believed, was a good thing; it discouraged jockeying for power and advantage, the very sort of gamesmanship most likely to bring forth partisanship, factionalism, and crises of authority.[7]

Significantly, Madison did not advance the most obvious, most devastating counter-argument at his disposal, one that drew power from recognition of Jefferson's basic premise. Living people think, and thinking people are sensitive to their environments; environments change, and so, therefore, do the thoughts of the living. Since environments change constantly, and minds change constantly, should not laws and constitutions change constantly? Why maintain them for 19 years? The form of government to which Jefferson's philosophy led, in essence, was not a checked and balanced representative republic but an absolute and absolutely direct democracy that rejected the delayed gratification promised by a constitutional compact. Maybe Madison, ever the firm unionist, did not even consider these questions, or maybe he realized that such a line of reasoning might have resulted in a logical triumph but strategic failure, for it might have led Jefferson further down the road toward the advocacy of political instability.

The States and the Union

This was not the first time that Jefferson discounted the risk of destabilizing the union, nor would it be the last. He had shrugged off news of Daniel Shays's rebellion in western Massachusetts, for example, with the sunny observation that, although the 13 states had been independent for 11 years, this was only the first armed uprising. "That comes to one rebellion in a century & a half for each state. What country before ever existed a century & [a] half without a rebellion? & what country can preserve it's [sic] liberties if their rulers are not warned from time to time that their people preserve the spirit of resistance?" The best remedy for popular insurrections, he thought, was not force but restraint—a principle, perhaps, that the British escalation of armed conflict after Lexington and Concord had taught him. The best response to insurrectionists, he maintained, "is to set them right as to facts, pardon & pacify them. What signify a few lives lost in a century or two? The tree of liberty must be refreshed from time to time," he contended, "with the blood of patriots and tyrants."[8]

Jefferson's belief that stability must sometimes be sacrificed to the cause of liberty—the essence of his "earth belongs to the living" letter—manifested itself even more clearly in the late 1790s, when the Federalist administration of John Adams responded to the notorious "XYZ affair" and the Quasi-War with France by creating a standing army, outfitting a navy, fortifying the coasts, imposing direct taxes, and—most ominous of all—signing into law the 1798 alien and sedition bills. Madison shared Jefferson's suspicion that these measures aimed less at national security than domestic oppression; he wrote that they would transform the government "into an absolute, or at best a mixed monarchy." Together they orchestrated a campaign of opposition resulting in the famous resolves of Kentucky and Virginia.[9]

Jefferson's resolutions, drafted in secrecy and originally intended for North Carolina, ended up in the hands of John Breckinridge, who put them before the Kentucky legislature. Similarly, Madison silently penned the Virginia Resolutions and handed them through Wilson Cary Nicholas to John Taylor of Caroline, who introduced them in the state's assembly.[10] Both sets of resolves claimed that the alien and sedition laws violated the Constitution; each called on other states to rise up in protest. But while the two men's drafts share much, a few of the differences illuminate crucial disjunctions between Jeffersonian and Madisonian modes of constitutional redress.

Jefferson's premise was that the union amounted to "a compact under the style and title of a Constitution for the United States . . . that to this compact each State acceded as a State," and that, "as in all other cases of compact among powers having no common judge, each party has an equal right to judge for itself, as well of infractions as of the mode and measure of redress." He then focused on the Tenth Amendment's assurance that "the powers not delegated to the United States by the Constitution, nor prohibited by it to the States, are reserved to the States respectively, or to the people." He noted that the authority to control political speech, for example, was not granted to the federal government; the First Amendment, in fact, explicitly prohibited such legislation.

In cases where office holders wrongfully exercised delegated powers, Jefferson continued, "a change by the people" of the men elected to serve them "would be the constitutional remedy." But "where powers are assumed which have not been delegated, a nullification of the act is the rightful remedy." Since the alien and sedition laws so clearly represented the second form of abuse, he called on other states to join Kentucky "in declaring these acts void, and of no force" and to ensure that "neither these acts, nor any others of the General Government not plainly and intentionally authorized by the Constitution, shall be exercised within their respective territories."[11]

Madison's much more brief, somewhat more temperate Virginia resolves made few such thunderous claims. While his draft agreed that "the states who are parties" to the Constitution "have the right, and are in duty bound, to interpose for arresting the progress of the evil, and for maintaining within their respective limits, the authorities, rights and liberties appertaining to them," he did not call for outright nullification. Instead, his draft adopted the fallback position of Jefferson's resolves: the hope "that the necessary and proper measures will be taken" by the other states "for cooperating with this State in maintaining unimpaired the authorities, rights, and liberties, reserved to the States respectively, or to the people."[12]

Madison's clear aversion to Jefferson's constitutional brinkmanship did not deter his disappointed friend from working to embolden the Virginia resolves. Monticello stood between Madison's Montpelier and Taylor's Caroline, and Nicholas stopped there to consult with Jefferson, who suggested that Madison's resolutions be amended to declare "that the said acts are . . . null, void and of no force, or effect." Nicholas and Taylor probably concurred, for Taylor submitted to the House of Delegates the altered version of Madison's resolves; the lines were withdrawn by Taylor only after Madison, who was visiting near Richmond, apparently learned of them. Madison explained to Jefferson that he employed more "general expressions" because of "the distinction between the power of the *State* and that of the *Legislature*" on constitutional questions. It was not the assembly, after all, that had ratified the Constitution: it was a special convention of citizens. Thus the legislature did not have the power to nullify. Were it to claim that prerogative it would expose itself to "the charge of Usurpation in the very act of protesting ag[ain]st the usurpations of Congress."[13]

It is not surprising that Madison resisted Jefferson's somewhat impetuous tinkering with the Constitutional process, a project that could lead, no less certainly than the Adams administration's constitutional improvisation, to the dissolution of his cherished union of states. The bases of the two men's arguments in the resolutions of Kentucky and Virginia place their differences in stark relief. Jefferson focused on his compact theory of government, which made the union the handmaiden of its constituent parts; from there, he resorted not to the heart of the Constitution but to the amendments—the Bill of Rights—that in 1787 he urged Madison to append to the new national charter.[14] Madison, on the other hand, concentrated on rescuing from Federalist license the "necessary and proper" clause, which he located near the core of the confusion over the Constitution. Even its wording, as he contended in his draft of the Virginia Resolutions, had been calculated to prevent misunderstandings, for it was borrowed from the Articles of Confederation.[15]

When the other states greeted Virginia's and Kentucky's resolutions with silence or scorn, Jefferson proposed to Madison a course of action that included communicating to the rest of the nation that we would "sever ourselves from the union we so much value, rather than give up the rights of self government which we have reserved, and in which alone we see liberty, safety and happiness."[16] We cannot say for sure how Madison responded to Jefferson's plan, for instead of writing to him he paid him a visit.[17] At Monticello, Madison apparently convinced his friend that the scheme rested on bad tactics and, perhaps, foolishness. When Jefferson finally penned a second set of resolutions for Kentucky, he assured other states that Kentucky's 1798 resolves aimed only "to escape the fangs of despotism" and that its resistance to odious laws would proceed only in a "constitutional manner" and with a firm "attachment to the Union."[18]

Nevertheless, Jefferson continued to glance serenely toward threats to the Union. When, after the purchase of Louisiana, he wondered if people west of the Mississippi would ever declare their independence from the government of the east, he indulged that future generation as if it were his own, which had declared its independence from another distant land. What mattered was not that Americans east and west of the Mississippi share the same republican government but that they share the same republican principles. America, in other words, was more than a nation-state; it was a state of mind. Even the very real and pressing Missouri Crisis of 1819–1821 may have failed to alarm him. Although historians have long cited his famous 1820 letter to Congressman John Holmes, in which he claimed that debate over the "momentous question" of slavery in Missouri "like a fire bell in the night, awakened and filled me with terror" because "I considered it at once the knell of the Union," one scholar has recently pointed out that such panicked pronouncements were sent only to northerners—whom Jefferson wanted to chasten—and to Virginians, whom Jefferson wanted to support his University of Virginia, which would provide an alternative to the colleges of the north for their state's youth. To others, such as the Marquis de Lafayette, Jefferson wrote that "the boisterous sea of liberty indeed is never without a wave," and that while the wave "from Missouri is now rolling towards us . . . we shall ride over it as we have over all others."[19]

Madison, however, remained a steady champion of the Union and the stability that it imparted. He winced at the Missouri Crisis and recoiled at John C. Calhoun's later doctrine of nullification—even though Calhoun linked his ideas to the legacy of the Virginia and Kentucky resolves of 1798. As he wrote in 1829, "the happy Union of these States is a wonder; their Constitution a miracle. . . . Woe to the ambition that would meditate the destruction of either!"[20]

If for Jefferson constitutional union was only a means to an end, for Madison it usually seemed the *only* means. Historian Peter Onuf recently noted that the "genealogy of secession—from 1861 back to 1798, and then to 1776—seems straightforward enough; it was a genealogy that Jefferson's words and deeds authorized, and that Madison, defending the legacy of 1787, resisted to his dying day."[21] But if Jefferson's ideas led to the carnage of the Civil War, the bloodiest conflict in American history, then Madison's led to the reconstructed but involuntary union that followed, based on force more than consent. It is unfair, of course, to ascribe to the thoughts of either man either outcome, for the earth—and the nation—really did belong to the living, and neither Jefferson nor Madison remained among them in 1861 or 1865.

Two Legacies

Do they remain among us today?

In the case of Thomas Jefferson, the answer seems clear. He has Mount Rushmore and the Tidal Basin memorial, the nickel, and the two-dollar bill. Americans remember him on the Fourth of July. Some celebrate him, others revere him, and a few—175 years after his death—still revile him. Everybody, it seems, regards him as important.

In 1998, when journalists learned of a DNA study suggesting that he had fathered at least one of the children of Sally Hemings—his slave, half sister-in-law, and probable mistress—he made the front pages of national newspapers. He earned features on evening newscasts, public radio, and weekly newsmagazines. Oprah Winfrey devoted an entire show to the Jefferson-Hemings relationship, and

CBS made it the subject of a mini-series. More recently, the closeness of the 2000 election reminded Americans of the contested nature of Jefferson's elevation to the presidency 200 years earlier. Politicians also remembered, and both Al Gore and George W. Bush approvingly quoted, the man who, as America's second vice president and third president, served as a predecessor for each. President Bill Clinton, in his final Oval Office address, also quoted Jefferson—this time disapprovingly, for the Virginian's proscription against "entangling alliances" with other nations could no longer apply, Clinton said, to a superpower with global responsibilities. One week later, retired General Colin Powell, speaking during his confirmation hearings to be Secretary of State, mentioned the man who first held the office no fewer than 11 times.

Jefferson, in sum, seems to be everywhere, not only in the stone of monuments but also in the living, breathing pageant of American popular culture and public life. Anyone skeptical of this claim need only look back through the issues of U.S. News and World Report, which in six months twice placed Jefferson on its cover.[22] What other dead (or living) American has ever been bestowed such a mark of relevance?

Sadly—but certainly—not Madison. Where are his monuments? Where is his currency? Scholars generally like him, and today generally they like him more than Jefferson. Yet academic publications and scholarly conferences do not directly affect the public mind.

These contrasting contemporary reputations suggest an irony. Historian Joyce Appleby recently observed that Jefferson opposed "the mindless transfer of laws, ideas—even words—from one generation to another. The true Jeffersonian legacy is to be hostile to legacies."[23] And that is the secret of its staying power, for members of every American generation have looked to Jefferson's effervescent ideals—some of which never have been, and probably never could be, put into practice—less for example than for inspiration.[24]

Madison, on the other hand, is nowhere because he appears to be everywhere. While Jefferson gives us license to determine what we want to be, Madison—more than any other member of the founding generation—made us what we are. No doubt he would have been saddened by the Civil War and the dissolution of his cherished Union, by the heavy-handed reconstruction of the Union and the usurpation of state's rights, and by the decline of limited government and the rise of the welfare state. Despite those departures from his plans, his ideas have remained vital enough for Americans to tell themselves that they remain true to them. People take his legacy for granted because, they think, they can.

Notes

1. James Morton Smith, ed., *The Republic of Letters: The Correspondence between Thomas Jefferson and James Madison, 1776–1826*, 3 vols. (New York: Norton, 1995), 1:xvii (quotation).

2. Joseph J. Ellis, *Founding Brothers: The Revolutionary Generation* (New York: Knopf, 2000), pp. 53 and 67; Drew R. McCoy, *The Last of the Fathers: James Madison and the Republican Legacy* (New York: Cambridge University Press, 1989), pp. 26–34. For Maclay's description, see Julian P. Boyd et al., eds., *The Papers of Thomas Jefferson*, 28 vols. to date (Princeton, N.J.: Princeton University Press, 1950), 16:381n.

3. Ibid., 12. The fullest comparative treatment of the two men remains Adrienne Koch, *Jefferson and Madison: The Great Collaboration* (New York: Knopf, 1950).

4. Jefferson to Madison, Sept. 6, 1789, in Smith, ed., *The Republic of Letters*, 1:631–36; Madison to Jefferson, Feb. 4, 1790, ibid., 1:650–53. Scholarly assessments of the exchange are numerous. The best include Lance Banning, *Jefferson and Madison: Three Conversations from the Founding* (Madison, Wis.: Madison House, 1995), pp. 27–55; Daniel J. Boorstin, *The Lost World of Thomas Jefferson* (New York: Henry Holt, 1948), pp. 204–13; Joseph J. Ellis, *American Sphinx: The Character of Thomas Jefferson* (New York: Knopf, 1997), pp. 110–15; Stanley N. Katz, "Thomas Jefferson and the Right to Property in Revolutionary America," *Michigan Law Review* 76 (1977): 1–29; David N. Mayer, *The Constitutional Thought of Thomas Jefferson* (Charlottesville, Va.: University Press of Virginia, 1994), 302-08; Merrill D. Peterson, "Mr. Jefferson's 'Sovereignty of the Living Generation,'" *Virginia Quarterly Review* 52 (1976): 437–47; Herbert E. Sloan, "The Earth Belongs in Usufruct to the Living," in Peter S. Onuf, ed., *Jeffersonian Legacies* (Charlottesville, Va.: University Press of Virginia, 1993), pp. 281–315; Garry Wills, *Inventing America: Jefferson's Declaration of Independence* (Garden City, N.Y.: Doubleday, 1978), pp. 132–48.

5. Robert M. S. McDonald, "Thomas Jefferson's Changing Reputation as Author of the Declaration of Independence: The First Fifty Years," *Journal of the Early Republic* 19 (1999): 169–95, esp. 188–89.

6. Jefferson to Madison, Sept. 6, 1789, in ibid., 631–36.

7. Madison to Jefferson, Feb. 4, 1790, in ibid., 650–53. For details on Jefferson's and Madison's payment of the national debt, see Mayer, *The Constitutional Thought of Thomas Jefferson*, p. 211.

8. Jefferson to William S. Smith, Nov. 13, 1787, in Merrill D. Peterson, ed., *Thomas Jefferson: Writings* (New York: Literary Classics, 1984), p. 911.

9. James Roger Sharp, *American Politics in the Early Republic: The New Nation in Crisis* (New Haven, Conn.: Yale University Press, 1993), pp. 163–200; Madison, The Virginia Resolutions, Dec. 21, 1798, in Banning, *Jefferson and Madison*, p. 216.

10. For a precise discussion of the provenance of both sets of resolves, see the introductory essay, "The Kentucky and Virginia Resolutions and American Civil Liberties," in *The Republic of Letters*, 2:1068–72.

11. Jefferson, Draft of the Kentucky Resolutions, October 1798, in *Thomas Jefferson: Writings*, pp. 449–56.

12. Madison, The Virginia Resolutions, Dec. 21, 1798, in *Jefferson and Madison*, pp. 215–17.

13. "Kentucky and Virginia Resolutions," in *The Republic of Letters*, 2:1071; Madison to Jefferson, Dec. 29, 1798, in ibid., 2:1085. One scholar's recent attribution to Madison of pro-nullification sentiments during this period results, in part, from the erroneous assumption that Jefferson's added words appeared in the original draft. See Constantine [Kevin R.] Gutzman, "A Troublesome Legacy: James Madison and 'The Principles of '98,'" *Journal of the Early Republic* 15 (1995): 581.

14. Jefferson to Madison, Dec. 20, 1787, in *The Republic of Letters*, 1:512–13.

15. Madison, The Virginia Resolutions, Dec. 21, 1798, in Banning, *Jefferson and Madison*, pp. 215–16.

16. Jefferson to Madison, Aug. 23, 1799, in *The Republic of Letters*, 2:1119.

17. Ibid., 1119n.

18. Koch, *Jefferson and Madison*, 199–201.

19. Stuart Leibiger, "Thomas Jefferson and the Missouri Crisis: An Alternative Interpretation," *Journal of the Early Republic* 17 (Spring 1997): 121–30, 124 and 127 (quotations).

20. Madison, Outline [for a speech in the Virginia State Convention of 1829–30], Sept. 1829, in Philip R. Fendall, ed., *Letters and Other Writings of James Madison*, 4 vols. (Philadelphia, 1865), 4: 20.

21. Peter S. Onuf, *Jefferson's Empire: The Language of American Nationhood* (Charlottesville, Va.: University Press of Virginia, 2000), p. 145.

22. See the Aug. 21, 2000, and Feb. 26, 2001, issues.

23. Joyce Appleby, "Jefferson and His Complex Legacy," in *Jeffersonian Legacies*, p. 2.

24. For a thoughtful analysis of how Americans after 1826 employed Jefferson's words, see Merrill D. Peterson, *The Jefferson Image in the American Mind* (New York: Oxford University Press, 1960).

6. Madison and Multiculturalism: Group Representation, Group Rights, and Constitutionalism

Tom G. Palmer

There is no doubt that James Madison envisioned a republic that encompassed many different interests. At least three questions present themselves:

1) Did Madison envision a "multicultural" republic?
2) Are contemporary advocates of various forms of group rights or group representation, often presented under the banner of "multiculturalism," advancing the Madisonian project, or undermining it?
3) Are group-differentiated rights a necessary and proper element of a constitutional order ordained and established to "form a more perfect Union, establish Justice, insure domestic Tranquility, provide for the common defence, promote the general Welfare, and secure the Blessings of Liberty to ourselves and to our Posterity"?

Madisonian Pluralism and the Common Good

Madison openly embraced a pluralistic constitutional order. Indeed, he believed such diversity was essential to maintain liberty. Madison's commitment to diversity in an extended republic directly contradicted the then widely held "small republic" theory forwarded by Montesquieu, who had famously declared,

> It is in the nature of a republic to have only a small territory; otherwise, it can scarcely continue to exist. In a large republic, there are large fortunes, and consequently little moderation in spirits: the depositories are too large to put in the hands of a citizen; interests become particularized; at first a man feels he can be happy, great, and glorious without his homeland; and soon, that he can be great only on the ruins of his homeland.

> In a large republic, the common good is sacrificed to a thousand considerations; it is subordinated to exceptions; it depends upon accidents. In a small one, the public good is better felt, better known, lies nearer to each citizen; abuses are less extensive there and consequently less protected.[1]

In contrast, Madison celebrated diversity and the extended republic. He believed that a wide diversity of what Montesquieu considered "particularized interests" supported, rather than threatened, liberty. In 1788 Madison declared, "Happily for the states, they enjoy the utmost freedom of religion. This freedom arises from that multiplicity of sects, which pervades America, and which is the best and only security for religious liberty in any society. For where there is such a variety of sects, there cannot be a majority of any one sect to oppress and persecute the rest."[2] Madison's remarks echo Voltaire, who wrote in his "Letter on the Presbyterians" that "if there were only one religion in England, there would be danger of tyranny; if there were two, they would cut each other's throats; but there are thirty, and they live happily together in peace."[3]

Madison's famous essay on the problem of faction, *Federalist* No. 10, is oft quoted but rarely carefully considered. Examine closely his definition of faction: "By a faction I understand a number of citizens, whether amounting to a majority or minority of the whole, who are united and actuated by some common impulse or passion, or of interest, adverse to the rights of other citizens, or to the permanent and aggregate interests of the community."[4] What is notable about that definition is that it presupposes:

A) that interests are not the same as rights,
B) that interests may be opposed to rights,
C) that citizens may be motivated by passions, as well as by interests, and
D) that there is a common good ("the permanent and aggregate interests of the community") to which particular interests or passions may be opposed.

Their critics often assert that classical liberals—among whom I count James Madison—believe that social and political life is merely a clash of particular interests, or even that there is no common good.[5] But this is not what classical liberals (including modern libertarians) believe. They are liberals because they believe that liberty is, if not the overriding common good, then at least a central element of the common good. If there are permanent and aggregate interests of a community, they will be shared by all of the particular interests, and it is the business of government to secure that public good. As Madison remarked, "It is too early for politicians to presume on our forgetting that the public good, the real welfare of the great body of the people is the supreme object to be pursued; and that no form of government whatever, has any other value, than as it may be fitted for the attainment of this object."[6]

For classical liberals such as Madison at least one permanent and aggregate interest of the community *is* the securing of a regime of equal rights for all citizens. Indeed, Madison proposed in a speech before the House of Representatives:

> That there be prefixed to the Constitution a declaration, that all power is originally vested in, and consequently derived from, the people.
> That Government is instituted and ought to be exercised for the benefit of the people; which consists in the enjoyment of life and liberty, with the right of acquiring and using property, and generally of pursuing and obtaining happiness and safety.[7]

One might claim Madison as an advocate of a multicultural republic because he accepted a wide variety of commitments ("passions") and interests in the new republic. He is decidedly not a "multiculturalist" in the sense of endorsing group-specific rights or the rights of groups to special representation. As he noted in his essay on "Parties":

> In every political society, parties are unavoidable. A difference of interests, real or supposed, is the most natural and fruitful source of them. The great object should be to combat the evil: 1. By establishing a political equality among all.[8]

Madison noted that the existence of parties, based on different interests, did not warrant the creation of "artificial parties."

> From the expediency, in politics, of making natural parties, mutual checks on each other, to infer the propriety of creating artificial parties, in order to form them into mutual checks, is not less absurd than it would be in ethics, to say, that new

vices ought to be promoted, where they would counteract
each other, because this use may be made of existing vices.[9]

Madison envisioned a political system oriented toward the common good, not toward "conflicting rights" or group warfare. The
common good consists of the maintenance of rules of conduct that
are the same for all citizens.[10]

Madison's commitment to the common good, that is, a good common to all citizens, is reflected in one of the most misunderstood
terms in the Constitution, the "general welfare." That term is found
in the preamble, wherein are stated the reasons for which the Constitution has been ordained and established: "in order to form a more
perfect Union, establish Justice, insure domestic Tranquility, provide
for the common Defense, promote the general Welfare, and secure
the Blessings of Liberty to ourselves and our Posterity." It is also
found in the first clause of Article I, Section 8, which states that
"The Congress shall have Power to lay and collect Taxes, Duties,
Imposts and Excises, to pay the Debts and provide for the common
Defense and general Welfare of the United States; but all Duties,
Imposts and Excises shall be uniform throughout the United States."
The Constitution does not authorize securing the welfare of some
at the expense of others; securing the welfare that is common to *both*
Peter and Paul is the purpose for which the Congress is granted its
limited powers. Article I, Section 1 ("All legislative Powers herein
granted shall be vested in a Congress of the United States") clearly
implies that some powers are *not* "herein granted" and therefore
cannot be legitimately exercised by the Congress.[11] The power to
rob Peter to pay Paul, today referred to as "redistribution," is not
a power granted to the Congress under the Constitution. The term
general welfare, which is so often interpreted as a blanket grant of
authority to the federal government to do anything and everything
(at least, anything that is not explicitly prohibited in the Constitution), is regularly cited to justify thousands upon thousands of acts
that promote the welfare of a few at the expense of others. But
reflection upon the meaning of the term general welfare suggests
that it is not merely *anyone's* "welfare" that is intended, but the
welfare that is general, that is, common to all.

The Constitution was proposed and ratified "in order to" secure
certain limited ends. It authorizes neither a regime of differentiated

caste privileges nor an unlimited power of majorities to impose their preferences upon minorities. Madison made that clear when he proposed in his speech of June 6, 1787, to the federal convention that drafted the Constitution that the proposed Constitution would be superior to the Articles of Confederation in "providing more effectually for the security of private rights and the steady dispensation of Justice" and asked, "In all cases where a majority are united by a common interest or passion, the rights of the minority are in danger. What motives are to restrain them?"[12] After noting that conscience rarely has much effect on large numbers of men, and cataloguing various forms of oppression experienced by polities ancient and modern, he asks, "What has been the source of those unjust laws complained of among ourselves?" and responds, "Has it not been the real or supposed interest of the major number?"[13] He concludes that:

> The lesson we are to draw from the whole is that where a majority are united by a common sentiment, and have an opportunity, the rights of the minor party become insecure. In a Republican Gov^t the majority if united have always an opportunity. The only remedy is to enlarge the sphere, and thereby divide the community into so great a number of interests and parties, that in the 1st place a majority will not be likely at the same moment to have a common interest separate from that of the whole or of the minority; and in the 2nd place, that in case they sh^d have such an interest, they may not be apt to unite in the pursuit of it. It was incumbent on us then to try this remedy, and with that view to frame a republican system on such a scale & in such a form as will controul all the evils wch have been experienced.[14]

In *Federalist* No. 10—itself largely an elaboration of his speech of June 6, 1787, before the Convention—Madison stated that "to secure the public good, and private rights against the danger of such a [majority] faction, and at the same time to preserve the spirit and the form of popular government, is then the great object to which our enquiries are directed."[15] Madison proposed, rather than democracy (the other form of "popular government"), a republic, "by which I mean a government in which the scheme of representation takes place," which differs from a democracy in "the delegation of the government . . . to a small number of citizens elected by the rest" and "the greater number of citizens, and greater sphere of country, over which [a republic] may be extended."[16]

The two solutions are, thus, first, to substitute representation for direct democracy, in order to "refine and enlarge the public views, by passing them through the medium of a chosen body of citizens," and second, to increase the transaction costs necessary to assemble a majority faction animated by a common interest contrary to that of the whole.[17] A system of representation, as distinct from direct democracy, would encourage deliberation and protect the public good from great swings in public opinion ignited by passion. It would also weaken the advantages of potential demagogues, as Madison noted in *Federalist* No. 58:

> In all legislative assemblies, the greater the number composing them may be, the fewer will be the men who will in fact direct their proceedings. In the first place, the more numerous any assembly may be, of whatever characters composed, the greater is known to be the ascendancy of passion over reason. In the next place, the larger the number, the greater will be the proportion of members of limited information and of weak capacities. Now it is precisely on characters of this description that the eloquence and address of the few are known to act with all their force. . . . On the same principle the more multitudinous a representative assembly may be rendered, the more it will partake of the infirmities incident to collective meetings of the people.[18]

The qualifications and election procedures for the membership of the United States Senate set out in Article I, Section 3 of the Constitution exemplify Madison's republican principles: "Immediately after they shall be assembled in Consequence of the first Election, they shall be divided as equally as may be into three Classes. . . . so that one third may be chosen every second Year" and "No person shall be a Senator who shall not have attained to the Age of thirty Years." Staggered elections insulate the Senate from the shifting passions of the electorate, and the age requirement seeks to limit the membership to a group more likely to have attained some wisdom, or at least to be less excited by the passions of the moment. The combination of the two is more likely to generate greater stability in the law, which is to say, a more consistent articulation and defense of the public good. As Madison noted in *Federalist* No. 62:

> The most deplorable effect of all [the effects of a mutable policy] is that diminution of attachment and reverence which steals into the heart of the people, towards a political system which betrays so many marks of infirmity, and disappoints so many of their flattering hopes. No government any more than an individual will long be respected, without being truly respectable, nor be truly respectable without possessing a certain portion of order and stability.[19]

Madison clearly stated the purpose of political representation:

> The aim of every political constitution is, or ought to be, first, to obtain for rulers men who possess most wisdom to discern, and most virtue to pursue the common good of the society; and in the next place, to take the most effectual precautions for keeping them virtuous, whilst they continue to hold their public trust. The elective mode of obtaining rulers is the characteristic policy of republican government. The means relied on in this form of government for preventing their degeneracy, are numerous and various. The most effectual one is such a limitation on the term of appointments, as will maintain a proper responsibility to the people.[20]

Madison focused attention upon the process of choosing representatives. Republican government relies on a democratic element ("the elective mode"), but it includes other elements, as well, such as the electoral college, apportionment of electors among the states, term limits, and the like.

Madison sought to create a stable system of government that can effectively promote the authentically common good and at the same time resist the natural tendency of human beings toward factional conflict. His political theory has little, if any, room for systems of group-specific or group-differentiated rights or representation. (There is an interesting exception, which is the rights of the politically organized Indian tribes, to which I will refer at the end of this essay, and which is considered at greater length in Jacob Levy's chapter in this volume.)

Multicultural Collectivism and Group Representation

Many political theorists now consider the idea of equality before the law to be old-fashioned or quaint. Others openly denounce it as a form of oppression. Some of those thinkers even claim the

Madisonian mantle, by which they mean a concern for protecting the interests of minorities within a broadly democratic (or, in Madison's term, popular) political framework. Those thinkers hope to protect minority interests not through guarantees of equal rights by a government of limited powers, but either by guaranteeing representation to groups as groups, or by erecting and continually adjusting a kaleidoscopic array of *unequal* group-specific rights, or by both.

Lani Guinier, an interesting and challenging defender of group representation, has set out an approach that she explicitly identifies with James Madison. She argues that Madison's concern with the protection of minorities from majority tyranny led him to embrace "the rule of shifting majorities, as the losers at one time or on one issue join with others and become part of the governing coalition at another time or on another issue." She calls "a majority that rules but does not dominate" a "Madisonian majority."[21] From the very beginning, however, Guinier mistakes what Madison means by representation, when she states that Madison objects to majority tyranny because "the majority may not represent all competing interests."[22] The majority, for Madison, does not represent interests; it *has* interests. Representatives deliberate about and attempt to secure the common interest and are answerable to those they represent. Guinier's misunderstanding of the role of representation sets the stage for a theory of political conflict in which the common good disappears as the goal of government. She claims that "including all sectors of society in government operation is consistent with Madison's vision" and offers as evidence *Federalist* No. 39, which she characterizes as "rejecting elitist plutocracy."[23]

Guinier does focus, however, on a problem with which a Madisonian should indeed be concerned: the permanent minority in a bipolar conflict. If there were a majority united by a common passion or interest that faced a minority that is both easily distinguished from the majority and incapable of becoming a majority, the minority would likely be systematically oppressed. In the case that Guinier considers, there are two major groups in America—blacks and whites—and one of them is an overwhelming majority. As such, it has been able to oppress the other systematically and brutally. Because of "the documented persistence of racial polarization . . . racism excludes minorities from ever becoming part of the governing coalition, meaning that the white majority will be permanent."[24]

Guinier's solution is what she calls, inspired by her young son's ideas about fairness, "the principle of taking turns."[25] She seeks not merely to secure the rights of black Americans to the suffrage, but also to obtain representation for blacks in the legislature by "authentically black" representatives. And she seeks not only representation of black voters by "authentically black" legislators, but also guarantees of particular legislative outcomes. She endorses the criterion of racial "authenticity," which for her "reflects the group consciousness, group history, and group perspective of a disadvantaged and stigmatized minority. Authenticity recognizes that black voters are a discrete 'social group' with a distinctive voice."[26] As such, representatives who are "descriptively black" but do not agree with the substantive policy agenda of Ms. Guinier either exhibit "false consciousness"[27] or are not authentically black. The "distinctive voice" of black America should be represented by authentically black representatives who represent authentic black policy preferences (which may or may not correspond to what the majority of descriptively black Americans say they prefer). Thus, "a theory of representation that derives its authority from the original civil rights' vision must address concerns of qualitative fairness involving equal recognition and just results. For those at the bottom, a system that gives everyone an equal chance of having their political preferences *physically represented* is inadequate. A fair system of political representation would provide mechanisms to ensure that disadvantaged and stigmatized minority groups also have a *fair chance* to have their policy preferences *satisfied*."[28]

Before considering Guinier's proposed means to ensure that minority groups have a fair chance to have their policy preferences satisfied, let's consider more carefully the issue of authenticity. In a discussion of authenticity that was cut from the version of her law review article that appeared in her book, Guinier states:

> Identifying "black representatives" raises several questions. For example, would descriptively black representatives who were also Republicans qualify as black representatives? More generally, is it the race of the representative that makes them part of the minority voting group? Although no one answer may suffice, the court should consider only a representative's status as the minority group's representative of choice. Therefore, only a representative sponsored by the black community and electorally accountable to it would count for purposes of a legislative bloc voting analysis.[29]

It is in this vein that opponents referred to current Secretary of the Interior Gale Norton during the period of her confirmation hearings as "James Watt in a skirt," apparently on the grounds that an authentic woman could not hold the views that she held.[30] Similarly, Margaret Thatcher's enemies in Britain repeatedly referred to her as a "female impersonator." Thus, members of a group who disagree with a self-appointed leadership of that group are labeled "inauthentic" if they disagree with that self-appointed leadership. For example, Andrew Sullivan is an openly gay man who, on grounds of justice, opposes legislation interfering with contractual relations by banning private discrimination on the basis of sexual orientation. He is routinely pilloried by self-appointed gay politicians as "not really gay" and as a traitor to the authentic gay community.[31] An implication of such claims is that whites who agree with Lani Guinier would not be "authentically white," men who support feminism would not be "real men," and heterosexuals who favor gay marriage would not be "authentically heterosexual." If the latter are absurd, so are the former. Such claims that ideas are determined by race, gender, or sexual orientation are not far from the claims of polylogism made by the National Socialists (race or nationality) and Marxists (class) in the last century, and are subject to criticism on the same logical grounds.[32]

In discussing legal solutions to cases raised by the Voting Rights Act, Guinier has proposed various forms of proportional representation to encourage group representation and the "fair chance" for the satisfaction of the authentic policy preferences of minorities. Although she is careful to hedge her proposals with various caveats, she prefers a form of proportional representation known as "cumulative voting," in which legislators are elected at-large (rather than in geographically separated districts) and voters are allocated a number of votes equal to the number of offices being chosen, which votes they can then cast in any manner they prefer, including casting all of them for one candidate. Similarly, she proposes cumulative voting as a method of legislation, in order to avoid marginalization of minority legislators. In this manner, voters and legislators can reveal not only the existence of their preferences, but also the intensity of those preferences. If a proportional representation scheme succeeds in electing more "authentically black" legislators, but they fail to achieve effective "proportional interest representation," the minority legislators could be given a "minority veto":

> If modifying the exclusion threshold alone did not yield
> proportionate interest representation, winner-take-all major-
> ity rule by a permanent, hostile legislative majority could be
> modified. Where majority representatives refuse to bargain
> with representatives of the minority, simple majority rule
> votes would be replaced. "A minority veto" for legislation
> of vital importance to minority interests would respond to
> evidence of gross "deliberative gerrymanders."[33]

What is at stake is the guarantee that authentically black preferences be satisfied: "If it is true, as I have argued, that representatives
are equal only if existing distribution of power, resources, and prejudices do not play an 'authoritative' role in their deliberations, then
it is not clear that the remedial goal of equal political participation
in the form of a fair and equal distribution of preference satisfaction
is realistic, especially within a litigation context."[34]

Guinier does not directly propose that votes be differently weight-
ed on the basis of race, but she does believe that black voters will
cast their votes as a bloc and thereby be represented as a group:
"As a discrete and insular minority, blacks may be able to take
maximum advantage of interest representation, in part because, as
a small group with group consciousness, they are better able to
organize collectively."[35]

Others have also endorsed replacing the dominant American form
of representation—geographically distinguished single-member districts that vote on a winner-take-all, first-past-the-post system—
with proportional representation as a means of representing racial
interests. Robert Richie and Steven Hill argue that proportional representation (PR) "provides better representation for racial minorities" and that "minorities would have greater opportunities to negotiate for influence because they could 'swing' among parties."[36]
Although they assert that "the case for PR is fundamentally nonparti-
san," they stake much of their case on their claim that "American
political progressives have a particularly urgent need to support PR
because of the growing problems created by a lack of a serious
electoral vehicle to the Democrats' left."[37]

Will Kymlicka generally endorses group representation as "not
inherently illiberal or undemocratic,"[38] but he does not try "to define
or defend any specific model of group representation," for he does
"not think it is possible to say much more at the general level."[39]

Among the alternatives he considers plausible are proportional representation as a means of securing group representation and guaranteeing seats for members of underrepresented or disadvantaged groups. In addition, Kymlicka and other writers endorse self government rights for indigenous national minorities, an issue that I will consider later. (I will deal at greater length with Kymlicka's endorsement of group-specific rights in the next section.)

Madison or Calhoun?

One of the most remarkable features of the case made for group representation by Guinier, Richie and Hill, Kymlicka, and others is not whom they cite, but whom they do not cite: John C. Calhoun. Rather than advancing Madison's project, they are advancing Calhoun's. The difference is significant, for Calhoun had effectively given up on the idea of a common good and replaced it with particular interests, each with the power to veto changes harmful to it. As Calhoun stated:

> If the whole community had the same interests, so that the interests of each and every portion would be so affected by the action of the government, that the laws which oppressed or impoverished one portion, would necessarily oppress and impoverish all others—or the reverse—then the right of suffrage, of itself, would be self-sufficient to counteract the tendency of the government to oppression and abuse of its powers; and, of course, would form, of itself, a perfect constitutional government.[40]

Calhoun explicitly rejected Madison's solution of an extended republic because "the more extensive and populous the country, the more diversified the condition and pursuits of its population, and the richer, more luxurious, and dissimilar the people, the more difficult it is to equalize the action of the government—and the more easy for one portion of the community to pervert its powers to oppress, and plunder the other."[41]

It may be obvious why Guinier would not cite a thinker who was one of America's most brilliant political theorists, but also a defender of slavery, the "peculiar institution" of the South. It is equally clear that Calhoun's work exercised a great influence on her.[42] In order to avoid systematic domination of one interest by another, Calhoun argued that interests themselves should be directly represented:

> There is ... but one mode in which this can be effected;
> and that is, by taking the sense of each interest or portion
> of the community, which may be unequally and injuriously
> affected by the action of the government, separately, through
> its own majority, or in some other way by which its voice
> may be fairly expressed; and to require the consent of each
> interest, either to put or to keep the government in action.
> This, too, can be accomplished only in one way—and that
> is, by such an organism of the government—and, if necessary
> for the purpose, of the community also—as will, by dividing
> and distributing the powers of government, give to each
> division or interest, through its appropriate organ, either a
> concurrent voice in making and executing the laws, or a veto
> on their execution.[43]

Thus, each interest should be guaranteed either a fair and equal
distribution of preference satisfaction or a veto on the actions of
the whole.

Calhoun, Guinier, Kymlicka, and other advocates of group representation have given up on the very idea of the common good,
which is central to the Madisonian enterprise. Calhoun distinguished
his approach precisely by eschewing the idea of a common interest:

> It results, from what has been said, that there are two
> different modes in which the sense of the community can
> be taken; one, simply by the right of suffrage, unaided; the
> other, by the right through a proper organism. Each collects
> the sense of the majority. But one regards numbers only, and
> considers the whole community as a unit, having but one
> common interest throughout; and collects the sense of the
> greater number of the whole, as that of the community. The
> other, on the contrary, regards interests as well as numbers—
> considering the community as made up of different and
> conflicting interests, as far as the action of the government
> is concerned; and takes the sense of each, through its majority
> or appropriate organ, and the united sense of all, in the sense
> of the entire community. The former of these I shall call the
> numerical, or absolute majority; and the later, the concurrent,
> or constitutional majority.[44]

Calhoun makes a strong case that even the normal functioning of
a constitutionally limited government entails differential impacts,
simply because of the value of the emoluments of office,[45] but slavery

weighed heavier in his overall case. As Calhoun noted, "We [the slave states] are already in a minority in the House of Representatives and the Electoral College; so that with the loss of the Senate, we shall be in a minority in every department of the Federal Government; and ever must continue so, if the non-slaveholding States should carry into effect their scheme of appropriating to their exclusive use all the territories of the United States. But, fortunately, under our system of government, mere numbers are not the only element of power. There are others, which would give us ample means of defending ourselves against the threatened danger, if we should be true to ourselves."[46]

Proportional representation may have its advantages, but I believe that it would be unwise to implement it, at least in the forms proposed by Guinier and by Richie and Hill, mainly for the very reasons that its advocates give for proposing it: it would lead to a fracturing of the American polity and would undermine the common good. Proportional representation would substitute for the *general* welfare a constitutional vision of opposing interests engaged in a zero sum competition for limited resources. A greater dedication to the common good, as instantiated by the Constitution, is far preferable to the Balkans-style politics that Guinier and other supporters of group representation envision. Proportional representation also has procedural disadvantages. It removes the search for consensus from the constituency to the legislature, with no obvious advantage to the republic as a whole. Tiny groups of extremists or single-issue zealots may find themselves in positions of exaggerated influence as swing votes. And governing coalitions and therefore policies may change dramatically, because of changing legislative coalitions, not changes in votes. Proportional representation has few advantages and several disadvantages. Since the United States is not in the midst of a political crisis, there is little reason to change what ain't (relative to the alternative) broke.

The advocates of group representation explicitly reject the Madisonian vision of the common good achieved through political representation of equal citizens in an extensive and pluralistic republic. Their vision is a war of all against all, not, to be sure, as the goal, but as the result. As the Lebanese Constitution rather innocently stated, "for the sake of justice and amity, the sects shall be equitably represented in public employment and in the composition of the ministry, provided such measures will not harm the general welfare of the state."[47] This commitment to "justice and amity" produced precisely the opposite, as Lebanon erupted into a veritable orgy of murder in 1975, when the Maronite Christians, who had been favored by the old constitutional order (based on the census of 1943), refused to cede power to the increasing portion of the population that followed Shiite Islam. A piece of paper may state that such representation is not to harm "the general welfare of the state," but once groups achieve representation they are typically loathe to surrender it in the name of the common good or the general welfare.[48]

Multicultural Collectivism and Group Rights

Group consciousness has brought about not only calls for group representation, but also calls for group-specific (or group differentiated) legal and personal rights and entitlements. This paper cannot deal with all the arguments for these theories, but a few common elements can be identified. They include: 1) a rejection of the ideal of legal equality as itself a form of oppression; 2) demands for reparations for historical injustices; and 3) a new interpretation of freedom as requiring that legal equality of rights be abolished in favor of complex sets of rights that are differentiated by membership in ascriptive groups. I will provide a brief excursion through a rather extensive literature, along with a Madisonian-influenced commentary and critique, followed by a statement of what I take to be the most plausible Madisonian response.

Equality as a Form of Oppression

Catharine MacKinnon, law professor at the University of Chicago, has become a prominent advocate of the idea that equality itself is a form of oppression. Thus, in her *Toward a Feminist Theory of the State*, she states, "Taking the sexes 'as individuals,' meaning one at a time, as if they do not belong to genders, perfectly obscures these collective realities and substantive correlates of gender group status behind the mask of recognition of individual rights."[49]

Although it is not entirely clear what remedies would flow logically from MacKinnon's pronouncements, the incoherence of her approach is indicated by the following statement:

> Under sex equality law, to be human, in substance, means to be a man. To be a person, an abstract individual with

85

abstract rights, may be a bourgeois concept, but its content is male. The only way to assert a claim *as* a member of the socially unequal group women, as opposed to seeking to assert a claim as *against* membership in the group women, is to seek treatment on a sexually denigrated basis. Human rights, including "women's rights," have implicitly been limited to those rights that men have to lose. This may be in part why men persistently confuse procedural and abstract equality with substantive equality: for them, they are the same. Abstract equality has never included those rights that women as women most need and never have had. All this appears rational and neutral in law because social reality is constructed from the same point of view.[50]

She rejects what she calls "abstract equality" and asserts that such equality does not include "those rights that *women as women* most need." To consider "women as women" is precisely to consider them abstractly, that is, in abstraction from their other characteristics (age, race, size, education, etc.). To treat both Catharine and Dorine as women is precisely to abstract from the fact that one is white and the other black. Although MacKinnon tries to offer a general critique of abstract individualism as merely an ideological front for masculine privilege and the oppression of women, her generic arguments destroy her own case for women-specific rights. That extreme incoherence marks many attempts to show how the ideas of abstract rights, that is, rights that apply to unspecified persons, and equality before the law are in fact merely especially invidious forms of oppression.

Writing also from a self-described feminist perspective, Iris Marion Young argues for differentiated rights for men and for women, as well as for ethnic and other groups, on the general grounds that:

where differences in capacities, culture, values, and behavioral styles exist among some groups, but some of these groups are privileged, strict adherence to a principle of equal treatment tends to perpetuate oppression or disadvantage. The inclusion and participation of everyone in social and political institutions therefore sometimes requires the articulation of special rights that attend to group differences in order to undermine oppression and disadvantage.[51]

More strongly, she claims that, "A general perspective does not exist which all persons can adopt and from which all experiences and perspectives can be understood and taken into account."[52]

In support of her strong claim that equality before the law is inherently oppressive, Young merely reports that "many" activists "struggling for the full inclusion and participation of all groups in this society's institutions and positions of power, reward, and satisfaction, argue that rights and rules that are universally formulated and thus blind to differences of race, culture, gender, age, or disability, perpetuate rather than undermine oppression."[53]

It is central to Young's case for assigning different rights to sexual genders (and to other ascriptive groups) that the very idea of a common good is a myth and that, in fact, it is impossible to "walk a mile in another's shoes" or to understand the claims that others may make. Thus:

> Instead of a universal citizenship in the sense of this generality, we need a group differentiated citizenship and a heterogeneous public. In a heterogeneous public, differences are publicly recognized and acknowledged as irreducible, by which I mean that persons from one perspective or history can never completely understand and adopt the point of view of those with other group-based perspectives and histories. Yet commitment to the need and desire to decide together the society's policies fosters communication across those differences.[54]

I do not believe that we should so readily accede to Young's claim that "persons from one perspective or history can never completely understand or adopt the point of view of those with other group-based perspectives and histories." If by "completely understand or adopt the point of view" she means actually become that other person, then her claim is correct but irrelevant. If to understand a play by Shakespeare I had to actually be Shakespeare (and be him at the very moment that he completed the play), then Young's words themselves would be incomprehensible to all but her. Similarly, if I had to have had the same experiences as another person to understand her claim of right, then acts of justice would be impossible.[55] That sets an erroneous standard of understanding, one that is as inappropriate for law and politics as it is for literature. To understand the claim for justice of another is not, in fact, impossible, just as it is not impossible to understand Young's writings; it is hardly absurd to seek to achieve an objective standpoint from which to judge claims of justice, as Young presumes.[56] Understanding a play, a foreign language, or a claim for justice may be difficult, but that is not the same as being impossible.[57] Furthermore, Madison and the other Founders understood quite well that one could not and should not expect citizens always to adopt the perspective of the common good; that would be a shaky foundation on which to build a republic. Madison in particular certainly understood that citizens are quite often motivated by both interests and passions that are contrary to the general interest. Madison's constitutional project assumed that the public would be, in Young's term, "heterogeneous." But the fact that citizens are diverse and that many or most of them fail to adopt the perspective of the common good entails neither that the system of rights and obligations secured by the Constitution cannot embody or secure the common good nor that we should abandon the idea of citizenship or republican virtue altogether. Some degree of republican virtue is required for a workable constitutional order, but Madison's defense of equal rights does not assume that all citizens will adopt a universal perspective or that citizenship requires that one "completely" understand or adopt the point of view of other citizens.

Young's position, like MacKinnon's, is fraught with problems of internal coherence, for if what she believes is true, how could she or those who join her in undermining the ideal of equality before the law know the histories or experiences of others, and therefore be able to determine what their rights should be? After all, she does not assert that seekers of differentiated rights may unilaterally assert them against the rights, interests, or passions of others; indeed, she specifically denies it. Instead, they must emerge out of some kind of democratic process; they must be "publicly recognized." But if that democratic process presupposes differential rights to input, then the argument is circular, for it requires to be already established what it purports to produce.

In a way that brings to mind Oscar Wilde's complaint about socialism (too many committee meetings), Young writes, "All citizens should have access to neighborhood or district assemblies where they participate in discussion and decision making. In such a more participatory democratic scheme, members of oppressed groups would also have group assemblies, which would delegate group representatives."[58] But which groups are to get these special rights? Which groups "count"? According to Young, "These principles do not apply to any persons who do not identify with majority language or culture within a society, but only to sizeable linguistic or cultural minorities living in distinct though not necessarily segregated communities."[59] So size matters when it comes to determining fundamental rights. In abandoning the highly salient ideal of equal individual rights before the law, Young plunges into a morass of circular argumentation and self-contradiction.[60]

Reparations to Groups for Historical Injustices

The second form of group-specific rights that I will consider is, at least superficially, based on adherence to a liberal concern with rights and restitution. It is clearly differentiated from the view articulated by MacKinnon, Young, and many other advocates of group-differentiated rights. As Young notes of her approach, "The goal is not to give special compensation to the deviant until they achieve normality, but rather to denormalize the way institutions formulate their rules by revealing the plural circumstances and needs that exist, or ought to exist, within them."[61]

In contrast, demands for reparations rest on background claims for equal justice, on the claim that what has been taken unjustly should be restored.[62] Human history is filled with examples of injustices against groups of people, and when they can be corrected, there is certainly at least a good case that they should be. The suffering of Jews and Roma under the National Socialists, to take perhaps the most well known example, has led to restitution and reparations of various kinds. Those whose property was expropriated under Communist rule have received compensation in some formerly Communist states. In the United States, surviving Japanese Americans who suffered loss of liberty and estate as a result of President Franklin D. Roosevelt's Executive Order 9066, issued on February 19, 1942,[63] received an official apology and payments of $20,000 each as a result of passage of the Civil Liberties Act of 1988, which President Ronald Reagan signed into law on August 10, 1988.[64]

As this essay is written, the primary claim in the United States for reparations from the United States government, or from all or some citizens of the United States, is the claim for reparations to black Americans.[65] Randall Robinson, founder and president of the TransAfrica Forum and author of *The Debt: What America Owes to Blacks*, argues that:

> there is much new fessing-up that white society must be
> induced to do here for the common good. First, it must

own up to slavery and acknowledge its debt to slavery's contemporary victims. It must, at long last, pay that debt in massive restitutions made to America's only involuntary members. It must help to rebuild the black esteem it destroyed, by democratizing access to a trove of histories, near and ancient, to which blacks contributed seminally and prominently. It must open wide a scholarly concourse to the African ancients to which its highly evolved culture owes much credit and gives none. It must rearrange the furniture of its national myths, monuments, lores, symbols, iconography, legends, and arts to reflect the contributions and sensibilities of all Americans. It must set afoot new values. It must purify memory. It must recast its lying face.[66]

Robinson offers a variety of arguments for reparations, but two are especially prominent. First, African Americans were robbed of the value of their labor, from which others benefited. The descendants of those who benefited are now richer than they would be otherwise, and the descendants of those who were robbed are poorer than they would be otherwise. Thus:

Through keloids of suffering, through coarse veils of damaged self-belief, lost direction, misplaced compass, shit-faced resignation, racial transmutation, black people worked long, hard, killing days, years, centuries—and they were never *paid*. The value of their labor went into others' pockets—plantation owners, northern entrepreneurs, state treasuries, the United States government.[67]

This argument has considerable appeal to liberals (and I count authentic Madisonians as such) because it claims restitution for what was unjustly taken. Such a claim certainly could have provided justification for the confiscation of the estates of slave-holders and their distribution to freed slaves, as was proposed in the famous Special Field Order No. 15 issued by Major-General W. T. Sherman on January 16, 1865.[68] However, a substantial amount of time has passed between the enslavement and exploitation that Robinson so forcefully describes and the present. There are no living persons who were either slaves or slave-holders. That fact does not dispense with claims for reparations; those who inherited less because the wealth of their ancestors was stolen could, after all, be compensated by those who inherited more because their ancestors stole. This argument, however, is difficult to maintain after the passage of so long a time. The populations are today so mixed and the strands so intertwined that we cannot determine the justice of inherited endowments. For example, consider the heirs of the hundreds of thousands of soldiers who died in the war that eliminated slavery. What should those heirs receive in compensation for the loss of the lives and the livelihood of their ancestors, who might otherwise have left them wealth?[69]

In principle, reparations arguments are acceptable within a liberal theory of justice, but such reparations must be tied to the actual harm suffered by some and the existence of benefits that are unjustifiably held by others. If someone harms another, the victim should be made whole. If the one who committed the harm is dead, his or her heirs do not bear any criminal responsibility. If, however, they materially benefited from the harm and the wealth can be transferred to the heir of the harmed, who has a greater claim, then there is an argument for making the transfer. But if the heirs of the one who harms did not benefit, then taking anything from them is itself criminal. For example, transferring resources from "the Russians" to Tatars, as reparations for the harms imposed on Tatars by the Soviet state, would be unjust, for the overwhelming majority of Russians did not benefit from that state, but were also victimized by it. The average white American is not, in fact, a beneficiary of the criminal enslavement of others, past or present, and it would be an injustice to hold him or her responsible.[70]

The second commonly offered reason for reparations payments is that the culture of African Americans has been systematically harmed, and this harm translates into systematic disadvantage for African Americans, disadvantages that are imposed on them by whites and for which they deserve compensation. Thus, as Randall Robinson formulates the thesis:

> Culture is the matrix on which the fragile human animal draws to remain socially healthy.[71]

> Contemporary discrimination alone does not explain the persistence of these income gaps. Another culprit is a mutant form of the coarse and visible old discrimination. This sneaky and invisible culprit can be called conditioned expectation.[72]

> By now, after 380 years of unrelenting psychological abuse, the biggest part of our problem is inside us: in how we have

come to see ourselves, in our damaged capacity to validate
a course for ourselves without outside approval.[73]

For those reasons, Robinson supports the proposal made by Robert
Westley that "a private trust be established for the benefit of all
African Americans. The trust would be funded out of the general
revenues of the United States" and would support programs
designed to expand and improve the educational opportunities of
African Americans and, notably, to fund political activities: "The
broad civil rights advocacy necessitated by a persistent climate of
American racism would be generously funded, as well as the political
work of black organizations seeking, as Ron Walters has suggested,
to 'own' the *politics* of the black community."[74]

Most advocates of reparations payments quickly dismiss the idea
of individual compensation. As Darrell L. Pugh notes, "The fact
that the reparations being suggested are prospective and primarily
benefit nonvictims argues against the individual payment approach."[75]
As with Robinson, Pugh (citing the authority of Boris I. Bittker, who
wrote on the issue in the 1960s and 1970s) suggests instead that
"creation of a national trust fund, administered by 'legitimate' representatives of the African American community with oversight by
Congress, might be one answer."[76] The point is not to compensate
individual harmed victims, but to rebuild a culture that has been
damaged. (Note that the representatives must be "legitimate," a
criterion that seems equivalent to the "authentic" criterion invoked
by Lani Guinier.)

How long might such a group entitlement last? Will Kymlicka
assumes that such race-differentiated entitlements would be remedial and time-limited: "A degree of short-term separateness and
colour-consciousness is needed to achieve the long-term goal of an
integrated and colour-blind society."[77] Others, however, make it
clear that the debt owed by whites to blacks has no time limit. As
Robinson argues, "The life and responsibilities of a society or nation
are not circumscribed by the life spans of its mortal constituents.
Social rights, wrongs, obligations, and responsibilities flow eternal."[78] Indeed, the debt can never be repaid until and unless the
understanding of African history is changed:

> This then is the nub of it. America's contemporary racial
> problems cannot be solved, racism cannot be arrested,

achievement gaps cannot be fully closed until Americans—
all Americans—are repaired in their views of Africa's role
in history.[79]

Setting such a standard, and specifically one that relies on a highly
contested account of the history of Africa, indeed implies a perpetual
debt and, correspondingly, a perpetual entitlement of "legitimate"
representatives of the African American community to enrich those
they believe worthy at the expense of others.

The fact that Robinson even mentions the possibility of "punitive
damages"[80] indicates that he believes that "whites" as a group have
interests implacably opposed to those of "blacks" as a group. Otherwise, why even consider the possibility of *punishment* of whites as
a group?

In addition to enriching and empowering a class of authentic or
legitimate representatives (authentic or legitimate as determined by
whom?), the most serious consequences of the perpetual status of
the debt (dare I say dependency) is made clear by a moving description of a young girl who is struggling in school:

> The profound consequences constitute still another particular
> in a long bill of them against the government of the United
> States and others who benefited from slavery. But this is
> why I have expended so much time here on the issue of
> reparations, for the very discussion engendered will help an
> embattled nine-year-old to know finally what happened to
> her, that she is blameless, that she has had something taken
> from her that has a far more than material value.[81]

Much more could be said both in favor of, and in criticism of,
reparations for the American descendants of enslaved Africans. But
current proposals would leave blacks perpetually in tutelage, second
class citizens lorded over by first class overlords, all of whom would
be "authentic" and "legitimate" representatives of their community.
It is certainly not a proposal for the protection of minority interests
of the sort that a Madisonian would envisage and bears greater
resemblance, instead, to the black Bantustans or "homelands" established under the tribalism of Afrikaner apartheid. In such homelands
the central state designated the ruling elites, funded them, and charged
them with supervising the development of their communities.[82]

Empowering elites to administer (in perpetuity) resources to a dependent class distinguished by their race is incompatible with virtually any recognizably liberal vision of politics, Madisonian or otherwise. Reparations to individual victims from those who have benefited may be justified, but a case for that has not been established by Robinson's arguments.

There might even be a case for reparations of some sort as a means of securing the stability of a republican political and legal order that is more conducive to justice than the most likely alternative. Such an admission may, however, cut several ways, depending on which group would be most likely to undermine republican institutions absent special consideration. That is the upshot of Madison's speech on the slave trade clause of the Constitution before the Virginia Ratifying Convention:

> I should conceive this clause to be impolitic, if it were one of those things which could be excluded without encountering greater evils. The southern states would not have entered into the union of America, without the temporary permission of that trade. And if they were excluded from the union, the consequences might be dreadful to them and to us. We are not in a worse situation than before. That traffic is prohibited by our laws, and we may continue the prohibition. The union is not in a worse situation. Under the articles of confederation, it might be continued forever: But by this clause an end may be put to it after twenty years. There is therefore an amelioration of our circumstances.[83]

Such arguments from expediency are, however, premised on the existence of a clear danger to the continued existence of the republic itself. No such danger exists at the present time. Further, they could just as easily cut against reparations for the heirs of slaves as in favor; which way it would cut would depend on the bargaining powers of the different parties, rather than on any claims to justice.

Inequality of Rights as a Precondition of Freedom

Will Kymlicka has argued effectively for group-differentiated rights.[84] Such rights are necessary, he claims, to protect the viability of groups that provide communal ties, without which individuals could not enjoy the range of "meaningful choices" necessary to be able to enjoy freedom. Such ties might be eroded without such special rights, obligations, and correlative powers of enforcement.

In the case of North American Indians, Kymlicka claims that "the viability of Indian communities depends on coercively restricting the mobility, residence, and political rights of both Indians and non-Indians."[85] (It should be noted in passing that Kymlicka does consider the role of federalism in the U.S. constitutional system as a means of protecting minorities and finds it wanting. His account, however, is unfortunately full of factual errors.[86] More importantly, Kymlicka relies on an implicit baseline, in comparison to which American federalism allegedly worsens the positions of minorities: "Federalism may well serve to worsen the position of national minorities, as has occurred in the United States, Brazil, Australia, and other territorial federalisms."[87] Worsened in comparison to what? Perhaps the U.S.S.R., which did institutionalize explicitly national political units? Or worsened in comparison to a non-existent fantasy world?)

Kymlicka derives this right to cultural membership indirectly from the framework outlined by John Rawls in his *A Theory of Justice*. Kymlicka highlights Rawls's notion of "self-respect" as a precondition for the pursuit of any rational plan of life (hence as a "primary good") and then tries to determine the preconditions for self respect. A cultural context within which choices can be made is such a precondition: "The decision about how to lead our lives must ultimately be ours alone, but this decision is always a matter of selecting what we believe to be most valuable from the various options available, selecting from a context of choice which provides us with different ways of life."[88] Thus, "Liberal values require both individual freedom of choice and a secure cultural context from which individuals can make their choices."[89] Furthermore, belonging replaces accomplishment as the focus of self-esteem: "national identity is particularly suited to serving as the 'primary foci of identification,' because it is based on belonging, not accomplishment."[90]

Kymlicka distinguishes between "internal restrictions" and "external protections": the former are restrictions placed by the group on its own members, and the latter are restrictions on the interaction of members of the wider society with members of the protected group or entitlements to benefits from the wider society.[91] He favors external protections and opposes internal restrictions. He opposes the latter on the ground that "protecting people from changes in the character of their culture can't be viewed as protecting their ability to choose."[92] But he cannot help but slide directly toward such paternalism and control on the members of minority groups: "The viability of Indian communities depends on coercively restricting the mobility, residence, and political rights of both Indians and non-Indians."[93]

Kymlicka believes that sets of group-differentiated rights pose no danger to social or political unity, since in the cases he considers the groups seek inclusion or integration: "Enabling integration may require some modification of the institutions of the dominant culture in the form of group-specific polyethnic rights, such as the right of Jews and Muslims to exemptions from Sunday closing legislation, or the right of Sikhs to exemptions to motorcycle helmet laws."[94] These examples could also be accommodated by a reformulation of the rule so that it would apply to all. Rather than propose exemptions, which means that some persons are empowered to decide who will be punished for infractions and who will not be punished, why not simply propose the abolition of compulsory shop closing laws and the elimination of compulsory helmet laws? It seems never to occur to Kymlicka that the state might have no business interfering in personal choice or voluntary transactions in this manner. If such foolish and paternalistic restrictions were removed for all, then no one would feel the exclusion that so concerns Kymlicka.

Moreover, compulsory shop closing laws in Europe and North America are usually defended as a requirement for the maintenance of the cultural and religious identity of the majority Christian community; some might argue that they are a precondition for the self-esteem of the members of that community. To be consistent, Kymlicka would have to argue that only non-Christians should be allowed to buy and sell on Sundays, whereas Christians should be forbidden by law from doing so. Perhaps special Christian police forces would enforce such group-specific restrictions. A more authentically liberal solution would be to propose the same rule— liberty—for all. That is true also of most of the other plausible examples that Kymlicka gives of means to avoid oppressing a minority, such as exemptions for the Amish from Social Security (which they erroneously believe is an actuarially sound insurance system) and compulsory education.[95]

Kymlicka's proposal for group-differentiated rights is flawed in other ways. Rights that are given and taken, and that have to be periodically revised by someone with power, are not rights at all.[96] Someone has to be in the position to grant, take away, or otherwise adjust Kymlickian differential rights, and that person or those persons will be, in effect, the real holders of the rights because they hold the powers to grant them or to take them away. Equality of rights for all has a salience that carefully tweaked inequalities do not. The latter require philosopher kings to create and administer them. Thus, the adoring newspaper headline about Will Kymlicka's worldwide crusade to eliminate equality before the law: "A Philosopher in Red Sneakers Gains Influence as a Global Guru."[97] But as Plato found during his disastrous mission to Syracuse, philosophers rarely get the final word on matters of political power. Establishing systems of unequal rights will probably foster intergroup conflict, not intergroup comity, and we have seen in the last century just how terrible such conflict can be. Stipulating that "such measures will not harm the general welfare of the state," as the Lebanese Constitution did, is about as effective as stipulating that socialism shall be imposed, provided that it works.

Further, the boundary between external protections and internal restrictions on which Kymlicka puts so much weight is less impermeable than he thinks. For example, a restriction on the rights of indigenous peoples to sell their land counts as an external protection, but it will certainly look to at least some members of the group as an internal restriction. Not only are outsiders restricted from contracting with them, but they are restricted from contracting with outsiders.[98] The unity of the community that emerges is likely to be manipulated by those with the power to control members of the group. And although this may in some cases (and in some sense) preserve a political community by restricting the rights of its members, it also ensures that opportunities for enrichment will be foregone, so that members of the community also share common poverty. Such poverty may bind a community together, but it is not usually so desirable for the non-elite members of the community who suffer from it. Such special rights are also often liabilities. For example, the inability to sell land means that one cannot get a mortgage on it. One has possession, but not capital.[99] Contrary to Kymlicka's assertions, the alleged protections for such groups have a poor historical record.

"Special rights" may also prove to be terribly disadvantageous in other ways. The special status of Jews in European history is instructive in this regard. In that case, R. I. Moore cogently points out:

> As so often in Jewish history special treatment was danger-
> ous, and what began as a privilege later became the means
> of oppression. Protection of the Jews and jurisdiction over
> them became one of the rights which the counts usurped
> from the crown in the tenth century, and the feudatories
> from the counts in the eleventh.[100]

In the *Leges Edwardi Confessoris* it is stated that "All Jews wherever they are in the kingdom must be under the guardianship of the king; nor may any of them be subject to any baron without the licence of the king, because Jews and all their property are the king's."[101] The special status of many American Indian bands and nations as "domestic dependent nations"[102] also does not present an especially happy picture of how group-differentiated rights may actually work in practice.[103]

Although Kymlicka repeatedly insists that the group-differentiated rights he endorses are individual rights, he consistently refers to "the group" making choices about whether or how their culture will change. Thus, "While indigenous peoples do not want modernization forced upon them, they demand the right to decide for themselves what aspects of the outside world they will incorporate into their cultures."[104] Who are the "they" here? If he means the individual members, their rights to decide what aspects of the outside world they wish to accept would be respected in a regime of equal rights. It seems clear that Kymlicka means the group as a whole, or at least its political leaders, in which case majorities (as a matter of practice, this means oligarchic elites) have the right, and he cannot assert that such rights are individual, rather than collective, rights. In virtually every case, despite his persistent denials, Kymlicka gives to the elite members of groups (frequently people who are articulate, like himself, or people who are brutal, violent, and ruthless in eliminating opposition) the right to determine how the other members of the group will live, and if that is not an "internal restriction," it is not clear what would be.[105] As Charles Taylor notes of restrictive laws in Quebec, "Restrictions have been placed on Quebeckers by their government, in the name of their collective goal of survival."[106] Kymlicka's approach follows the general trend of declarations, conventions, and covenants governing indigenous people, most of which do not mention individual rights of the members of indigenous nations, such as the right to own land individually or freely in association with others, but consistently refer only to the right of "peoples" to "lands" and "territories." A philosophical defense of such restrictions is offered by Michael McDonald, who complains of "the distorting force of individual mobility rights" and asserts "such rights can intentionally or unintentionally lead to the destruction of worthwhile groups."[107] The approach is decidedly collectivist, rather than individualist. Thus, Article 17, Section 2 of the Convention concerning Indigenous and Tribal Peoples in Independent Countries states, "The peoples concerned shall be consulted whenever consideration is being given to their capacity to alienate their lands or otherwise transmit their rights outside their own community."[108] Such "rights" are explicitly collective rights, founded on race or ethnicity, and not, *pace* Kymlicka, individual rights. They subject individuals to the rule of the collectivity to which they are assigned, which quite often means in practice subordination to the rule of parasitic and predatory elites who have attained preeminence or power within and therefore over their own national or ethnic group.

Kymlicka rests his case on the alleged unavoidability of the mixture of state and ethnicity: "The state cannot help but take an active role in the reproduction of cultures."[109] To avoid oppression and to guarantee each group the recognition its members need as a primary good necessary for the pursuit of rational plans of life, the state should interact with the members of each ethnic group differently. Thus, since "there is no way to have a complete 'separation of state and ethnicity,'" it follows that "the only question is how to ensure that these unavoidable forms of support for particular ethnic and national groups are provided fairly—that is, how to ensure that they do not privilege some groups and disadvantage others."[110] Further, he argues that "the most plausible reason" for not granting automatic citizenship to each and every human who might desire it is "to recognize and protect our membership in distinct cultures," and this, in turn, "is also a reason for allowing group-differentiated citizenship within a state."[111]

Such reasoning is compatible with nationalist or socialist thought but not with liberalism. The liberal approach recognizes the inevitability of conflicts over common goods among people with different ends and therefore limits the state to those things necessary to the maintenance of a civil society, to what is in fact a good common to all. That is the most plausible interpretation of the "necessary and proper" clause of the United States Constitution, a clause that is usually misinterpreted to mean "convenient and not clearly prohibited." If government schools inevitably impart some set of moral values (which, of course, includes the currently dominant null set promulgated in most government schools), we may consider alternatives to monopoly state schooling, rather than trying to fine-tune the curriculum so that each and every ethnic group will not feel excluded. The result of the latter has turned out to be (in the United States, at least) a curriculum remarkably devoid of moral and other content. Kymlicka never considers whether individuals may have a right to withdraw from coercive state-imposed systems; exemptions may be "granted" by the state, but they should always be understood to be gifts or dispensations made by those with the power and the right to grant or to deny them. They are not rights.[112]

Kymlicka and others start with the fixed point of national borders and restrictions on freedom of movement and trade, assuming that nothing could be less controversial than protectionism and controls on the movement of people. They treat the relatively recent invention of the passport and of controls on movement in European history as if they were an inheritance of the ages.[113] As Kymlicka writes of group-differentiated rights, "they are logically presupposed by existing liberal practice."[114] By this he means restricting rights to work, travel, own property, and the like to citizens. The statement is true only if we consider shooting people who try to sneak across the borders in search of opportunities to offer their services to willing employers to be part of "liberal practice." But Kymlicka does have a thin wedge to open the door to group-differentiated rights: even if borders were open to trade and travel, one legal right at least would not be open to any and all who desired it. One right that should be reserved for citizens is the right to vote. That is an important limitation on the scope of a legal right, but voting is hardly a natural right like the right to own property or the right to choose one's profession; it is a procedural right that is useful as a means of protecting our fundamental rights, such as the right to freedom of religion or the right to choose one's profession or spouse. And it is a very, very, very thin wedge to use to create a general theory of group-restricted rights. "To recognize and protect our membership in distinct cultures" is hardly "the most plausible reason" for limiting the franchise to citizens and limiting citizenship to those who are a part of the civic culture of liberalism. Further, the idea that citizenship should be limited to members of distinct ethnic or cultural groups is hardly widely accepted as a part of liberalism. Kymlicka puts a great deal of weight on the alleged intuitive plausibility of his thesis, but his intuition is not shared by many other contemporary liberals.[115]

Unlike Madison and other classical liberals, Kymlicka is willing or even eager to jettison legal stability in favor of an ever changing kaleidoscope of rights and obligations. The very variety and flexibility of rights regimes that Kymlicka endorses—a plurality that requires wise supervisors, adjudicators, and assigners of rights to and among groups—has terrible consequences for the rule of law generally. Rather than being a condition of freedom, as Kymlicka asserts,[116] these regimes require subjection to the arbitrary will of others who are empowered to tweak, adjust, change, and rearrange rights as they see fit. Traditional liberalism defined that subjection as the very condition of tyranny, rather than of liberty.[117]

It seems that the one fixed point for Kymlicka is the existence of national state borders, protectionism, immigration controls, and armed border guards, not an especially promising point for an allegedly liberal theory of rights. Yet Kymlicka's own argument for group-differentiated rights can just as easily be used against him, by identifying groups with common identities and interests that transcend national state borders and whose claims or rights, therefore, to be protected, would require that those very borders be eliminated. One obvious example is the travel of nomadic peoples across state borders; examples include the Somali of the Ogaden, the Sami of Scandinavia, Finland, and Russia, and others. Other groups whose "identities" transcend national borders include religious groups and gay people. In the case of religion, Jeremy Waldron brings up the helpful example of a Catholic Breton who considers her religion, which is shared by people in many other national communities, as more important to her sense of self than her Celtic ethnicity: "That feature of her life—that as a Breton she shares a faith and a church with Irish, Italians, Poles, Brazilians, and Filipinos—may be much more important to her identity than anything which (say) a Tourist Board would use to highlight her cultural distinctiveness."[118] Barring her from freedom of travel, trade, and interaction with her fellow Catholics in the name of her Celtic ethnicity would likely be far

101

more damaging to her than Kymlicka seems willing to admit. Taking border guards and protectionism as a given is to constrain the liberty that she would see as most instrumentally valuable to the fulfillment of her identity.

Another case overlooked by Kymlicka is that of gay people. As Carl Stychin points out, "If we accept the possibility of group based identity and rights," then the theories of multiculturalism and diversity advanced by Charles Taylor and Will Kymlicka "are going to be more complicated than we (and they) might first have considered."[119] Stychin's critique is not, however, based on a call for equal individual rights; he agrees fundamentally with thinkers such as Taylor and Kymlicka but carries their project to its own absurd conclusion. Stychin shows how a serious commitment to group-differentiated rights on Kymlickian foundations (self-esteem, recognition, etc.) ultimately destroys the very national borders that Kymlicka considered determined starting points. As Stychin argues, "lesbians and gays (and, for that matter, many others) are skeptical when they read Kymlicka's arguments about culture. For many of us, an important cultural reference point is queer culture, which seems more than capable of surviving (and thriving) in the current cultural conditions."[120] But he concludes from the fact that such identities and communities are transnational that "lesbian, gay, bisexual, and queer politics and culture can bring to a study of national identities a framework in which identity is self-consciously contingent and in process, characterized by reinvention and an ongoing questioning of borders and membership."[121] Stychin finds that prospect exciting, but one wonders whether people who have suffered through border changes in the past—those in Poland, for example—are likely to be as excited about an ongoing questioning of borders and membership. Stychin takes the multicultural project of Kymlicka and others seriously enough to bring it to its absurd conclusion: all the rules, all the time, are always open to "reinvention." As he says, "As nations struggle with their sense of self, they could do well to appropriate this excitement of reconstitution, which I would describe as a queering of the nation itself."[122] An authentically liberal perspective would simply recognize the equal individual rights of gay people, including the rights to travel and work where they wish, to marry, and so on, so that gay partners who are citizens of different countries would not be separated by odious border controls, residence permits, and work permits. Group-differentiated rights, when taken seriously, lead to both logical and legal instability. Equal individual rights, on the other hand, are stable, predictable, salient, and knowable by and to all and do not rest on such odious and immoral practices as terrorizing those who wish to cross state borders for peaceful purposes.

Madison's vision of "establishing a political equality among all"[123] provides a much more stable foundation from which to secure the common good than do any of the innumerable variety of systems of inequality proposed by multiculturalists. Madison envisioned a constitutional order encompassing a wide variety of factions living together under a regime of equal rights. He defended such a republican order in the name of liberty, for he did not think that liberty would be as secure in the small republic that Montesquieu and some of the anti-Federalists believed was the only secure repository of liberty.[124] For example, "Brutus," writing in opposition to adoption of the Constitution, argued that:

> History furnishes no example of a free republic, any thing like the extent of the United States. The Grecian republics were of small extent; so also was that of the Romans. Both of these, it is true, in process of time, extended their conquests over large territories of country; and the consequence was, that their governments were changed from that of free governments to those of the most tyrannical that ever existed in the world.[125]

> In a republic, the manners, sentiments, and interests of the people should be similar. If this be not the case, there will be a constant clashing of opinions; and the representatives of one part will be continually striving against those of the other. This will retard the operations of government, and prevent such conclusions as will promote the public good.[126]

Madison drew precisely the opposite conclusion:

> The lesson we are to draw from the whole is that where a majority are united by a common sentiment, and have an opportunity, the rights of the minor party become insecure. In a Republican Gov^t the majority if united have always an opportunity. The only remedy is to enlarge the sphere, and thereby divide the community into so great a number of interests and parties, that in the 1st place a majority will not be likely at the same moment to have a common interest

> separate from that of the whole or of the minority; and in
> the 2^d place, that in case they sh ^{d} have such an interest, they
> may not be apt to unite in the pursuit of it. It was incumbent
> on us then to try this remedy, and with that view to frame
> a republican system on such a scale & in such a form as will
> controul all the evils wch have been experienced.[127]

Kymlicka and others are trying to replicate within each extended or multicultural republic a set of little republics, each ethnically (relatively) homogeneous, and each, therefore, more likely to experience the tyranny by majorities over minorities. Madison sought to prevent such tyranny by expanding the scope of the American republic. The establishment of such little republics is likely to generate conflicts among those with group-differentiated rights about what the ultimate decisionmakers of the state are going to put into each Christmas stocking of rights.[128]

A fairly obvious example of the possible conflicts among groups that are made inevitable by such schemes of group-differentiated rights is presented by the conflict between feminist and multiculturalist approaches. Feminist theorist Susan Moller Okin has raised the problem of the treatment of women in cultural, ethnic, religious, or national groups whose traditions incorporate or rest upon the subordination of women.[129] In response, Will Kymlicka noted that "Okin says she is concerned about the view that the members of a minority 'are not sufficiently protected by the practice of ensuring the individual rights of their members,' and minority group members are demanding 'a group right not available to the rest of the population.' But many feminists have made precisely the same argument about gender equality—i.e., that true equality will require rights for women that are not available to men, such as affirmative action, women-only classrooms, gender-specific prohibitions on pornography, gender-specific health programs, and the like. Others have made similar arguments about the need for group-specific rights and benefits for the disabled, or for gays and lesbians. All of these movements are challenging the traditional liberal assumption that equality requires identical treatment."[130] The very fact of the limitless variety of group-differentiated rights may be the strongest argument for equal rights.

Madison and the Indians

There is one exception to the general argument for equal rights under the rule of law, and that is the status of the native American nations, on whose behalf Madison devoted much effort and whose status is recognized in the Constitution of the United States of America. (For Madison's views and efforts on behalf of the American Indians, see Jacob Levy's contribution to this volume.) Thus, Article I, Section 8, Clause 3 of the Constitution vests in the Congress of the United States the power "To regulate Commerce with foreign Nations, and among the several States, and with the Indian tribes." Article VI, Clause 2 further specifies that "This Constitution, and the Laws of the United States which shall be made in Pursuance thereof; and all Treaties made, or which shall be made, under the Authority of the United States, shall be the supreme Law of the Land; and the Judges in every State shall be bound thereby, any Thing in the Constitution or Laws of any State to the Contrary notwithstanding." This clearly means that all of the treaties with the Indian tribes that preceded the new Constitution of the United States were part of the "supreme law of the land," for it specifically refers to "all Treaties *made*, or which shall be made" (emphasis added). On the basis of the historical facts and the law of the land, Chief Justice Marshall declared in *Worcester v. Georgia*, "The Cherokee nation, then, is a distinct community, occupying its own territory, with boundaries accurately described, in which the laws of Georgia can have no force. . . ."[131] Thus, the new Constitution did not completely wipe out the preexisting political independence of the Indian tribes, although Marshall's denomination of them as "domestic dependent nations" in "a state of pupilage" to the United States government implied something less than independence. Whether Marshall's reading of the status of the Indian tribes is tenable, the United States government is obligated to respect all of the particular rights and obligations specified in the 367 ratified treaties between Indian tribes and the American government.[132] Adherence to all such treaties is justified not only by the preexisting status of the Indian tribes, but more importantly, by the fundamental legal obligation to fulfill the terms of the Constitution. Arguments about securing a higher kind of freedom by "recognizing" the special status of groups are irrelevant to adherence to the law of the land.

Special legal and political status for Indian tribes and bands is justified by the fact of their preexisting political status and the requirement that treaties already entered into be respected. To do otherwise would be to violate fundamental requirements of justice, and to replace law with brute force and power. For the same reasons that new group-differentiated rights should not be conjured up by legislative fiat, legally binding treaties should not be unilaterally abrogated (unless the treaty itself provides for such abrogation).

The variety of regimes of group-differentiated rights that are presented as realizations of multiculturalism is too great to catalogue or to rebut in this essay.[133] The above remarks merely rebut some of the more prominent variants and should point the way to a general liberal defense of the idea of equality before the law.

Conclusion

The project that Madison and his colleagues (both those who supported and those who opposed the Constitution) launched has proven itself quite attractive in comparison to other existing regimes. Despite its many flaws and failings, it has secured more liberty and more prosperity for more people than any other regime in the history of humanity. I see no reason to replace a regime of equal individual rights, itself the result of heroic struggles familiar to students of American history, with any of the variety of mutually incompatible regimes of group-differentiated rights. Equality is unique; inequality is not. That fact alone should indicate to us that any proposed regime of unequal rights will be opposed by all the advocates of other competing regimes of unequal rights. Each group (or, more precisely, the elite self-appointed leaders of each group who expect to benefit) will struggle for maximum advantage, to the detriment of the common good.

In every case, advocates of unequal rights reject the common good, whether explicitly in theory or implicitly in practice. In place of Madison's attempt to protect "the rights of other citizens, or the permanent and aggregate interests of the community,"[134] advocates of group-differentiated rights have adopted Calhoun's vision of legal and political processes as "considering the community as made up of different and conflicting interests, as far as the action of government is concerned."[135] The common good is a central element of the classical liberal/libertarian tradition of thinking. The common good, at least under the normal circumstances of justice, is liberty and the rule of law. Advocates of group-differentiated rights reject both by subjecting citizens to those empowered to change the rules, reallocate rights, and create caste distinctions among them.

We may, then, answer the three questions with which I opened this essay:

1. Did Madison envision a "multicultural" republic?
   Yes, if by multicultural we mean encompassing a wide variety of passions and interests. No, if by multicultural we mean regimes of group-differentiated rights.
2. Are contemporary advocates of various forms of group rights or group representation, often presented under the banner of "multiculturalism," advancing the Madisonian project, or undermining it?
   Such thinkers are undermining Madison's project and advancing Calhoun's radically different vision of the Constitution.
3. Are group-differentiated rights a necessary and proper element of a constitutional order ordained and established to "form a more perfect Union, establish Justice, insure domestic Tranquility, provide for the common defence, promote the general Welfare, and secure the Blessings of Liberty to ourselves and to our Posterity"?
   Such group-differentiated rights are neither necessary to securing the goods listed in the preamble, nor proper, for they violate fundamental principles of republican government and the rule of law, and are therefore not authorized under the Constitution.

Madison's vision of an extended republic as the framework for liberty remains inspiring. Millions of people, from virtually every nation, race, ethnicity, and religion still seek to become citizens of the United States of America. They seek to live in a nation in which "government is instituted and ought to be exercised for the benefit of the people."[136] For pursuit of the common good to be institutionally stable, it should not encompass too many goals. The more goods that are claimed to be common, the less likely that the entire bundle will, in fact, amount to the common good. That is why the Founders excluded supporting religion from the common good; not because they discounted the importance of religion, but because the variety of religions meant that no one religion could be considered the common good among practitioners of many religions. As Madison noted, the benefit of the people "consists in the enjoyment of life and liberty, with the right of acquiring and using property, and generally of pursuing and obtaining happiness and safety."[137]

Accordingly the Constitution does not establish particular religion; it prohibits the Congress from making any law "respecting an establishment of religion, or prohibiting the free exercise thereof." The common good—for Christians, Jews, Muslims, Buddhists, Hindus, atheists, and others—is liberty of religion. And the particular goods that people pursue are quite simply not the business of government. The Declaration of Independence asserts rights to "Life, Liberty, and the *Pursuit* of Happiness," just as Madison identifies the common good with *"pursuing* and obtaining happiness and safety" (emphasis added). Just as for religion, so for cultural goods and identity, education, preferences for material goods and all the other means of pursuing happiness, government may secure our *right to pursue* those goods by providing for justice and defense but is not authorized to provide the goods themselves. That is the proper responsibility of the citizens themselves, acting in their capacities as private persons.

A legal order that can secure a framework within which a great variety of persons who are members of many different cultural, ethnic, religious, or national groups can pursue and obtain happiness and safety *is* the common good, and that legal order is undermined by attempts to use it to secure the concrete good of this or that group, or to tweak it to fulfill the preferred arrangements of entitlements and obligations of this or that activist or philosopher. Americans should do as Madison's friend Thomas Jefferson urged them in his First Inaugural Address,

> Let us then, with courage and confidence pursue our own federal and republican principles, our attachment to our union and representative government.[138]

Notes

1. Montesquieu, *The Spirit of the Laws*, trans. and ed. Anne M. Cohler, Basia Carolyn Miller, and Harold Samuel Stone (Cambridge: Cambridge University Press, 1989), Part I, Chapter 16, "Distinctive Properties of the Republic," p. 124.

2. James Madison, "Speech in the Virginia Ratifying Convention on Taxation, a Bill of Rights, and the Mississippi," in *James Madison: Writings*, ed. Jack N. Rakove (New York: Penguin Putnam, 1999), pp. 381–82. The context of Madison's remarks is that a bill of rights formally guaranteeing religious freedom is not necessary to the enjoyment of such liberty.

3. François-Marie Arouet Voltaire, *Candide and Philosophical Letters* (1734; New York: Random House, 1992), p. 141.

4. *The Federalist* No. 10 (James Madison).

5. See, for example, Amitai Etzioni, "The Responsive Community: A Communitarian Perspective," Presidential Address, American Sociological Association, August

20, 1995. *American Sociological Review*, (February 1996), 1–11: "Most important for the point at hand is that libertarians actively oppose the notion of 'shared values' or the idea of 'the common good,'" (available at www.gwu.edu/~ccps/etzioni/A241.html). Further, Etzioni asserts in "Libertarian Follies," *The World & I*, May 1995, pp. 365–77, "Libertarians seem to fear that the recognition of the common good as a value that is co-equal with personal freedom will endanger the standing of that liberty." For an attempt to set the record straight, and to articulate a classical liberal conception of the common good, see Tom G. Palmer, "Myths of Individualism," *Cato Policy Report* 18, no. 5 (September/October 1996) (available at www.cato.org/pubs/policy_report/cpr-18n5-1.html). For a nuanced statement of the liberal idea of "self-interest," see "The Secret History of Self-Interest," in Stephen Holmes, *Passions and Constraint: On the Theory of Liberal Democracy* (Chicago: University of Chicago Press, 1995).

6. *The Federalist* No. 45 (James Madison).

7. James Madison, "Speech in the House of Representatives, June 8, 1789," in *The Mind of the Founder: Sources of the Political Thought of James Madison*, ed. Marvin Meyers (Hanover, N.H.: University Press of New England, 1981), p. 164.

8. Madison, "Parties," in *James Madison: Writings*, p. 504.

9. Ibid., p. 505.

10. Not only should the rules be common, but they must be stable if they are to be just and compatible with the order of a free society. Madison described the effects of a "mutable policy" starkly: "It poisons the blessings of liberty itself. It will be of little avail to the people that the laws are made by men of their own choice, if the laws be so voluminous that they cannot be read, or so incoherent that they cannot be understood; if they be repealed or revised before they are promulgated, or undergo such incessant changes that no man who knows what the law is today can guess what it will be tomorrow. Law is defined to be a rule of action; but how can that be a rule, which is little known and less fixed?

"Another effect of public instability is the unreasonable advantage it gives to the sagacious, the enterprising, and the moneyed few, over the industrious and uninformed mass of the people. Every new regulation concerning commerce or revenue; or in any manner affecting the value of the different species of property, presents a new harvest to those who watch the change and can trace the consequences; a harvest reared not by themselves but by the toils and cares of the great body of their fellow citizens. This is a state of things in which it may be said with some truth that laws are made for the *few* not for the *many*." *The Federalist* No. 62 (James Madison).

11. As Madison noted in opposing on the floor of Congress the establishment of a national bank, "No argument could be drawn from the terms 'common defence, and general welfare.' The power as to these general purposes, was limited to acts laying taxes for them; and the general purposes themselves were limited and explained by the particular enumeration subjoined. To understand these terms in any sense, that would justify the power in question, would give to Congress an unlimited power; would render nugatory the enumeration of particular powers; would supercede all the powers reserved to the state governments. These terms are copied from the articles of confederation; had it ever been pretended, that they were to be understood otherwise than as here explained?" James Madison, "Speech in Congress Opposing the National Bank," in *James Madison: Writings*, p. 483.

12. *Notes of Debates in the Federal Convention of 1787 Reported by James Madison*, ed. Gaillard Hunt and James Brown Scott (New York: W. W. Norton & Co., 1987), p. 76.

13. Ibid., p. 77. It is worth noting that just prior to these questions, Madison states "We have seen the mere distinction of colour made in the most enlightened period of time, a ground of the most oppressive dominion ever exercised by man over man." Madison, like many of the other Founders, was acutely aware of the injustice of slavery and saw it as one form of the oppression that their innovative approach to government was to eliminate. See also his "Memorandum on Colonizing Freed Slaves," in *James Madison: Writings*, pp. 472–73, in which he argued that incorporation of a freed black population into American society would be "rendered impossible by the prejudices of the Whites, prejudices which proceeding principally from the differences of colour must be considered as permanent and insuperable." He proposed colonization of Africa, for "an experiment for providing such an external establishment for the blacks might induce the humanity of Masters, and by degrees both the humanity and policy of the Governments, to forward the abolition of slavery in America."

14. Ibid., p. 77.

15. *The Federalist* No. 10 (James Madison).

16. Ibid.

17. Here Madison seemed not to consider the possibility of a tyranny of special interests that, having smaller transaction costs than the majority, can impose diffuse microburdens on the majority, the aggregate of which, when concentrated in the hands of a minority, provide a substantial incentive to organize factions against the common interest. This is the phenomenon of "diffused costs, concentrated benefits" with which students of rent-seeking in modern polities are so well acquainted. Second, such particular interests may engage in logrolling, in which legislators trade votes on issue A for votes on an unrelated issue B, to create legislative majorities that are systematically opposed to the common interest.

18. *The Federalist* No. 58 (James Madison).

19. *The Federalist* No. 62 (James Madison).

20. *The Federalist* No. 57 (James Madison).

21. Lani Guinier, *The Tyranny of the Majority* (New York: The Free Press, 1994), p. 4.

22. Ibid., p. 3.

23. Ibid., pp. 57, 216. A careful reading of *The Federalist* No. 39 did not reveal to me any connection of Madison's ideas to Guinier's statement that "all sectors of society" should be included in "government operation."

24. Ibid., p. 103.

25. Ibid., p. 5.

26. Ibid., p. 58.

27. Ibid., p. 227, footnote 154, and p. 245, footnote 42.

28. Ibid., p. 70.

29. Lani Guinier, "No Two Seats: The Elusive Quest for Political Equality," *Virginia Law Review* 77 (1991), p. 1514, footnote 299. Henry Louis Gates Jr. endorses *The Tyranny of the Majority* on the back cover of the book as "At last . . . the public hearing she was denied. . . . It doesn't matter where you think you stand; it's all here, to argue or agree with." Stephen L. Carter, in his foreword to the book, stated that "the debate, after all, was about her written record. It is high time, then, for the record to be available for all to view. Let readers make up their own minds, without the intercession of media experts and electronic sound bites." Apparently, Gates and Carter were deceived, for a number of the more startling claims that appeared in her law review articles did not make it into the book.

30. See, for example, Doug Kendall, "Gale Norton Is No James Watt; She's Even Worse," *Los Angeles Times*, January 9, 2001: "The more you learn about Norton, the more the label 'James Watt in a skirt' seems unfair to Watt."

31. See, for example, the remarks of gay writer Charles Kaiser, quoted in the *New York Times*: "I certainly think that Andrew's popularity, especially on the talk-show circuit has a lot to do with his own self-hatred, which makes him an especially attractive kind of homosexual to a certain kind of talk-show host. Which is the reason that his prominence is so infuriating to the rest of the community." "Conservative Gay Columnist Is under Fire," by Felicity Barringer, *New York Times*, August 6, 2001. The main topic of the essay is the firestorm of criticism attracted by Norah Vincent, a columnist for the *Village Voice* and the *Los Angeles Times* who is a lesbian and a libertarian, and therefore a prime target for collectivist gay writers. As one dissident editor at the *Village Voice*, Richard Goldstein, put it, "The liberal press needs to ask itself why they consistently promote the work of gay writers who attack other gay people." Note that the "other gay people" whom Norah Vincent and Andrew Sullivan have on occasion criticized are collectivists and statists, but their collectivism and statism are implicitly equated by Goldstein with their homosexuality, so anyone who criticizes them is criticizing "gay people," and not "collectivist statists." In Goldstein's view, it is an essential property of being homosexual that one favor state power over individual rights.

32. See, for example, Ludwig von Mises, *Human Action* (Chicago: Henry Regnery Company, 1966), pp. 75–91.

33. Lani Guinier, "The Triumph of Tokenism: The Voting Rights Act and the Theory of Black Electoral Success," *Michigan Law Review* 89 (1991): 1140. This discussion, too, was deleted from the version of the essay that appeared in her book *The Tyranny of the Majority*.

34. Lani Guinier, *The Tyranny of the Majority*, p. 113.

35. Ibid., p. 254.

36. Robert Richie and Steven Hill, *Reflecting All of Us: The Case for Proportional Representation* (Boston: Beacon Press, 1999), pp. 14, 15.

37. Ibid., p. 18.

38. Will Kymlicka, *Multicultural Citizenship* (Oxford: Clarendon Press, 1995), p. 151.

39. Ibid., p. 150.

40. John C. Calhoun, *A Disquisition on Government*, in *Union and Liberty: The Political · Philosophy of John C. Calhoun*, Ross M. Lence, ed. (Indianapolis: Liberty Fund, 1992), p. 14.

41. Ibid., p. 15.

42. Guinier's discussion of what she calls a "Madisonian majority" (*The Tyranny of the Majority*, p. 4) is strikingly parallel to Calhoun's discussion of how "a minority might become the majority" (*A Disquisition on Government*, p. 20) and is rejected as a solution to the problem of majority domination for the same reasons, namely, that (for Guinier) blacks as a bloc facing another racial bloc cannot transform themselves into the majority and (for Calhoun) the minority bloc of slave states cannot transform itself into a majority bloc, at least given the demographic trends in the United States in Calhoun's time.

43. Calhoun, p. 21.

44. Ibid., pp. 23–24.

45. Ibid., pp. 16–19. Here Calhoun makes a powerful point that is fully consistent with a Madisonian approach; the more Madisonian solution, however, would seem

to be to strive for strictly limited government and for strict economy in those functions best discharged by government, rather than to attempt to guarantee a system of group representation that would, in any case, be more likely to generate collusion among groups represented to capture disproportionate shares of such emoluments.

46. John C. Calhoun, "Speech at the Meeting of the Citizens of Charleston" (March 9, 1847), in *Union and Liberty: The Political Philosophy of John C. Calhoun*, p. 526. In his *A Discourse on the Constitution and Government,* Calhoun presented an interpretation of the United States Constitution through his theory of the concurrent majority, and asserted that the United States was "preeminently a government of the concurrent majority." In *Union and Liberty: The Political Philosophy of John C. Calhoun,* p. 121.

47. Lebanese Constitution, Article 95, cited in Enver M. Koury, *The Crisis in the Lebanese System: Confessionalism and Chaos* (Washington, D.C.: American Enterprise Institute, 1976), p. 5. Article 95 was added by the constitutional law of November 9, 1943. It effectively abrogated Article 7: "All the Lebanese are equal before the law. They enjoy equal civil and political rights and are equally subjected to public charges and duties, without any distinction whatsoever."

48. In the Lebanese case, the rough proportion between demography and political office was upset by an enormous demographic change; unsurprisingly, those who were favored by the old scheme did not want to give it up in favor of the new, and the result was a savage civil war that is still not fully over.

49. Catharine MacKinnon, *Toward a Feminist Theory of the State* (Cambridge, Mass.: Harvard University Press, 1989), p. 228.

50. Ibid., p. 229.

51. Iris Marion Young, "Polity and Group Difference: A Critique of the Ideal of Universal Citizenship," in *Feminism and Political Theory,* Cass R. Sunstein, ed. (Chicago: University of Chicago Press, 1990), p. 118.

52. Ibid., p. 129.

53. Ibid., p. 134.

54. Ibid., p. 125. One might wonder why someone with Young's general philosophical presuppositions would favor "communication across those differences." Communication across difference presupposes something common, which seems to be what Young is rejecting.

55. These issues, in the context of the written word, are carefully explored by Roman Ingarden in *The Literary Work of Art: An Investigation on the Borderlines of Ontology, Logic, and Theory of Literature,* trans. by George R. Grabowicz (Evanston, Ill.: Northwestern University Press, 1973). See also Roman Ingarden, *The Cognition of the Literary Work of Art,* trans. by Ruth Ann Crowley and Kenneth R. Olson (Evanston, Ill.: Northwestern University Press, 1973) and *The Work of Music and the Problem of Its Identity,* trans. by Adam Czerniawski (Berkeley, Calif.; University of California Press, 1986). Ingarden offers a powerful general critique of the sort of claim of incommensurability and incomprehensibility that Young makes.

56. On the issue of objectivity in general, see Thomas Nagel, *The View from Nowhere* (Oxford: Oxford University Press, 1986).

57. Note also that Young asserts the inability to "completely understand or adopt the point of view of those with other *group-based* perspectives and histories" (italics added), but certainly if this claim is true, it would be even more the case for communication among individual members of the same groups, for individual life histories among group members differ. Young has smuggled into the discussion a remarkable

set of implausible ontological claims about groups and their relationships to both the individuals who comprise them and to other groups.

58. "Polity and Group Difference," p. 133. Nowhere does Young mention or consider the tremendous advantage in such meetings held by the articulate over the inarticulate. College professors, who live by the spoken and written word, are often quite eager to center the power over others in forums where—mirabile dictu!—it is they who have the greatest advantage; in this, they are no different from other minority factions and should be treated with the same suspicion as are all other special interest groups.

59. "Polity and Group Difference," p. 139–40.

60. The incipiently authoritarian nature of her case is indicated in her reference to the Nicaraguan state: "Reports of experiments with publicly institutionalized self-organization among women, indigenous peoples, workers, peasants, and students in contemporary Nicaragua offer an example closer to the conception I am advocating." Iris Marion Young, "Polity and Group Difference," p. 132. (The essay originally appeared in 1989; no mention is made of the war waged by the Sandinistas on the Mosquito Indians and other indigenous groups.) "Polity and Group Difference: A Critique of the Ideal of Universal Citizenship."

61. Young, p. 140.

62. As Bartolomé de las Casas concluded his defense of the American Indians in 1550, "The Indians are our brothers, and Christ has given his life for them. Why, then, do we persecute them with such inhuman savagery when they do not deserve such treatment? The past, because it cannot be undone, must be attributed to our weakness, provided that what has been taken unjustly is restored." Bartolomé de las Casas, *In Defense of the Indians*, trans. by Stafford Poole (DeKalb, Ill.: Northern Illinois University Press, 1992), p. 362.

63. See "Executive Order 9066: Authorizing the Secretary of War to Prescribe Military Areas," in *When Sorry Isn't Enough: The Controversy over Apologies and Reparations for Human Injustice*, Roy L. Brooks, ed. (New York: New York University Press, 1999), pp. 169–70.

64. Civil Liberties Act of 1988, *U.S. Statutes at Large* 102 (1988): 903. In addition, the act authorized the establishment of a special education fund.

65. For a representative statement on the issue, see the transcript of a TransAfrica Forum program at www.transafricaforum.org/reports/print/reparations_print.shtml.

66. Randall Robinson, *The Debt: What America Owes to Blacks* (New York: Penguin Putnam, Inc., 2000), pp. 107–08.

67. Ibid., p. 207.

68. See "Special Field Order No. 15," in *When Sorry Isn't Enough: The Controversy over Apologies and Reparations for Human Injustice*, pp. 365–66. The order does not specify the reasons for the settlement (beyond encouraging enlistment in the United States military) and merely refers to "The islands from Charleston south, the abandoned rice-fields along the rivers for thirty miles back from the sea, and the country bordering the St. John's River, Florida." This reflects its status as a document of war, rather than a postwar settlement of accounts or reparations.

69. For statements of some of the problems inherent in an attempt to make such endowment-based compensation, see John McWhorter, "Blood Money: Why I Don't Want Reparations for Slavery," and Deroy Murdock, "A Bean Counting Nightmare to Avoid," both in *American Enterprise*, July/August 2001.

70. Some of these points were made in a somewhat inflammatory manner by David Horowitz in newspaper advertisements in college papers. See www.frontpagemag. com/horowitzsnotepad/2001/hn01-03-01.htm for a list of Horowitz's ten reasons to oppose reparations. I find numbers eight and nine on the list to provide very weak arguments against reparations, namely that transfer payments (welfare) to black Americans have already paid any putative debt and that the fact that American-born black people are richer than African-born black people indicates that they are better off than they would be if their ancestors had remained in Africa. The first is problematic because more white people have received transfer payments than have black people, and certainly many blacks have paid taxes to support nonworking whites, indicating that the system is hardly a just answer to the injustice of slavery. That the second is irrelevant is clear when we consider the following case: a Jewish family in Bratislava loses their liberty, their home, and their business when the National Socialists take power; the children survive the concentration camps and move to New York; they prosper in New York; after the fall of the Communist government in Slovakia there is a debate about the home and business establishment that were confiscated by by the National Socialists and then by the Communists. Is it relevant to the proper allocation of the property that those who remained behind in the village, Jew and non-Jew alike, are poorer than those who later prospered in New York? The fact that someone did relatively well after suffering an injustice is a poor argument against compensation for the injustice.

71. Robinson, p. 218. For a meticulous statement of the principle of culture as a foundation for group-differentiated rights claims, see Will Kymlicka, *Liberalism, Community and Culture* (Oxford: Oxford University Press, 1989). Robinson notes that of other terrors visited on peoples, including the Jews, Cambodians under the Khmer Rouge, Native Americans, Rwandan Tutsis, and the peoples of the Belgian Congo under King Leopold II (the period of the so-called Free State), "All of these were unspeakably brutal human rights crimes that occurred over periods ranging from a few weeks to the span of an average lifetime. But in each of these cases, the cultures of those who were killed and persecuted survived the killing spasms." p. 215.

72. Robinson, p. 62.

73. Ibid., p. 206.

74. Ibid., pp. 244, 245–46.

75. Darrell L. Pugh, "Collective Rehabilitation," in *When Sorry Isn't Enough*, p. 373.

76. Ibid., p. 373. As he notes on the same page, "The prospect of reparations to African Americans is an exciting one." If you hope to be on the board of a multi-billion-dollar fund with discretion to award funds, that would certainly be true.

77. Will Kymlicka, *Politics in the Vernacular: Nationalism, Multiculturalism, and Citizenship* (Oxford: Oxford University Press, 2001), p. 184.

78. Robinson, p. 230.

79. Ibid., p. 16.

80. Ibid., p. 209: "If one leaves aside the question of punitive damages to do a rough reckoning of what might be fair in basic compensation . . ."

81. Ibid., pp. 239–40.

82. See Ralph Horwitz, *The Political Economy of South Africa* (New York: Frederick A. Praeger, 1967), esp. pp. 380–86.

83. James Madison, "Speech in the Virginia Ratifying Convention on the Slave Trade Clause," in *James Madison: Writings*, p. 39. It should be pointed out that Madison goes on to point out that the compromise not only allows for abolition of the slave

trade, but protects the interests of current owners of slaves. Madison argues, again, that the compromise represented an amelioration of the situation, and concluded, "Great as the evil is, a dismemberment of the union would be worse. If those states should disunite from the other states, for not indulging them in the temporary continuance of this traffic, they might solicit and obtain aid from foreign powers." Ibid., p. 392.

84. Such proposals, although dressed up in new language, are hardly new. The idea of special national or confessional privileges has an ancient history, but it is largely *pre*-liberal, rather than liberal. That is to say, the recognition of rights, immunities, and privileges—or of liberties, with the emphasis on the plural—is a step to the recognition of the right to *liberty*, as a general right. But the liberal contribution lay in stepping from a mass of particular rights, privileges, and immunities for particular individuals and groups to an abstract principle of individual liberty for every individual person. One close observer described the results of differential rights based on religion in Europe thusly: "For a confession to secure its position against the oppression by others and through establishment of the sphere of right of every individual to eliminate the occasion for frictions—that was the reason, whereby—as today the particular nationalities, so then the particular confessions—their demands were motivated. In catholic countries the Protestants were allotted particular territories; there were particular forts equipped, which were to serve as fortified places for the religion; the number of churches was determined by law; it was determined, how many individuals for a particular office from which confession were to be allowed to be candidates, what the determinate portion of the city council from these or those communities of belief should be;—and what was the result of all these rules and measures, where the solution of the religious question was sought in this way? What else, than endless frictions between the various confessions, the suppression of those who were in the minority on a particular territory, unbounded intolerance on the side of each of those, to which opportunity was offered, and as result of all of this, a century of continuous bloody struggle, which shook the most powerful states, created in one of the greatest nations of Europe a split that has not yet been filled [healed] and everywhere hindered the progress of civilization! In particular states the struggle was bloodier, in others it led to complete suppression of one confession, but everywhere, where this did not succeed and the reconciliation of the confessions was sought in the determination through law of the spheres of rights and the privileges of each, the result was the same, namely that *the citizens of each such country, split up by confessions, stood in hostility against each other and religious peace and harmony was the less achieved the more numerous and detailed were the laws created to achieve it.*" (Josef Freiherrn von Eötvös, *Die Nationalitätenfrage*, trans. from the Hungarian by Dr. Max Falk [Pest, Hungary: Verlag von Moritz Ráth, 1865], pp. 146–47).

85. Kymlicka, *Liberalism, Community and Culture*, p. 146.

86. For example, he asserts that "because residents of Puerto Rico have special self-governing powers that exempt them from certain federal legislation, they have reduced representation in Washington. They help select presidential candidates in party primaries, but do not vote in presidential elections. And they have only one representative in Congress, a 'commissioner' who has a voice but no vote, except in committees." (*Politics in the Vernacular*, p. 108.) In fact, Puerto Rico has no congressional representation because it is not a state, not because it is exempt from federal legislation. And participation in presidential primaries is entirely a matter of the rules of political parties, not of constitutional law. Puerto Ricans are accorded U.S.

citizenship, but Puerto Rico is not a political unit of the United States of America. Kymlicka also makes no mention of the treatment of Indian tribes or Indian population in Article I, Section 2 ("Representatives and direct Taxes shall be apportioned among the several States which may be included within this Union, according to their respective Numbers . . . excluding Indians not taxed"; this provision was changed by the Fourteenth Amendment, but the exclusion of "Indians not taxed" was retained), Article I, Section 8 ("The Congress shall have Power . . . To regulate Commerce with foreign Nations, and among the several States, and with the Indian tribes"), and Article VI ("This Constitution, and the Laws of the United States which shall be made in Pursuance thereof; and all Treaties made, or which shall be made, under the Authority of the United States, shall be the supreme Law of the Land"; this clause includes under the "supreme Law of the Land" the treaty rights of Indians under treaties already made or to be made).

87. *Politics in the Vernacular*, p. 101.

88. Kymlicka, *Liberalism, Community and Culture*, p. 164.

89. Ibid., p. 169.

90. Kymlicka, *Multicultural Citizenship* (Oxford: Clarendon Press, 1995), p. 89.

91. See Ibid., pp. 34–48.

92. Kymlicka, *Liberalism, Community and Culture*, p. 167.

93. Ibid., p. 146.

94. Kymlicka, *Multicultural Citizenship*, p. 97. (He also mentions military service and compulsory education of children on p. 177.)

95. Oddly enough, Kymlicka interprets the exemption from compulsory education for the Amish and other Christian sects as a form of an "internal restriction." He also regards the practice of shunning as putting "severe restrictions on the ability of group members to leave their group." (*Multicultural Citizenship*, pp. 41–42). It is true that a high cost is borne by those who wish to leave, in the form of the loss of family and friends, but to my knowledge there are no restrictions placed on exit. Indeed, the Amish, Mennonites, and others like them are very clear about the liberty of members to leave the group and embrace the wider world. The term "cost" and "restriction" should not be used interchangeably, as Kymlicka does, for a failure to make such distinctions would require us to say that not returning friendship to friends who betray us is to "restrict" their ability to leave our friendship, rather than to say that they would bear the cost of losing our friendship if they were to betray us. Such distinctions are needed if the variety of human relationships is to be properly understood and grasped.

96. I have dealt with this issue in a far more extensive and thoroughgoing manner in Tom G. Palmer, "Saving Rights Theory from Its Friends," in *Individual Rights Reconsidered: Are the Truths of the U.S. Declaration of Independence Lasting?*, Tibor Machan, ed. (Stanford: Hoover Institution Press, 2001).

97. *Wall Street Journal*, March 28, 2000, p. B1.

98. See Kymlicka, *Multicultural Citizenship*, p. 43.

99. See Hernando de Soto, *The Mystery of Capital* (New York: Basic Books, 2000), for an explanation of why the ability to alienate is so important to the development of capital and therefore of wealth.

100. R. I. Moore, *The Formation of a Persecuting Society* (Oxford: Basil Blackwell, 1987), p. 40.

101. Cited in ibid., p. 40.

102. They were so denominated by Chief Justice John Marshall, who stated that "Though the Indians are acknowledged to have an unquestionable, and, heretofore unquestioned, right to the lands they occupy, until that right shall be extinguished by a voluntary cession to our government; yet it may well be doubted, whether those tribes which reside within the acknowledged boundaries of the United States can, with strict accuracy, be denominated foreign nations. They may, more correctly, perhaps, be denominated domestic dependent nations. They occupy a territory to which we assert a title independent of their will, which must take effect in point of possession, when their right of possession ceases. Meanwhile, they are in a state of pupilage; their relation to the United States resembles that of a ward to his guardian." 30 U.S. (5 Pet.) at 17. Cited in William C. Canby Jr., *American Indian Law* (St. Paul, Minn.: West Group, 1998), p. 15.

103. That is not to say that all of the problems or injustices faced by American Indians have been the result of such group-differentiated rights; the story is, at least, a very complicated one. But it should be kept in mind that merely asserting that such rights are intended to benefit the members of a group does not guarantee that they will have beneficial effects. The intention of the lawgiver is irrelevant to the outcome.

104. Kymlicka, *Multicultural Citizenship*, p. 104.

105. Charles Taylor has criticized Kymlicka for not fully understanding the demands implicit in the politics of difference: "Where Kymlicka's interesting argument fails to capture the actual demands made by the groups concerned—say Indian bands in Canada, or French-speaking Canadians—is with respect to their goal of survival. Kymlicka's reasoning is valid (perhaps) for *existing* people who find themselves trapped within a culture under pressure, and can flourish within it or not at all. But it doesn't justify measures designed to ensure survival through indefinite future generations. For the populations concerned, however, that is what is at stake." Charles Taylor, *Multiculturalism: Examining the Politics of Recognition* (Princeton: Princeton University Press, 1994), p. 41.

106. Ibid., p. 53. Taylor himself, however, tries to have his liberal cake and eat it, too, by asserting "invariant defense of *certain* rights," exemplified by Taylor by the right of habeas corpus, but allowing that these can be distinguished from "the broad range of immunities and presumptions of uniform treatment that have sprung up in modern cultures of judicial review." Ibid., p. 61. His claims seem to be simply drawn from a philosophical hat. And, like Kymlicka, he is sometimes careless with alleged historical facts, such as that "the Americans were the first to write out and entrench a bill of rights" (p. 54), ignoring a remarkably rich history of bills of rights in European and transatlantic jurisprudence, from Magna Carta to the Golden Bull of Hungary to the English Bill of Rights to the various bills of rights of the American states.

107. Michael McDonald, "Reflections on Liberal Individualism," in *Human Rights in Cross-Cultural Perspectives: A Quest for Consensus*, Abdullahi Ahmed An-Na'im, ed. (Philadelphia: University of Pennsylvania Press, 1992), p. 147. McDonald seems to rest his views on an implicit theory of the natural or "undistorted" development of groups in the absence of individual mobility rights.

108. International Labor Organization (ILO No. 169), 72 ILO Official Bull. 59, entered into force Sept. 5, 1991, available at www1.umn.edu/humanrts/instree/r1citp.htm. See also Section 17, "Traditional forms of ownership and cultural survival: Rights to land, territories and resources," of the Proposed American Declaration on

the Rights of Indigenous Peoples (Approved by the Inter-American Commission on Human Rights on February 26, 1997, at its 1333rd session, 95th Regular Session), OEA/Ser/L/V/.II.95 Doc.6 (1997), available at www1.umn.edu/humanrts/instree/indigenousdecl.html. Many other examples can be cited, some of which can be found at www.umn.edu/humanrts.

109. Kymlicka, *Politics in the Vernacular*, p. 50.

110. Kymlicka, *Multicultural Citizenship*, p. 115.

111. Ibid., p. 125.

112. Kymlicka refers to the "Amish and Mennonites who emigrated to the United States and Canada early in [the 20th] century, as well as the Hasidic Jews in New York. For various reasons, when these immigrant groups arrived, they were given exemptions from the usual requirements regarding integration, and were allowed to maintain certain internal restrictions." (*Multicultural Citizenship*, p. 170) The historical claim is an odd one; I am unaware of any collective negotiations by Jews in eastern Europe or Anabaptists in central Europe that resulted in their migration to North America on the condition that they were to be allowed to practice their religions. Further, to my knowledge, no one is forced to be Amish, Mennonite, or Hasidic, and the cost of exit is no greater than is the cost of exit from the Roman Catholic Church, which entails denial of the Beatific Vision, than which no worldly cost could be greater. When an acquaintance of mine had his name struck from the Book of Life by his own father, an Old Order Mennonite minister, on the grounds of the son's homosexuality, the loss of religious companionship and of family relations enormously painful and certainly imposed a high cost on him. But that does not qualify as some kind of special dispensation "to maintain certain internal restrictions." It's a requirement of the First Amendment to the United States Constitution that the state not interfere with such processes, and the Constitution was not negotiated especially for the groups that Kymlicka mentions, but for all Americans.

113. See, in contrast, John Torpey, *The Invention of the Passport: Surveillance, Citizenship, and the State* (Cambridge: Cambridge University Press, 2000).

114. Kymlicka, *Multicultural Citizenship*, p. 124.

115. Maintaining liberty and justice is surely more important than recognizing one's membership in a distinct culture, a goal that can be achieved in a multitude of nonpolitical ways. It is not only classical liberals who are unlikely to embrace Kymlicka's view. The redistributionist "egalitarian liberal" Brian Barry subjects such views to withering criticism in his *Culture and Equality* (Cambridge, Mass.: Harvard University Press, 2001).

116. See especially *Multicultural Citizenship*, chap. 5, pp. 75–106.

117. In this Locke and Kant, although in many other ways offering different approaches to political morality and justice, were in agreement: "*the end of Law* is not to abolish or restrain, but *to preserve and enlarge Freedom*: For in all the States of created beings capable of Laws, *where there is no Law, there is no Freedom*. For *Liberty* is to be free from restraint and violence from others which cannot be, where there is no Law: But Freedom is not, as we are told, *A Liberty for every Man to do what he lists*: (For who could be free, when every other Man's Humour might domineer over him?) But a *Liberty* to dispose, and order, as he lists, his Person, Actions, Possessions, and his whole Property, within the Allowance of those Laws under which he is; and therein not to be subjected to the arbitrary Will of another, but freely follow his own." (John Locke, *Two Treatises of Government*, ed. Peter Laslett [Cambridge: Cambridge

University Press, 1988], II, chap VI, §57, p. 306, italics in original); "Freedom (independence from the constraint of another's will), insofar as it is compatible with the freedom of everyone else in accordance with a universal law, is the one sole and original right that belongs to every human being by virtue of his humanity." (Immanuel Kant, *The Metaphysical Elements of Justice*, trans. John Ladd [New York: Macmillan Publishing Co., 1985], pp. 43–44.)

118. Jeremy Waldron, "Multiculturalism and Mélange," in Robert Fullinwider, ed., *Public Education in a Multicultural Society* (Cambridge: Cambridge University Press, 1996), p. 100.

119. Carl F. Stychin, *A Nation by Rights: National Cultures, Sexual Identity Politics, and the Discourse of Rights* (Philadelphia: Temple University Press, 1998), p. 111.

120. Ibid., p. 110.

121. Ibid., p. 113.

122. Ibid., p. 114.

123. James Madison, "Parties," in *James Madison: Writings*, p. 504.

124. See Herbert J. Storing, *What the Anti-Federalists Were For* (Chicago: University of Chicago Press, 1981), esp. chap. 3, "The Small Republic," pp. 15–23.

125. Brutus, "To the Citizens of the State of New York, 18 October 1787," in Herbert J. Storing, *The Anti-Federalist: Writings by the Opponents of the Constitution* (Chicago: University of Chicago Press, 1985), p. 113.

126. Ibid.

127. *Notes of Debates in the Federal Convention of 1787 Reported by James Madison*, p. 77.

128. As Hillel Steiner notes of such schemes of unequal and incompatible rights claims, "such group rights are highly likely to generate claims incompatible with the rights of other groups, to say nothing of individuals' rights." *An Essay on Rights* (Oxford: Basil Blackwell, 1994), p. 165.

129. Susan Moller Okin with respondents, *Is Multiculturalism Bad for Women?* (Princeton: Princeton University Press, 1999).

130. Will Kymlicka, "Liberal Complacencies," in *Is Multiculturalism Bad for Women?*, pp. 33–34.

131. 31 U.S. (6 Pet.) at 561 (cited in William C. Canby Jr., *American Indian Law*, pp. 16–17).

132. For a full list, see Francis Paul Prucha, *American Indian Treaties: The History of a Political Anomaly* (Berkeley: University of California Press, 1997), pp. 446–502. Prucha appends a list of six agreements that could plausibly be added to the list. William C. Canby Jr., notes that "in 1871, Congress passed a statute providing that no tribe thereafter was to be recognized as an independent nation with which the United States could make treaties. Existing treaties were not affected." *American Indian Law*, p. 18. Reservations created thereafter were created by statute, rather than by treaty. In reading for this paper, I was surprised to find that Indians born within the United States were made citizens only in 1924, by act of Congress (8 U.S.C.A. § 1401(b)).

133. A thorough survey is offered by Jacob Levy in his *The Multiculturalism of Fear* (Oxford: Oxford University Press, 2000).

134. *The Federalist* No. 10 (James Madison).

135. John C. Calhoun, *A Disquisition on Government*, in *Union and Liberty: The Political Philosophy of John C. Calhoun*, pp. 23–24.

136. Madison, "Speech in the House of Representatives, June 8, 1789."

137. Ibid.

138. Thomas Jefferson, First Inaugural Address (1801), in *Jefferson: Political Writings*, Joyce Appleby, ed. (Cambridge: Cambridge University Press, 1999), p. 174.

7. Indians in Madison's Constitutional Order

Jacob T. Levy

Next to the case of the black race within our bosom, that of the red on our borders is the problem most baffling to the policy of our country.[1]

—James Madison

"What"—they [the Indians] may say—"have we to do with the Federal Constitution, or the relations formed by it between the Union and its members? We were no parties to the compact and cannot be affected by it." And as to a charter of the King of England—is it not as much a mockery to them, as the bull of a Pope dividing a world of discovery between the Spaniards and Portuguese, was held to be by the nations who disowned and disdained his authority?[2]

—James Madison

One portion of Madison's views (and of his life) receives too little attention: his views about and his activity regarding American Indians, specifically the conflict between states and the federal government over Indians.[3] Madison had, I suggest, a consistent view over the course of decades as to Indians and the constitutional order.

Besides biographical interest, there are two purposes in laying out those views and the circumstances in which he held them. First, I contend that contemporary law and practice violate Madison's understanding, and that we are today moving in an anti-Madisonian direction with regard to Indian policy.

Second, I believe that *Federalist* No. 10, though important, does not exhaust Madison's views on the management of diversity. Madison himself did not, and we should not, treat *Federalist* No. 10 as a kind of hammer that makes every instance of diversity look like a nail. There is room within the Madisonian system to recognize a kind of plurality that should not be assimilated to the analysis of faction.

Constitutional designers today, confronting states with significant ethnic divisions, misunderstand Madison's legacy by treating every division in a society as if it could be solved and dissolved by the alchemy of *Federalist* No. 10.

The Articles and the Constitution

Over the course of at least some 40 years, Madison consistently thought that the federal government ought to have absolute priority over the states in dealing with Indian nations, that the states were far too prone to undertake greedy and unjust actions, and that the national government should protect the rights of Indians against the states. He persevered in his opinion under the Articles of Confederation and under the Constitution, in peace and in war, as well as before, during, and after his presidency. It held so firmly that Madison did not abandon it even when it required him to agree with John Marshall. Madison always thought that Indian nations had a place in a well-designed constitutional order, a place that was governed almost exclusively by treaties with the central government and not by the states. He held that those federal treaties appropriately guaranteed Indians not only their lands but also a separate order of government, neither state nor federal.

Madison acted on his belief at the Constitutional Convention. Article VI of the Articles of Confederation reads, in part, "The United States in Congress assembled shall also have the sole and exclusive right and power of . . . regulating the trade and managing all affairs with the Indians, not members of any of the States, provided that the legislative right of any State within its own limits be not infringed or violated." As early as 1784, when he and the Marquis de Lafayette negotiated with New York Indians on behalf of the Continental Congress, Madison noted with disapproval the separate negotiations being carried on by New York State. During the Philadelphia convention, Madison proposed, as part of a new enumeration, that the legislature be given the power "to regulate affairs with the Indians as well as without the limits of the United States"—that is, to regulate the affairs with *all* Indians and to do so *without qualification*, without worrying about intruding on the states.[4] Article I, Section 8 of the Constitution provides that Congress shall have the power "to regulate Commerce with foreign Nations, and among the several States, and with the Indian Tribes."

In *Federalist* No. 42 Madison argues for the superiority of the Philadelphia clause over that in the Articles:

> The regulation of commerce with the Indian tribes is very properly unfettered from two limitations in the articles of Confederation, which render the provision obscure and contradictory. The power is there restrained to Indians, not members of any of the States, and is not to violate or infringe the legislative right of any State within its own limits. What description of Indians are to be deemed members of a State, is not yet settled, and has been a question of frequent perplexity and contention in the federal councils. And how the trade with Indians, though not members of a State, yet residing within its legislative jurisdiction, can be regulated by an external authority, without so far intruding on the internal rights of legislation, is absolutely incomprehensible. This is not the only case in which the articles of Confederation have inconsiderately endeavored to accomplish impossibilities; to reconcile a partial sovereignty in the Union, with complete sovereignty in the States; to subvert a mathematical axiom, by taking away a part, and letting the whole remain.

The Articles allowed Congress the power to regulate such commerce only with Indians who were not members of the state, and only insofar as it could avoid any infringement on the legislative capacity of the state. Madison points out that which Indians were members of the states was precisely one of the vexed questions of Indian policy, and that it was impossible to make any agreement with Indians that did not infringe the ability of the states to subsequently do something different. Neither of these absurd limitations is placed on Congress in the Constitution: Congress will have the ability to regulate relations even between a state and Indians who are citizens of that state (or if their citizenship is under dispute), and even if that limits the state's own freedom of action.

It is often hazardous to attribute the views of Madison-as-Publius directly to Madison. Publius was far less of a centralist and far more of a federalist[5] than was Madison himself (at least in the 1780s). Publius defended the careful balance of powers between the center and the states in the Constitution, but Madison had advocated a far more powerful center, notably one that had the power to veto any law of any state. Indeed, even after ratification he privately worried that the lack of that power could doom the entire system. But the argument that the federal government and not the states had to be given charge of Indian relations was Madison's, not only Publius's. Madison gave an identical assessment of the inadequacy of the Congressional Indian power in a private letter to James Monroe as early as 1784: "No act of Congress within the limits of a state can be conceived which will not in some way or other encroach on the authority of the state," and therefore the limitation if "taken in its full latitude must destroy the authority of Congress altogether."[6]

The question of who would manage relations with Indian tribes blends two aspects of Madison's criticisms of government under the Articles: the lack of a unified foreign policy, and the violation of individual and minority rights by state governments. If each state conducted its own foreign policy, and thus were able to undermine the foreign policy of Congress, then Americans would have a badly weakened ability to protect themselves and to pursue common international interests. Relations with Indians were, throughout the central decades of Madison's career, inextricable from relations with Britain and Spain. It would be impossible to settle frontier questions with the European powers if the central government could not also make its own agreements with Indians, and be sure that they would be in force. A coherent foreign and defense policy required exclusive federal rights to make treaties with Indians.

But Indians were also, unlike European states, vulnerable to predatory behavior by state governments. The possibility that local majorities would act in biased ("interested," in the language of the 1780s) and, ultimately, tyrannical ways was a major concern of Madison's, and of Publius's. According to the argument in *Federalist* No. 10, the possibility of such majority factions was much diminished in a large or extended republic, since assembling a self-interested majority of a large heterogeneous population would be more difficult than doing so out of a small and homogenous population. But Madison never suggested that this remedy would be sufficient to protect Indians, the treatment of whom by the states was so unacceptable as to create "much danger that the character [i.e. reputation] of our country will suffer."[7] Local white majorities might be more passionately anti-Indian and hungry for land than the republic-wide majority; but the white majority would not be quantitatively diminished by the move to an extended republic.

The project of consolidating Indian policy in the hands of the federal government—a project that included not only Article 1, Section 8 of the Constitution but also the Federal Trade and Intercourse Act of 1790 forbidding state purchases of Indian lands without federal approval—never fully succeeded, of course. During the first decade that the Constitution and the Act were in effect, New York state began to seize and (often fraudulently) purchase lands from the tribes of the Iroquois Confederacy.[8] The project more or less collapsed during Madison's lifetime, when Georgia gained the de facto right to make Indian policy in violation of federal treaties.

Land, Cultivation, and the Cherokee

Madison, like his friend Thomas Jefferson, had a special interest in encouraging Indians to take up agriculture and a system of private property. He accepted an honorary membership in a controversial society founded by Yale geographer Jedediah Morse dedicated to bringing about such a switch.[9] In 1812, when by far his most pressing concern with regard to Indians was that they not join the British in the new war, he gave an important address to a group of chiefs in Washington. Even in that address, he interrupted his appeals for peace to stress that whites have "good houses to shelter them from all weathers, good clothes, suitable for all seasons, and food enough and to spare" while "the condition of the red people" was that "their lodges are cold, leaky and smoky" and "they have hard fare, and not enough of it" because "the white people breed cattle and sheep. They plow the earth, and make it give them everything they want." He mentioned the project of encouraging cultivation and Europeanization among the Indians in his first Inaugural Address and in four of his eight Annual Messages to the Congress (what we now call State of the Union addresses). In his final such speech, he made special mention of the prospect for "extending that divided and individual ownership, which now exists in movable property only, to the soil itself, and thus of establishing in the culture and improvement of it the true foundation for a transit from the habits of the savage to the arts and comforts of social life."[10]

Despite his Lockean conviction that the adoption of cultivation and private property was crucial for Indian welfare, Madison did not share the common view that Indians needed to take up farming in order to enjoy property rights that whites must respect. This was a sharp break with other Lockeans of his era. Then-President Monroe articulated the general position in one Annual Message, saying that "the hunter state can exist only in the vast uncultivated desert. It yields to the more dense and compact form and greater force of civilized population; and of right it ought to yield, for the earth was given to mankind to support the greatest number of which it is capable, and no tribe or people have a right to withold from the wants of others more than is necessary for their own support and comfort."[11]

Madison argued in reply that such a principle "might imply a right in a people cultivating it with the spade to say to one using the plough, either adopt our mode or let us substitute it ourselves. It might also not be easy to repel the claims of those without land in other countries, if not in our own, to vacant lands within the U.S. likely to remain for a long period unproductive of human food."[12] If land could be seized from the unproductive and given to the productive, then no property was safe. Monroe insisted that his position was supported by the history of American colonization and by natural law and advocated "*compelling* them [Indians] to cultivate the earth," a proposition Madison pointedly declined to endorse.[13]

Madison did once suggest that "the plea with the best aspect, for dispossessing Indians of the lands on which they have lived, is that, by not incorporating their labor and associating fixed improvements with the soil, they have not appropriated it to themselves, nor made the destined use of its capacity for increasing the number and the enjoyments of the human race." This, however, was far from saying that this "plea" was *sufficient* to justify dispossession; he did not endorse the argument. He mentioned it only to make the point that it did not apply to the case then at hand—that of the Cherokees.[14]

That "meritorious tribe of Indians"[15] was the exception to the general failure of the liberal-republican project of encouraging agriculture and Europeanization among Indians. Christianity made deep inroads into some tribes, but agriculture typically did not. The Cherokees adopted a written version of their language, took up farming and individual private property, created a republican government modeled on the U.S. Constitution, and created a free and independent press. Moreover, the Cherokees were reliable allies of the United States. To Jefferson, Madison, and others who thought like them, the Cherokees were exemplary. Unfortunately, the admiration of the authors of the Declaration and of the Constitution proved insufficient to protect the Cherokee nation.

In the War of 1812 America largely wanted Indians to stay neutral, assuming that if they took up arms they would fight against the locals and for the British. The Cherokees, though, fought as a group on the American side. They contributed greatly to the U.S. victory in the southwestern theater of the war. They fought alongside General Andrew Jackson's Tennessee militia against the Creek Indians and the British. In the winter of 1813 they fed that militia, when supplies were unable to reach it. Beyond what they supplied voluntarily, the Cherokee lost crops and livestock to militiamen committing what federal Cherokee agent Colonel Return Meigs later called "wanton maraudings and depradations" against the tribe.[16]

Jackson opposed any postwar compensation for these damages. Worse, in the final peace settlement with the Creek, he insisted that the Creek cede to the United States some 2.2 million acres of land south of the Tennessee River that in fact belonged to the Cherokees. As the historian William McLoughlin describes it, "Not only had [the Cherokees] had settlements there since 1777 without challenge from the Creeks, but in the Treaty of Washington in 1806 the federal government had conceded their ownership of this southern side of the Tennessee River below Muscle Shoals. Both Meigs and [federal Agent for Indian Affairs South of the Ohio Benjamin] Hawkins agreed with their claim. The Creeks, fearing that Jackson would take more land from them elsewhere if they conceded that this area near the Tennessee River belonged to the Cherokees, refused to make any statement."[17]

The Cherokees appealed directly to Madison for redress. Cherokee leaders met with Madison in Washington in February 1816. He agreed with them on virtually every point. The lands had been illegally and unjustly seized, and had to be returned, not merely compensated for. The government was liable for the spoilage the army had committed, to the tune of $25,000. He even agreed to their request for full veterans' and survivors' benefits equal to those for white soldiers. Madison was convinced that justice was on the side of the Cherokees, and so he took their side as well. On March 22 the Cherokee nation and the federal government signed two treaties, one selling a piece of Cherokee land in South Carolina, the other confirming Cherokee ownership of the Alabama territories seized by Jackson.

Madison seems to have been entirely unprepared for the political maneuvering that followed. Jackson led fierce resistance to the new treaties and against the payment for damages. He encouraged settlers and squatters to occupy the disputed territory, creating what in the Middle East today are referred to as new "facts on the ground." He maintained, in public and in private, that it was an insult to his men to claim that they had done anything that required compensation. Westerners protested that Madison had sided with savages against the wildly popular Hero of New Orleans. Jackson's political campaign succeeded. Madison backed down, and the administration informed the Cherokee that they would have to give up the land.

Jackson had himself appointed as one of three commissioners charged with negotiating a new treaty, one that would buy back the disputed territory. The general was annoyed at having to purchase land that he thought he had already gained for the United States, but the Cherokee were devastated to see their victory turn to defeat. Jackson negotiated with a delegation of Cherokees who were specifically instructed to sell no land. Jackson and his fellow commissioners threatened them with the withdrawal of protection against settler violence, and with the possibility that the government would hand-pick a different set of Cherokees with whom to negotiate. Moreover, Jackson distributed about $5,000 in bribes. Eventually, the delegation accepted Jackson's terms.

Jackson's freelance policymaking as a general was to continue, most spectacularly with his unilateral invasion and annexation of Spanish Florida. Jackson's career as a general may have been the most important failure of civilian control over the military in U.S. history. Douglas MacArthur ultimately lost in his standoff with the Truman administration and, despite widespread speculation, did not reach elected office himself. Neither Madison nor Monroe ever publicly stood up to Jackson or stopped his string of successes, which paved the way for him to take the White House, with disastrous consequences for the Cherokee. Madison's defeat was the beginning of the end of the Cherokee republic, with the final blow coming after John Marshall's Supreme Court upheld the Cherokees' rights against Georgia; Andrew Jackson is alleged to have said, "John Marshall has made his decision, now let him enforce it." Jackson ignored the law and evicted the Cherokee to west of the Mississippi on what came to be known as the Trail of Tears.

Madison was not a major actor in the end of this story, but he never abandoned his sense that the Cherokee had both justice and the Constitution on their side. The federal treaties with Indians were the supreme law of the land, with clear priority over the actions and laws of Georgia. The Cherokees hired as one of their primary attorneys William Wirt, formerly Madison's attorney general. Madison approved of Wirt's efforts, saying that "the views you have presented of the question between Georgia and the Cherokees are a sufficient pledge, if there were no others, to those sons of the forest, now the pupils of civilization[,] that justice will be done to their cause, whether the forum for the final hearing be a federal court, the American public, or the civilized world."[18] In the event, of course, justice was done their cause in federal court and perhaps in the historical record of the civilized world, but decidedly not by the American public or then-president Andrew Jackson.

Two Contemporary Errors

What remains of Madison's sense of the place Indians had in the constitutional order? Something, but very much less than he might have hoped. For the most important of the three Marshall Cherokee cases, Wirt's clients were actually two whites, members of one of the associations that went among the Cherokees to spread agriculture, republicanism, and Christianity. Georgia claimed the right to criminally punish them for doing so. The Court, and friends of the Cherokee, maintained that Georgia's criminal law did not reach inside the territory of the Cherokee nation, and that non-Indians who entered Indian territory were accepting Indian jurisdiction.

Since 1978, by contrast, the Court has held that the criminal justice systems of Indian reservations have no jurisdiction over non-Indians, treating those courts' jursidictions as racially rather than territorially bounded.[19] A non-Indian committing crimes on an Indian reservation may be arrested only by federal marshals and tried in federal courts, neither of which has much time for or interest in robberies and assaults committed in the middle of the New Mexico desert. As an unsurprising result, Indians are the only (so-called) racial group in the United States that suffers more interracial violence and crime than intraracial violence and crime. Most crime against blacks is committed by blacks; most crime against whites is committed by whites; but most crime against Indians is also committed by whites, despite the relative geographic isolation of much of the Indian population.

Perhaps more important is the strange revival of the 11th Amendment (the first which Madison did not help to draft), immunizing the states from lawsuits in federal court. One of the crucial cases in the contemporary line of 11th Amendment cases was *Seminole vs. Florida*, decided in 1996.[20] In *Seminole* the Supreme Court held that even the special constitutional relationship between the federal government and Indian tribes did not permit tribes to sue states to enforce their rights under federal law, and that Congress lacked the power to make such suits possible.

The Supreme Court's new federalist jurisprudence has proceeded along two tracks. One has at least started to return the United States to a constitution of delegated and limited powers, a constitution in which the 10th Amendment means something and "commerce" does not mean everything. This is all to the good, even if so far the Court has taken only very small steps. By contrast, the new 11th Amendment jurisprudence sweepingly removes constraints on state governments. It cripples Congress' ability to exercise even its clearly legitimate and delegated powers, like regulation of Indian relations and protection of intellectual property, by saying that persons or tribes cannot sue the states to enforce their rights under federal law. The 11th Amendment was arguably misguided to begin with, but recent jurisprudence has gone much farther than the text or any precedent requires.[21] Among much other damage, it has brought the Supreme Court into line with Andrew Jackson's view that the states may ignore Indian treaties with impunity, and taken it decisively away from Madison's understanding of the constitutional order, in regard to Indians.

A General Lesson

Does any of this matter for more than just Indian law? I think it does. In the past decade there has been a revival of interest both in Madisonian constitutional design, as emerging democracies seek to become constitutional states, and in institutions that entrench and protect rights of ethnic minorities, driven by events from Quebec to Rwanda. These two interests have generally been taken to be in conflict. Those who self-identify as Madisonians have sometimes suggested that all that needs to be said about minorities and diversity and pluralism is said in *Federalist* No. 10. But even Madison himself did not think that. Not all divisions can be treated as if they represented *Federalist* No. 10 factions. Sometimes the threat posed by local majorities to local minorities requires special institutions to protect against those majorities, and sometimes those institutions will be a kind of ethnic self-government.

This should not, after all, surprise us. Debtors and creditors were among the factions of greatest interest to Madison, and protecting creditors against local majorities of debtors, as in Rhode Island, was one of his central concerns. But he did not rely *exclusively* on the move to an extended republic and the multiplication of interests to protect the rights of creditors. The Constitution specifically entrenched such protection, forbidding states from impairing the obligation of contracts or making paper money legal tender for the payment of debts. Not all majority factions will disappear by expanding the republic, and everything we've learned about ethnic politics says that ethnic majority factions are a prime example. They capture the central state and use it as a tool to attack minorities, to violate their rights. This happens from France to Rwanda and from Turkey to Australia. Protecting minority rights—the basic liberal individual rights of members of ethnic minorities, including their freedom of religion, of speech, of the press, and their right to hold their property—requires more than just allowing pluralist democratic politics. It requires institutional, constitutional design to keep the ethnic majority faction in check. And there is nothing anti-Madisonian in this. It is precisely in the spirit of the Madisonian constitutional project and solidly in line with Madison's own defense of Indian rights.

Notes

I thank Chad Cyrenne for valuable research assistance, and the Social Philosophy and Policy Center at Bowling Green State University for a visiting fellowship during which much of this chapter was written.

1. James Madison, letter to Thomas L. McKenney, February 10, 1826.

2. Letter to William Wirt, October 1, 1830.

3. For example, the story I relate below about Madison, Jackson, and the Cherokee is not related in Drew McCoy, *The Last of the Fathers: James Madison & The Republican Legacy* (Cambridge: Cambridge University Press, 1989); Ralph Ketcham, *James Madison: A Biography*, (Charlottesville: University Press of Virginia, 1990); Lance Banning, *The Sacred Fire of Liberty: James Madison and the Founding of the Federal Republic* (Ithaca,

Cornell University Press, 1998); or Gary Rosen, *American Compact: James Madison and the Problem of Founding* (Lawrence: University Press of Kansas, 1999).

4. From Madison's Convention notes of Saturday, August 18, 1787. James Madison, *The Debates in the Federal Convention of 1787 Which Framed the Constitution of the United States of America,* Gaillard Hunt and James Brown Scott, eds. (Buffalo: Prometheus Books, 1987 [1840]) p. 420.

5. By "federalist" I mean a supporter of federalism, not a supporter of the federal government against the states. In other words, federalist and Federalist are closer to being antonyms than to being synonyms, as in general the Anti-Federalists were more federalist than their opponents. The proper noun or adjective "Federalist" means, depending on context, the supporters of ratification of the Philadelphia Constitution or the political party to which John Adams and Alexander Hamilton later belonged.

6. Letter to James Monroe, November 27, 1784. Madison then offered a construction of the clause that did not take it "in its full latitude," but rather sharply narrowed the protected "legislative right" of the states to pre-empting private purchases of Indian lands.

7. Letter to William Wirt, October 12, 1830.

8. The illegality of those transfers under federal law, and their violation of a number of federal-Indian treaties including the 1794 Treaty of Canandaigua, has left great swaths of upstate New York open to current Indian land claims. These most prominently include an Oneida claim to over 270,000 acres, a Seneca claim to 100,000 acres, and a pending Onondaga claim to 100 square miles, including all of the city of Syracuse.

9. Jefferson himself refused the affiliation. See Madison to Jedediah Morse, February 16, 1822; Madison to Jefferson, March 5 1822; Jefferson to Morse, March 6, 1822; and Jefferson to Madison, February 25, 1822.

10. Eighth Annual Message to the Congress, December 3, 1816.

11. James Monroe, First Annual Message to the Congress, December 2, 1817.

12. Madison to Monroe, December 27, 1817.

13. Monroe to Madison, December 22, 1817, emphasis added.

14. "But this plea, whatever original force be allowed it, is here repelled by the fact that the Indians are making the very use of that capacity which the plea requires. . . ." Madison to Wirt, October 12, 1830.

15. Letter to the Secretary of War John Armstrong, May 20, 1814.

16. Quoted in Thurman Wilkins, *Cherokee Tragedy: The Ridge Family and the Decimation of a People* (Norman, Okla.: University of Oklahoma Press, 1986), p. 84. My account of the Madison-Jackson-Cherokee events draws heavily on Wilkins, pp. 80–96, and William McLoughlin, *Cherokee Renascence in the New Republic* (Princeton: Princeton University Press, 1986), pp. 186–205.

17. McLaughlin, p. 198.

18. Madison to Wirt, October 1, 1830.

19. *Oliphant vs. Suquamish Tribe,* 435 U.S. 191 (1978).

20. *Seminole v. Florida,* 517 U.S. 44 (1996).

21. For more on Madison and the 11th Amendment, see Mark Strasser, "Chisholm, the Eleventh Amendment, and Sovereign Immunity: On Alden's Return to Confederation Principles," *Florida State University Law Review,* 28 no. 605. For more on the turn in 11th Amendment jurisprudence and its diminution of both Indian sovereignty and the priority of the federal over state governments in regulating Indian affairs,

see John P. LaVelle, "Sanctioning a Tyranny: The Diminishment of Ex Parte Young, Expansion of Hans Immunity, and Denial of Indian Rights in Coeur d'Alene Tribe," *Arizona State Law Journal* 31 no. 3 (1999): 786.

8. James Madison on Religion and Politics

Walter Berns

Everyone who ought to know does know that James Madison is often described as the father of the Constitution. They ought also to know that he rightly deserves to be known as the father of the Bill of Rights, for, although he thought them unnecessary, it was he who succeeded in getting a reluctant First Congress to propose the 10 amendments that we know as the Bill of Rights.

The first (or what emerged as the first) of these amendments provides, in part, that "Congress shall make no law respecting an establishment of religion, or prohibiting the free exercise thereof; or abridging the freedom of speech, or of the press...." Less well known, although part of the public record, is that Madison proposed another amendment that, had it been adopted, would have imposed similar restrictions on the states. It read, in part, "No State shall infringe the equal rights of conscience, nor the freedom of speech, or of the press...." Madison called it "the most valuable amendment on the whole list,"[1] most valuable almost surely because he anticipated that what we have come to see as our most fundamental rights would more likely be abridged by the states than by the national government. He may have been thinking of something that had already happened in his own state of Virginia.

In 1784, Patrick Henry, with the initial support of George Washington and John Marshall, introduced a bill in the Virginia House of Delegates authorizing "a moderate tax or contribution annually for the support of the Christian religion." Henry assured the House that his purpose was purely secular: "The general diffusion of Christian knowledge," he said, has "a natural tendency to correct the morals of men, restrain their vices, and preserve the peace of society." Under the bill, taxpayers would have been permitted to designate the church, or the seminary of learning, to which their tax dollars would be paid, with the proviso, introduced by Washington, that exemptions should be granted to "Jews, Mahometans, or otherwise."[2]

In opposition, Madison wrote his famous *Memorial and Remonstrance Against Religious Assessments*, a paper that not only aroused public sentiment against Henry's bill and paved the way for the subsequent adoption of Jefferson's Statute for Religious Liberty but was destined to have, as we say, a long shelf life. Even today it is thought by some, including some justices of the Supreme Court, to be the authoritative statement of the intent of the First Amendment. But this can be said to be true only by ignoring the major premise of his final argument.

Madison's case against Henry's bill consists, in part and secondarily, of an argument that appealed especially to the state's Baptists and Presbyterians, the long-time opponents of the once-upon-a-time Episcopal establishment in Virginia. "Who does not see," he asks, "that the same authority which can establish Christianity, in exclusion of all other Religions, may establish with the same ease any particular sect of Christians, in exclusion of all other Sects? That the same authority which can force citizens to contribute three pence only of his property for the support of any one establishment, may force him to conform to any other establishment in all cases whatsoever?"[3] As one of his biographers said, "this classic defense of the principle of religious freedom pointed toward the sharp separation of church and state that Madison would later write into the federal bill of rights."[4] True as far as it goes, but Madison was not content to rest his case upon this rhetorically exaggerated but otherwise sensible argument.

Henry and company had left no doubt of their purpose in sponsoring the bill. They were concerned with what they perceived to be a decay of civic spirit and public morality, but Madison, incorrectly but deliberately, attributes a religious purpose to them. This allowed him to say (as if he were primarily concerned with the health of the churches) that ecclesiastical establishments, instead of maintaining the purity and efficacy of Religion, have, instead, caused its corruption. "During almost fifteen centuries, has the legal establishment of Christianity been on trial. What have been its fruits? More or less in all places, pride and indolence in the Clergy, ignorance and servility in the laity; in both superstition, bigotry and persecution" (sec. 7).

Turning to the political situation in Virginia, he argued that the proposed bill is a departure from the state's traditional policy of "offering asylum to the persecuted and oppressed of every Nation and Religion," a policy that "promised a lustre to our country, and an accession to the number of its citizens." Not only is the bill a departure, but it is "a signal of persecution." He even goes so far as to liken it to the Spanish Inquisition, differing from it, he says, only in degree. "The one is the first step, the other the last in the career of intolerance" (sec. 9). Usually so moderate a politician, Madison proved to be as radical as Tom Paine on religious matters— and not only in his rhetoric.

Like Paine, but not only Paine, Madison appealed to natural rights. "The equal right of every citizen to the free exercise of his Religion according to the dictates of conscience is," he said, "the gift of nature" (sec. 15) and, as such, takes precedence "both in order of time and degree of obligation, to the claims of Civil Society" (sec. 1).

No one at that time, and certainly not anyone attached to the principles of the Declaration of Independence, would have taken exception to this; they had all been schooled in the thought of John Locke and were familiar with his writings on religion. As Locke said, "liberty of conscience is every man's natural right [and] nobody ought to be compelled in matters of religion either by law or force"; which is to say, the powers of government do not rightly extend to matters of faith and the care of souls.[5] "The care, therefore, of every man's soul belongs unto himself, and is to be left unto himself."[6]

But what has that to do with Henry's general assessment bill? In what way does Henry's proposal violate anybody's liberty of conscience? Nobody would be compelled to believe anything respecting the care of souls. The Christians in Virginia would be compelled to pay a tax, the proceeds of which were to be devoted to supporting the church of their choice, but others ("Jews, Mahometans, or otherwise") would not be compelled to do anything. But Madison insisted that public support of religion—of religion in general and in particular—and in whatever form it takes, violated the natural right of freedom of religion. It is a violation because, by supporting religion, the government takes cognizance of religion, and this it is forbidden to do; by doing it the government abridges the natural right to worship, or not to worship, as one pleases. But how can this be? In what way does a tax on Christians, to support the salaries of ministers and teachers of every Christian denomination, deprive anyone of his freedom of religion?

Madison's argument, such as it is, goes as follows: Everyone agrees that the right of freedom of conscience is unalienable, which means that men retain it when entering civil society—or as he put it, "no man's right is abridged by the institution of Civil Society"—but from this, unlike Henry, Washington, and Marshall, Madison draws the conclusion that "Religion is wholly exempt from its cognizance" (sec. 1). Only the most doctrinaire civil libertarian would argue that this principle is part of the First Amendment.

Generally speaking, government takes cognizance of religion by imposing penalties on practices unique to it, for example, forbidding the Hindu practice of suttee (whereby a widow accepts cremation with her husband's remains), or by granting religion special favors, such as subsidizing it, as the Virginia bill proposed to do, or by not taxing religious property, or by making it a crime to commit what a particular religion regards as blasphemy, or by exempting religious believers from the general requirement to obey the law. The ways of cognizance are many, and it is only with respect to some of them that Madison's prohibition makes sense, by which I mean, can be said to be a requirement of natural right.

Locke addressed this question in his *Letter on Toleration*:

> What if some congregation should have a mind to sacrifice infants, or (as the primitive Christians were falsely accused) lustfully pollute themselves in promiscuous uncleanliness, or practice any other such heinous enormities, is the magistrate obliged to tolerate them because they are committed in a religious assembly? I answer, No. These things are not lawful in the ordinary course of life, nor in any private house; and therefore neither are they so in the worship of God, or in any religious meeting.[7]

In short, to punish the religious practice of infanticide is not to take cognizance of religion because the offense is a heinous enormity, and is so regarded by the law, whoever commits it.

So far as I know, no religious sect in this country has had "a mind to sacrifice infants," but—as our legal records attest—we do have sects that, for religious reasons, kill chickens (Santerians), ingest hallucinogenic drugs (Native Americans), carry daggers to school (Sikhs), keep their children out of the schools (the Amish), or, for one more example, refuse to serve in the military (originally the Quakers, Mennonites, and Schwenckfelders, but now anyone who has a "sincere" objection to serving).[8] May the government, state or federal, take cognizance of these various religious beliefs by exempting believers from the requirement to obey the law that applies to everyone?

Again, Madison could have found support in Locke's writings. As Locke made clear, the freedom to worship and the requirement to obey the law come together, connected by the principle from which they both derive: the separation of church and state, or of the private and the public, specifically of religious belief and the law, with the understanding that, when they conflict, the law prevails and must be obeyed. A severe command, perhaps, but obeying it brings a considerable benefit. As Locke said in his *Second Treatise of Government*, by excluding all private judgments, "the community comes to be [governed] by settled standing rules, indifferent and the same to all parties, and by men having authority from the community for the execution of those rules."[9] Whether a law is just or unjust is a judgment that belongs to no "private man," Locke writes, however pious or learned or, as we say today, sincere he may be. This means, and I believe Madison meant, we are first of all citizens, and only secondarily Christians—or "Jews, Mahometans, or otherwise." By lending no support to sectarian opinions, the community avoids sectarian strife, and the result is peace or, in the words of the Constitution's preamble, "domestic tranquility." That, at least, is what Locke and Madison had in mind.

In the event, however, it is difficult, and among a democratic people probably impossible, for the government to avoid taking cognizance of religion, not, in the typical case, by imposing a penalty on a religious practice or tenet, but by granting exemptions from the requirement to obey the law. One of these—having to do with the requirement to bear arms—deserves further attention because, despite his constitutional scruples, Madison, too, favored exempting those with religious scruples.

Conscientious objection, as we have come to call it, has a long history in this country. As early as 1775, the Continental Congress adopted a resolution recognizing, and advising the various colonies to recognize, that there are people whose religious principles forbid them to "bear arms in any case." Delaware, New York, New Hampshire, and Pennsylvania responded by making conscientious objection a state constitutional right. A few years later, and in flat violation of his no-cognizance principle, Madison proposed that "no person religiously scrupulous of bearing arms shall be compelled to render military service in person."[10] This proposal was defeated, but the debate over the issues it raised continued well into the 20th century, ceasing only when Congress, by repealing the Selective Service Act, decided that no one was required to bear arms.[11]

The issue that has not been resolved in this country, and the one uppermost in the minds of Patrick Henry and the other sponsors of the Virginia general assessment bill, is whether government, particularly state government, may use religion to support civic spirit or public morality.

A few years later, the issue arose in the ratification debates; in fact, the Anti-Federalists opposed ratification in part because the Constitution made no provision for education, by which they meant moral education. Some of them saw this as its major defect. For example, Charles Turner of Massachusetts said that "without the prevalence of *Christian piety and morals*, the best republican constitutions can never save us from slavery and ruin." He followed this by expressing the hope that the states (if not the national government) would institute such means of education "as shall seem *adequate* to the *divine, patriotick purpose* of training up the children and youth at large, in that solid learning, and in those pious and moral principles, which are the *support*, the life and SOUL of republican government and liberty, of which a free Constitution is the body."[12] But Madison rejected the idea that the government "may employ Religion as an engine of Civil policy."[13]

He said this more than once, even though he knew very well that republican government especially depended on a virtuous people; he said as much in *Federalist*, No. 55. "There is," he wrote, "sufficient virtue among men for self-government," but he nowhere wondered whether this would continue to be the case. Nor, unlike the political philosopher he called "the celebrated Montesquieu," did he wonder how it might be transmitted from one generation to the next.[14] For this, the Anti-Federalists depended on religious education, and called upon the states to provide it in their schools. And this they did.

During the colonial period and continuing into the 19th century— to the extent that it existed at all outside the family (or the wealthy families employing tutors for the purpose)—education was the direct responsibility of the various churches. The states assumed it when they established the public schools, but, except that it ceased to be sectarian, the education they provided continued to be religious in character, consisting, as one historian said, "largely in the Bible and moralizing based on it."[15] The founders of these schools believed, with George Washington—on this, see his Farewell Address—that belief in God and attachment to country go together, and that to promote the one is to promote the other. Indeed, according to Alexis de Tocqueville, this was the opinion of Americans generally. As he put it, "The Americans combine the notions of Christianity and of liberty so intimately in their minds that it is impossible to make them conceive the one without the other."[16]

Madison disagreed; he apparently believed that a purely secular education would suffice. This, at least, is the import of a letter he wrote in 1822, to a friend in Kentucky.

The young had to be educated, he said, and to that end, in addition to reading, writing, and arithmatic, he favored "some knowledge of Geography [and of] the Solar system [and of] the Globe we inhabit, the Nations among which it is divided, and the characters and customs which distinguish them." This might, he added, "weaken local prejudices, and enlarge the sphere of benevolent feelings [and] create a taste for Books of Travels and Voyages; out of which might grow a general taste for History, an inexhaustible fund of entertainment and instruction." Then, as if to show that he was not completely indifferent to their moral character, he closed by saying, "any reading not of a vicious species must be a good substitute for the amusements too apt to fill up the leisure of the labouring classes."[17]

Madison died in 1836, the year that saw the publication of William McGuffey's *Eclectic Readers*. Originally published in four volumes, with the third and last edition coming in 1879, they sold more than 120 million copies in the years 1836 through 1920. The principal historian of American education estimates that half the schoolchildren of America "drew their inspiration and formulated their codes of morals and conduct from this remarkable series of readers."[18]

In the first edition, young children were enjoined to "pray to God to keep [them] from sin and harm," and to ask God to fill [their] hearts with love for him," and to obey his commandments because "you cannot steal the smallest pin without being seen by that eye which never sleeps." The sinful were told that they would go to hell and were left in no doubt of its existence. Many of the readings were taken directly from the Old and New Testaments, and the children were asked to read them aloud, and told how to read them. ("Hold your book up well and do not bend forward. Speak each word distinctly and be careful to pronounce correctly. Endeavor to understand what you read.") And all this, mind you, to the end of preparing the young to be good citizens under Madison's Constitution.

In the 1879 edition, published after McGuffey's death, the Bible makes only an occasional appearance, sin almost never, and nothing is said about piety and salvation. Children are told not to covet their neighbors' riches, not because of God's commandment forbidding it, but because "God makes everybody rich." Still present are the edifying tales—such as "Perseverance," "Beware of the First Drink," and "Dare to Do Right"—and, here and there, the admonition to pray before going to sleep. But mostly children are enjoined to be industrious, loyal to their employers, as well as frugal, reliable, and truthful.

A Presbyterian minister and a professor of moral philosophy at the University of Virginia, McGuffey would have deplored this shift from religious to merely moral instruction, but, given the changes in the demographic character of the population and the spread of the Madisonian-Jeffersonian principles, a "watering down" of the public school curriculum was both inevitable and required. How could the states promote religious belief if, as Madison anticipated, and as in fact was increasingly the case as the 19th century proceeded, they had to deal with a plurality of sects, and not all of them Christian?

But it was not inevitable that the states get out of the religion business altogether, or to be more precise, that they cease to promote religion in general, or on an ecumenical basis, as Patrick Henry had proposed in 1784. It is only in our own time—at least, in *my own* time—that the states have ceased to do this. In fact, they had no choice in the matter. In a pair of decisions handed down in the 1940s, the Supreme Court, citing Madison as the authority, held that the First Amendment prohibited the states from making any law "respecting the establishment of religion." This was a momentous decision; it was also erroneous.

142

Previously, everyone having anything to do with the subject understood that the prohibitions of the First Amendment did not apply to the states, and that to change this would require a constitutional amendment. This, as I have indicated, was Madison's view in 1789, during the debates on the Bill of Rights, when he proposed the amendment forbidding the states to "violate the equal rights of conscience." It was also the general view in 1876 when Senator James G. Blaine, at the behest of President Ulysses S. Grant, proposed a somewhat similar amendment. Blaine's amendment passed in the House, but, like Madison's, went down to defeat in the Senate, coming two votes short of the required two-thirds majority.[19] But what Madison could not do in 1789, or Grant and Blaine in 1876, a divided Supreme Court, without so much as a by-your-leave, effectively did in the 1940s.

The first of the 1940 cases involved a New Jersey statute that, leaving aside complications, allowed parents to be reimbursed for the cost of transporting their children to school, parochial as well as public; the second, from Illinois, involved a "released-time" program in which public-school children, with the consent of their parents, received religious instruction during school hours, in the school building, from unpaid religious teachers (Protestant, Catholic, or Jewish).[20] It was in the New Jersey case that Justice Wiley B. Rutledge declared, citing Madison and Jefferson as his authorities—indeed, he reprinted in an appendix the entire text of Madison's *Memorial and Remonstrance*—that the purpose of the First Amendment "was to create a complete and permanent separation of the spheres of religious activity and civil authority by comprehensively forbidding every form of public aid or support for religion."[21] Unless intending deliberately to deceive, no one with any knowledge of American history could have written this.

What is of interest in these cases, aside from the judgments rendered and the specious arguments used to support them, is the heedless manner in which they were decided. Not one of the Supreme Court justices gave any thought whatever to the role of religion in republican government, specifically, the connection, or even the possibility of a connection, between religious training and the sort of citizen required by a self-governing republic. They simply did not address the issue, as if the cases being decided had nothing to do with it, or as if Madison had said everything there was to be said on the subject.

As a consequence, moral education, which had traditionally been understood to be partly a public responsibility, became exclusively a private one, to be performed, in part by the churches, but mostly by parents in the home. Presumably, they will want to teach their children "values," as we now say, but, if so, they will get little or no help from government. This is how Madison would have it, and we are in the process of learning whether he was right.

Notes

1. Helen E. Veit, Kenneth R. Bowling, and Charlene Bangs Bickford, eds., *Creating the Bill of Rights: The Documentary Record from the First Federal Congress* (Baltimore: Johns Hopkins University Press, 1991), p. 188.

2. A. James Reichley, *Religion in American Public Life* (Washington: The Brookings Institution, 1985), p. 87.

3. James Madison, "A Memorial and Remonstrance," sec. 3. Marvin Meyers, *The Mind of the Founder: Sources of the Political Thought of James Madison* (Hanover and London: The University Press of New England, rev. ed., 1981), p. 8.

4. Meyers, p. 6.

5. John Locke, *Letter on Toleration,* ¶ 70 (Indianapolis and New York: The Library of Liberal Arts, Bobbs-Merrill, Co., 1955), p. 52.

6. Ibid., p. 30.

7. Ibid., p. 39.

8. *Church of the Lukumi Babalu Aye v. City of Hialeah,* 508 U.S. 520 (1993); *Employment Division v. Smith,* 494 U.S. 872 (1990); *Wisconsin v. Yoder,* 406 U.S. 205 (1968); *United States v. Seeger,* 380 U.S. 163 (1965).

9. John Locke, *Treatises of Government,* II, sec. 87.

10. *The Debates and Proceedings in the Congress of the United States (Annals of Congress),* vol. 1, p. 434 (June 8, 1789).

11. Unlike conscientious objection, blasphemy has never been much of an issue in this country, not because prohibiting it was declared unconstitutional, but because various state courts redefined the offense. This was done by the New York Supreme Court in 1811, in the first case tried after independence, and then again in Delaware in 1837. The Delaware defendant, one Thomas Jefferson Chandler, was charged with making an unlawful, wicked, and blasphemous attack on the Christian religion, insofar as he did pronounce, in a loud voice and "in the presence and hearing of diverse citizens of [the] state . . . that the virgin Mary was whore and Jesus Christ a bastard." Chandler admitted the utterance—he was in no position to deny it—but protested his innocence by citing certain letters written by his famous namesake. The court found him guilty, nevertheless. It agreed that blasphemy was a crime under the common law, but only because blasphemy was likely to cause a breach of the peace. This was not, the court said, a case of taking cognizance of the Christian religion, or of protecting Christianity or any of its precepts; it was merely a matter of taking judicial notice of the fact that Delaware was inhabited largely by Christians, that the blasphemy was an attack on their faith, and that they could be expected to react to it in a violent manner. Alter these facts, and the ruling would be the same. Suppose, the court said, the people of Delaware were to "repudiate the religion of their fathers," and adopt Judaism or Islam; it would then be a crime to revile the

name of Moses or the prophet Muhammad. Thus, rather than declaring the blasphemy law unconstitutional as a denial of the rights of conscience, these early state courts stripped it of its religious character, making it an offense against the state rather than against the Christian (or any other) religion. See *People v. Ruggles,* 8 Johns. (N.Y.) 290 (1811); *State v. Chandler,* 2 Harr. (Del.) 553 (1837).

12. Charles Turner, *Speeches in the Massachusetts Ratifying Convention,* February 5, 1788, in Herbert J. Storing, *The Complete Anti-Federalist* (Chicago: The University of Chicago Press, 1981), vol. 4, p. 221 (emphasis in original).

13. Madison, *Memorial and Remonstrance,* sec. 5.

14. Montesquieu, *The Spirit of the Laws,* Book IV, especially chapter 5.

15. Leo Pfeffer, *Church, State and Freedom,* rev. ed. (Boston: Beacon Press, 1967), p. 325.

16. Alexis de Tocqueville, *Democracy in America,* vol. 1, ch. XVII, Vintage Classics ed., p. 306.

17. Madison to William T. Barry, Aug. 4, 1822, quoted in Meyers, pp. 346–7.

18. Elwood B. Cubberley, *Public Education in the United States: A Study and Interpretation of American Educational History,* rev. ed. (Boston: Houghton Mifflin, 1934), p. 294.

19. Reichley, p. 139.

20. *Everson v. Board of Education,* 330 U.S. 1 (1947); *McCollum v. Board of Education,* 333 U.S. 203 (1947).

21. *Everson v. Board of Education,* at 31-2.

9. James Madison on Religion and Politics: Conservative, Anti-Rationalist, Libertarian

Michael Hayes

Before writing this essay, I shared with many other Christians a general sense that America had drifted away from its religious roots. I suspected that Supreme Court rulings over the years had enshrined a secular vision of the public realm that limited my freedom of expression. I had gleaned from contemporary conservative polemics that the Framers meant something very different by the wording of the First Amendment than the activist courts mean now. I took the separation of church and state to be a secular liberal ideal aimed at forcing religion out of the public square and advancing a pro-abortion, anti-family social agenda. All these moves toward the secular and the liberal bothered me.

After writing this essay, however, I see Madison's vision of the separation of church and state as a position that should be embraced by thoughtful Christians. Moreover, I view it as a quintessentially conservative idea. This conclusion is not obvious, however. Conservative Christians have offered compelling criticisms of Madison's view of religion and politics. Richard Weaver, for example, holds that the separation of church and state necessarily leads to a false, secular vision of the culture that must, sooner or later, degenerate into a pathological form of pluralism and ethical relativism. By contrast Michael Oakeshott offers a strong defense of Madison based on a different understanding of conservatism.

To grasp these two kinds of conservatism better, I will begin by developing a typology of four different worldviews. I will argue that Oakeshott's "adaptive conservatism," not Weaver's "nostalgic conservatism," captures Madison's vision and should appeal to conservative Christians.

Worldviews

The worldviews I will develop here are rooted in different assumptions about human nature; these different starting points lead to different conclusions regarding what it is possible to achieve through politics, the uses and abuses of political power, the proper role of the state, and the meanings of such important terms as freedom, equality, and justice.[1] Worldviews are not full-blown theories of human behavior; rather, they are pre-theoretical or pre-analytical visions of how the world works.

My typology builds on the earlier work of Hayek, Sowell, and Spicer, each of whom distinguished between two distinctive worldviews, which may be termed rationalist and anti-rationalist, although one could just as easily call these two groups utopians and anti-utopians, or idealists and realists.[2] Rationalists take an optimistic view of human nature. They believe man is basically good and that it is possible to solve social problems completely and comprehensively through the use of human reason. Sowell calls this view "articulated rationality."

By contrast, anti-rationalists are pessimistic about human nature; they view man as both fallible and fallen. Anti-rationalists give reason a much less heroic role in human affairs. Within this vision, good public policy outcomes emerge (if at all) from the interaction of many actors and institutions—through the working of the economic market or the operation of a political system of checks and balances, for example. Sowell calls this process of rationality via social interaction "systemic rationality." Anti-rationalists believe fallible and sinful human beings can achieve only limited ends through systemic rationality; social problems can only be ameliorated, not fully solved.

The Framers of the American constitution were clearly anti-rationalists, as Spicer has convincingly shown, and Madison's view of the proper relationship between church and state is quintessentially anti-rationalist. All factions should be expected to pursue their narrow interests at the expense of other groups. Even groups pursuing what they view as the larger public interest should be subject to check inasmuch as they will be tempted to impose their private vision of the good society on others who do not share it. Religious groups are particularly prone to this temptation, and they are likely to be characterized by more passion (and even intolerance) than groups pursuing economic advantage. Fortunately, the same system of checks and balances that helps to control the effects of economic or political factions checks the excesses of religious factions as well.[3]

These two worldviews also differ on the proper place of political power in society. Rationalists believe intellectuals can design utopian social and economic systems, and they see political power as natural and normal—something to be used for good. Because they take a benign view of human nature, they see no need for checks on political power. To the contrary, they see politics as an attempt to turn a private dream into a public and compulsory manner of living,[4] as Michael Oakeshott recognized:

> They tell us that they have seen in a dream the glorious, collisionless manner of living proper to all mankind, and this dream they understand as their warrant for seeking to remove the diversities and occasions of conflict which distinguish our current manner of living. Of course, their dreams are not all exactly alike; but they have this in common: each is a vision of a condition of human circumstance from which the occasion of conflict has been removed, a vision of human activity co-ordinated and set going in a single direction and of every resource being used to the full.[5]

Not surprisingly, rationalists tend to favor reforms that would make the American political system more like the British parliamentary system, where the party that was victorious in the last election has the votes to pass and implement its platform.

In contrast, anti-rationalists see political power as potential tyranny and thus as something dangerous that needs to be checked and balanced. The anti-rationalists' emphasis on subjecting power to checks at every point encourages deliberation on public policy proposals, minimizes the role of coercion, and thus elevates the importance of persuasion.[6] Deliberative government, defined in this way, is the political embodiment of systemic rationality.

While there can be little doubt how to classify Madison's views where the choice is confined to two alternative worldviews, we also need to distinguish individuals with a strong disposition to reform (liberals, or progressives) from those who just as consistently seek to conserve or preserve the inheritance."[7] Liberals doubt the existence of objective truth, and if it did exist, they doubt that we are anywhere close to having apprehended it. They refuse to accept any institution or practice merely because it is ancient or venerated; to

Table 9.1
A TYPOLOGY OF WORLDVIEWS

	Anti-Rationalists: See man as fallible and doubt that objective truth can be identified	Rationalists: Believe in existence of objective truth
Liberals: Progressives who would subject all institutions to reason and reform	*Meliorative liberals*	*Holistic social engineers*
Conservatives: Traditionalists who seek to preserve some aspects of "the inheritance"	*Adaptive conservatives*	*Nostalgic conservatives*

the contrary, they believe all knowledge is partial and incomplete, and they believe all existing institutions are subject to potential improvement and must, therefore, be subjected to reason.[8] By contrast, while conservatives do not all agree on what elements of the inheritance should be preserved or restored, they all share a sense that the forces of modernity have eroded something precious from the past.

Table 9.1 comprises a typology of four worldviews based on these outlooks. The first dimension distinguishes between rationalists and anti-rationalists. For the purposes of this typology, the defining characteristic of the rationalists is their belief in the existence of objective truth, whether this is identified through human reason or divine revelation. As Oakeshott observed, they see politics as an arena for imposing their vision of truth on the entire society. By contrast, anti-rationalists emphasize human fallibility; they are profoundly skeptical that objective truth can be identified or agreed upon, and they see politics as properly limited to the amelioration of problems that will never be fully resolved. The second dimension distinguishes between conservatives and liberals. Conservatives are defined here as traditionalists who seek to preserve "the inheritance." By contrast, liberals are defined as congenital reformers who would subject all inherited institutions and practices to reason and reform.

The resulting typology identifies four distinct worldviews. The first category consists of rationalist reformers—utopian visionaries who are drawn to large-scale policy experiments. Following Karl Popper, we might term these individuals "holistic social engineers."[9] Because they believe it is possible to attain objective truth through the operation of articulated rationality, they are utopian idealists, not liberals.

By contrast, meliorative liberals are the genuine liberals. Although they share with the utopian visionaries an emphasis on social reform, they view mankind as fallible and see all knowledge as tentative and incomplete. They are thus anti-rationalist, melioristic reformers. Because they see error as inevitable, they favor political systems (like democracies) that facilitate the peaceful correction of error and prefer incremental or piecemeal social change to the holistic approach advocated by the holistic social engineers.[10]

The typology also distinguishes between two kinds of conservatism. Adaptive conservatives are anti-rationalists, with a strong sense of the moral and intellectual limits of man. They acknowledge a need to adapt to changing circumstances to preserve what is truly precious from the past. Frank S. Meyer, who regarded all conservatism as necessarily adaptive, succinctly captured this worldview:

> In any era the problem of conservatism is to find the way to restore the tradition of the civilization and apply it in a new situation. But this means that conservatism is by its nature two-sided. It must at one and the same time be reactionary and presentist. It cannot content itself with appealing to the past. The very circumstances that call conscious conservatism into being create an irrevocable break with the past.[11]

By contrast, nostalgic conservatives are rationalists inasmuch as they believe in the existence of objective truth. However, where holistic social engineers expect to discover truth through the exercise of human reason, the nostalgic conservatives believe that some revealed truth underlay the organization of society before being eroded by modernity. The nostalgic conservative wants above all to restore this revealed truth.

The Nostalgic Conservative Critique of Religious Pluralism

Richard Weaver stands squarely within the nostalgic conservative tradition. He believes conservatism acknowledges objective truth:

> It is my contention that a conservative is a realist, who believes that there is a structure of reality independent of

151

his own will and desire. He believes that there is a creation which was before him, which exists now not just by his sufferance, and which will be here after he's gone. This structure consists not merely of the great physical world but also of many laws, principles, and regulations which control human behavior. Though this reality is independent of the individual, it is not hostile to him. It is in fact amenable by him in many ways, but it cannot be changed radically and arbitrarily. This is the cardinal point. The conservative holds that man in this world cannot make his will his law without any regards to limits and to the fixed nature of things.[12]

Weaver grounded conservatism in religion. The conservative accepts that creation is the work of an entity larger than himself. Because the nature of physical reality and the laws that govern human behavior stem from an external source, man is not the center of things.[13] To Weaver, religion is not just a philosophy or worldview to be accepted by some and rejected by others; it is always about facts, about the true nature of reality. If God exists, that is a *fact*, with certain consequences and implications that the realist must reckon with. Assuming that God does not exist when in fact He does starts human reasoning from a flawed foundation: "If the disposition is wrong, reason increases maleficence; if it is right, reason orders and furthers the good."[14]

Weaver believes liberals inherently assume a false view of reality. The liberal rejects the existence of anything or anyone higher than man, thus placing man at the center of things, which ultimately has the effect of divinizing man. If man is the only source of value in the universe, his will is supreme; there are no higher standards by which human behavior may be judged. Man can develop his own theories of ethics and subject physical reality to his will.[15] This is why the holistic social engineer can envision a glorious, collisionless manner of living in which every resource is utilized to the fullest, in Oakeshott's terms.

Denying the existence of anything higher than man necessarily leads, sooner or later, to denying the existence of objective truth, followed by a short slide down a slippery slope towards philosophical relativism. Thus, although better educated than any previous generation, contemporary man is a "moral idiot." Each person has been "not only his own priest but his own professor of ethics, and the consequence is an anarchy which threatens even that minimum consensus of value necessary to the political state."[16] The nearest thing we possess to a common culture is a rampant materialism that places emphasis on comfort and immediate experience. Weaver's project, in *Ideas Have Consequences,* was to call attention to this development and to characterize it accurately for a generation that did not even realize it was in decline.[17]

In defining culture, Weaver distinguished among three levels of conscious reflection. The lowest level consists of the specific ideas people hold about the things in their immediate environment. The second level consists of tentative generalizations about what factors are important and how they are related to one another to explain social or political or other phenomena. The highest level consists of intuitive ideas of the immanent nature of reality. This level serves as the standard of verification for ideas about things and generalizations about cause-and-effect relationships. Weaver defines culture as a consensus at this highest level, which he refers to as "a shared metaphysical dream of reality." Those who cannot affirm the shared metaphysical dream are outside the culture.

In *Ideas Have Consequences* Weaver was trying to reverse the decline of a culture that had come to deny the reality of God's existence. In this early work, Weaver thought this denial would lead to the complete disintegration of culture in favor of a pathological pluralism in which relativism reigns supreme. Under such circumstances, materialism, defined as a desire for material comfort, security, and a steady increase in the standard of living, is the closest thing we have to a shared culture.

Culture Wars and Tyrannizing Cores

Weaver's mid-century description of America as a nation in which each person invented his own ethics would still ring true today, but this kind of disintegration of culture may not persist. In a later work, *Visions of Order,* Weaver suggests that the human need for meaning is so powerful that it is impossible to persist for any great length of time without some shared vision of who we are as a people. Culture is not optional, according to Weaver; some larger vision of who we are will eventually emerge; the only real question is what that larger vision will be.[18]

While the emergence of a new culture might seem preferable to the disintegration of culture into a kind of hyper-pluralism, Weaver suggested that ultimately every culture will necessarily have a "tyrannizing idea" at its core:

> The truth is that if the culture is to assume form and to bring the satisfactions for which cultures are created, it is not culturally feasible for everyone to do everything "any way he wants to." There is at the heart of every culture a center of authority from which there proceed subtle and pervasive pressures upon us to conform and to repel the unlike as disruptive.[19]

The "tyrannizing idea" at the core of a culture defines who we are as a people, vis-à-vis each other, the outside world, and the supernatural world. Culture inevitably affirms some roles and activities while denigrating others.[20]

Weaver would not be surprised to find contemporary America caught in the middle of a culture war. James Davison Hunter has characterized that culture war as a clash between two diametrically opposed worldviews; while adherents of the orthodox vision recognize the existence of an external, definable, and transcendent authority, progressives derive their moral authority from "the spirit of the modern age, a spirit of rationalism and subjectivism."[21]

Both sides in this culture war certainly act as if they believe a tyrannizing idea defines every culture. The divisions between these two groups are firm and unyielding, and the rhetorical conflict between them is so intense and untempered that Hunter fears social peace requires the eventual triumph of one side or the other. This victory would constitute the emergence of a new culture, in Weaver's terms. Unfortunately, Hunter's analysis (and the nation's experience since Hunter's book was published) suggests that neither side is likely to surrender anytime soon.

The stakes are very high for both sides in this culture war. Were the secular, progressive vision of the culture to prevail, religious believers would be viewed as superstitious enemies of progress. Traditional families would be viewed as just one of several possible family structures. Public schools would address matters like sex education in ways the orthodox would not choose. And so on.[22] However, the triumph of the orthodox worldview would be every bit as calamitous for a different set of people: non-patriarchal families would be viewed as aberrant, nonbelievers would become "pagans," and practicing homosexuals would be stigmatized as an abomination in the eyes of God.

The divide between the orthodox and progressive visions concerns not just secularists and the religious, as the foregoing argument would seem to imply. To the contrary, religious activists populate both sides of this divide. Culturally conservative Protestants, Catholics, and Jews espouse the orthodox vision, while liberal or modernist denominations affirm the progressive vision. Among Protestant Christians (the group I know best), progressive denominations view the Bible as the product of fallible authors. Progressives see God's revelation to man through the Bible as cumulative, with God telling his people only as much as they could comprehend at any time, culminating with the incarnation of Jesus Christ, who embodied the very mind of God. God's revelation to man, within this vision, is incomplete and ongoing.[23] By contrast, orthodox denominations view the Bible as God's revelation to man and accept it as authoritative and inerrant. Within this view, the Bible is both sufficient (everything we need to know for holy living is contained there) and complete (everything God really wants to say to us is contained there). Suggestions that God's revelation continues today represent a heretical denial of the authority and inerrancy of scripture.[24]

Clearly, these contrasting views of the Bible are more than a minor difference of opinion among members of a common faith committed to loving one another as Christ commanded. Too often contemporary Christians vindicate Madison's insight that opposing religious factions are more intense and intolerant than groups pursuing mere economic advantage.

These sharp doctrinal divisions among Christian denominations, along with the increasing pluralism of religious life within the United States, render unlikely any return to an authentic Christian culture, by which I mean one that arises naturally rather than being imposed by the state. This is almost surely good, although it saddens me as a Christian to say this, because the revival of a religious consensus some conservatives long for would pose, in direct proportion to the extent of its hegemony, a real threat to those minorities (religious or not) that remained outside the mainstream. Nostalgic conservatives are ultimately rationalists, no less tempted than secular utopians to turn private dreams into public and compulsory ways of living.

Once again we find ourselves grateful for Madison's insights. In *Federalist* No. 51, Madison held that the threat of tyranny rises when a single faction dominates a particular constituency. He sought protection against tyranny in the extended republic and its multitude of factions, a beneficial diversity that certainly characterizes contemporary religious life as much as any other area.[25]

Religious Pluralism within a Spontaneous Social Order

Michael Oakeshott's essay "On Being Conservative" provides the best exposition of adaptive conservatism. Oakeshott sees conservatism as a disposition, not an ideology. Oakeshott's conservatives recognize the unanticipated consequences of social action and ask reformers to show that anticipated benefits outweigh the costs of disruption. They support change as a response to some specific defect rather than a utopian attempt to attain some abstract vision of perfection.[26]

Oakeshott emphatically rejects any connection between conservatism and religious beliefs or the desire to restore some vision of revealed truth. To Oakeshott, the conservative disposition in politics has "nothing to do with natural law, a providential order, morality, or religion."[27] To the contrary, any government imposing a vision of truth on its subjects will surely forfeit its legitimacy, and a government which does not sustain the loyalty of its subjects is worthless. A wise government will choose instead to focus on the maintenance of social peace through general rules of conduct that temper passions, moderate behavior, and buffer individuals from inevitable collisions as they pursue their own ends and enterprises, including religious worship and evangelism.[28]

Under the rule of law individuals are subject to laws rather than to men. Good laws are specific enough to minimize, if not fully eliminate, discretion in enforcement. Within such a regime, individuals can formulate and act on plans because they know what the law permits and what it proscribes. Moreover, good laws are general and impersonal, applying equally to all citizens rather than singling out specific individuals or groups for privileges or punishments. Such a regime, which Friedrich Hayek has termed a "spontaneous social order,"[29] defines justice as equality under the law, which really means, in practical terms, equal treatment under the law.

This adaptive conservatism marks Madison's view of the proper relationship between church and state. As Madison saw it, all men must be considered to have entered into the social contract on equal conditions, with each relinquishing natural rights to the same degree. Each must retain an equal title to the free exercise of religion according to conscience:

> Whilst we assert for ourselves a freedom to embrace, to profess and to observe the Religion which we believe to be of divine origin, we cannot deny an equal freedom to those whose minds have not yet yielded to the evidence which has convinced us.[30]

Scrupulous neutrality among religious denominations as well as between religious believers and nonbelievers does not impose a secular agenda but rather extends to the religious sphere the larger principle of equal treatment under law.[31]

Madison's vision of the proper relationship between church and state can be fully realized only within a pluralistic polity where government is limited to enforcing general rules in support of a spontaneous social order.[32] Where the state takes on more and more functions, as it has in the contemporary United States, the sphere of the spontaneous social order shrinks and the distinction between private and public morality blurs. By contrast, where the business of government is ". . . not the management of an enterprise, but the rule of those engaged in a great diversity of self-chosen enterprises,"[33] the realm of private morality (and religious freedom) expands.

Religious Pluralism and the Christian Intellectual

Is there a role for the Christian intellectual within a spontaneous social order that accepts the need for religious pluralism? If Weaver is correct that all cultures have a tyrannizing core at their center, then no secular vision of the political realm imposed by the Constitution or the courts could ever be truly neutral between religious believers and nonbelievers. As Stephen Monsma has observed:

> The bottom line is that the Supreme Court's decisions are supportive of a secularized public sphere that is not neutral on religion and nonreligion. Those who seek to live out a religious faith in all walks of their lives (in the education of

their children, in the public policies they advocate, and in the acts of charity and social responsibility they take) face insistent direct and indirect hindrances and discouragements. The free exercise of their religious faith has been compromised. Secularism as a diffuse cultural ethos is in a privileged position, implicitly endorsed and supported by various public practices and ceremonies.[34]

By this reasoning, admitting only secular arguments to the public square forces the religious to pose as secularists, taking on a false identity when engaged in political advocacy.[35]

Weaver responded by going on the offensive, calling on right-minded intellectuals (e.g., intellectuals in touch with the immanent nature of reality) to diagnose the malady enervating the culture. Like a physician, the intellectual can say, "This is a disease, this is a poison, this is bad diet."[36] While nostalgic conservatives are free to make this argument within a Madisonian republic, Christian intellectuals are not limited to criticizing culture. There is good reason to believe that efforts to restore a religious foundation to our culture will ultimately fail. Weaver concedes as much when he observes that whether the patient listens or not, he will at least have been warned.

Certainly within academia, the target of Weaver's polemic, Christian intellectuals face a daunting task. Many of the academics I know do not see religion as a subject that even warrants their attention. As Paul Tillich observed, intellectuals are not asking the questions for which the gospel is the answer.[37] In his view, the most important problems of the mid-20th century concerned estrangement and meaninglessness, and the central questions common to all mankind involve the search for healing and meaning. Before Christian intellectuals can persuade most academics that our culture is in decline, we first need to convince them that these questions are worth asking:

> No mature scholar is humanly mature who has not asked the question of the meaning of his existence. A scholar who rightly takes nothing for granted in his scholarly work, but who takes his being as a scholar and his being as a man for granted is immature.[38]

That is a very different task from cultural criticism; it is an evangelical task. As such, it will be successful (if at all) only in the very long run, and much of the hard work will be done in the churches by pastors and laypersons rather than by intellectuals, which is to say within the private realm of the spontaneous social order rather than through the public square.[39]

Of course, Christians have the same rights other groups do to enter the public square in defense of our unique group interests. We need not suppress our identities as Christians when we approach government to say that some government action or societal development interferes with our constitutional right to worship as we please or to make important choices that are consistent with our faith.

The wall of separation between church and state comes into play, however, when Christians move beyond defending group interests and advocate general public policies. It is hard to see why nonreligious Americans should find religious arguments for policy positions compelling when Christians disagree over doctrine and dispute the authenticity of one another's faith. As Glenn Loury observed, where there is a "cacophony of religious voices," their "very discordant inconsistency ought to deny any one of them a claim to *public* authority."[40]

I recently attended a debate at my university that illustrates both the problems Christians face in trying to bring their faith to bear on public policy and the legitimacy of injecting that faith into the debate where it is done for the right reasons. That debate pitted Richard J. Neuhaus, a Catholic priest, against Peter Singer, a college professor who advocates (among other things) voluntary euthanasia.[41] Singer stated that religious arguments should be excluded from the debate because they are ultimately based on assumptions about the existence of God that really cannot be proved to the satisfaction of all the participants involved. The real issue, in my judgment, is whether religious arguments can be invoked to trump other arguments in an intellectual discussion—for example, "There is a God and he says we shouldn't kill, so you're just wrong and that's all there is to it." If the participants are to make any progress at all, in Singer's view, arguments must be secular, where all involved share a common vocabulary.

While Christians may have to compete on the same intellectual turf as their opponents if they are to persuade non-Christians, Singer's ground rules eliminated from the discussion the very arguments I find most compelling. I may agree with Singer that life doesn't seem worth living for terminal cancer patients or infants with particularly severe birth defects. I may even agree that it is necessary (or at least defensible) to end human life in extreme cases—and acknowledge that in fact we already do this now in the really hard cases. At the same time, I remain profoundly uncomfortable terminating human life, an action reserved to God, and I would feel better if I knew that the people terminating human life viewed human life as sacred.

This Singer-Neuhaus debate illustrates that cultures rooted in shared metaphysical dreams have tyrannizing cores. Where voluntary euthanasia is permitted (and the libertarian in me wants to extend the realm of human freedom even here), those who opt not to terminate their lives can come under severe pressure to conform to the new norm. Terminally ill patients are often a physical burden to caregivers, and they are also a financial burden to family members and health insurance providers. These burdens go away where terminally ill patients decide to "die with dignity." As more and more terminally ill patients make that choice, those with contrary beliefs will come to be seen less as normal and more as exceptions, and pressure on them will inevitably grow. National health care does not solve the problem by relieving the financial burden on caregivers; where the government funds medical care, political pressures to contain spending will inevitably make resistance to voluntary euthanasia seem selfish and even cowardly. While Christian arguments cannot be invoked here to trump other arguments, the erosion of an old religious norm and its replacement with a new secular alternative would make it increasingly difficult for Christians or other religious believers to make important life choices in a way that is consistent with their faith; as such, it is a legitimate interest affecting Christians as a group that should be admitted to the public square.

There is another potential role for the Christian intellectual, the role of prophet or social critic as exemplified by the libertarian historian Lord Acton. Both a historian and a moralist, Acton saw the verdict of history as necessarily including an element of moral judgment. Although a devout Catholic, he uncovered a wide variety of crimes—torture, persecution, even murder—committed by agents of his church. Acton was appalled that previous church historians had covered up these crimes, and he was determined to tell the whole truth about the Church's mendacity. When Acton came under attack from religious authorities seeking to suppress his findings, he was protected by the state, which scrupulously respected academic freedom. When Acton's later research demonstrated that absolute monarchies had also engaged in persecution and murder, he criticized the state as well, eventually advocating the broad intellectual liberty for which he is remembered.[42]

While individual Christians may see scripture as God's revealed truth and thus long for a prior era in which that truth provided the foundation for the culture, Lord Acton's experience shows just how tyrannical the church can be in suppressing criticism. Whether they choose to criticize the culture, the church, or the state, Christian intellectuals need to understand how desperately dependent we are on the freedom of expression embraced by Madison. Our culture must be founded not on a metaphysical dream of reality, but rather on a renewed commitment to Madison's principles of liberty, equality under the law, and religious toleration. Given the natural tendency for Christians to view religious pluralism and secularism as necessarily offensive to God, Christian intellectuals have a special responsibility to articulate the case for this conception of the culture. Religious liberty and diversity should be understood as symptoms of public health rather than cultural disintegration.

Notes

1. Michael T. Hayes, *The Limits of Policy Change: Incrementalism, Worldview, and the Rule of Law* (Washington: Georgetown University Press, 2001); Michael W. Spicer, *The Founders, the Constitution, and Public Administration: A Conflict in Worldviews* (Washington: Georgetown University Press, 1995), pp. 9–10.

2. See Friedrich A. Hayek, *Individualism and Economic Order* (Chicago: University of Chicago Press, 1948), pp. 1–32; Thomas Sowell, *A Conflict of Visions: Ideological Origins of Political Struggles* (New York: William Morrow, 1987); and Spicer.

3. Spicer, pp. 45–46.

4. Michael Oakeshott, "On Being Conservative," in his *Rationalism in Politics and Other Essays* (Indianapolis: Liberty Fund, 1999), p. 426.

5. Ibid.

6. Joseph M. Bessette, *The Mild Voice of Reason: Deliberative Democracy and American National Government* (Chicago: University of Chicago Press, 1994).

7. Joseph Cropsey, "Conservatism and Liberalism," in *Left, Right, and Center: Essays on Liberalism and Conservatism in the United States*, ed. Robert A. Goldwin (Chicago: Rand McNally, 1965), p. 43.

8. For a particularly good example of this kind of thinking, see Gary Hart, *The Good Fight: The Education of an American Reformer* (New York: Random House, 1993).

9. Karl Popper, *The Poverty of Historicism* (London and New York: Routledge and Kegan Paul, 1994).

10. For an excellent statement of the case for this form of liberalism, see Popper, op. cit. See also David Spitz, "A Liberal Perspective on Liberalism and Conservatism," in Goldwin, pp. 18–41.

11. Frank S. Meyer, *In Defense of Freedom and Other Essays* (Indianapolis: Liberty Fund, 1996), p. 188. For more examples of Meyer's thought, see Frank S. Meyer, *The Conservative Mainstream* (New Rochelle, N.Y.: Arlington House, 1969).

12. Richard M. Weaver, "Conservatism and Libertarianism: The Common Ground," in *In Defense of Tradition: Collected Shorter Writings of Richard M. Weaver, 1929–1963*, ed. Ted J. Smith (Indianapolis: Liberty Fund, 2000), p. 477.

13. Ibid., pp. 486–87.

14. Richard M. Weaver, *Ideas Have Consequences* (Chicago: University of Chicago Press, 1948), p. 19.

15. Weaver, "Conservatism and Liberalism," p. 487.

16. Weaver, *Ideas Have Consequences*, p. 2.

17. Ibid., p. 10.

18. Richard M. Weaver, *Visions of Order: The Cultural Crisis of Our Time* (Wilmington, Del.: Intercollegiate Studies Institute 1995), pp. 3–21.

19. Ibid., p. 11.

20. Ibid., pp. 11–12.

21. James Davison Hunter, *Culture Wars: The Struggle to Define America* (New York: Basic Books, 1991), p. 44.

22. On this point see Thomas Sowell, *The Vision of the Anointed: Self-Congratulation as a Basis for Social Policy* (New York: Basic Books, 1995), pp. 172–82.

23. For a particularly clear statement of this perspective, see Harry Emerson Fosdick, *The Modern Use of the Bible* (New York: Macmillan, 1924).

24. For a good statement of this view, see J. I. Packer, *Truth and Power: The Place of Scripture in the Christian Life* (Wheaton, Ill.: Harold Shaw Publishers, 1996).

25. *The Federalist* No. 51 (James Madison). To his credit, Weaver did recognize this danger. Although Weaver's celebration of the ante-bellum South as a social system rooted at every point in his vision of culture would seem to suggest that he was calling for the state to embrace that lost metaphysical dream of reality and impose it on society, his later works make clear that his instincts were decisively libertarian and that he viewed freedom of expression (particularly for artists and intellectuals) as indispensable within any culture. See Richard M. Weaver, *The Southern Tradition at Bay: A History of Post-Bellum Thought* (Washington: Regnery Gateway, 1989); "Conservatism and Libertarianism," p. 481; and "The Importance of Cultural Freedom," in *The Paleoconservatives: New Voices of the Old Right*, ed. Joseph Scotchie (New Brunswick, N.J.: Transaction Publishers, 1999), pp. 79–94.

26. Oakeshott, pp. 408–12. Charles Lindblom makes much the same argument in his various works on incrementalism. However, to Lindblom, a quintessential meliorative liberal, this conception of policy change as necessarily remedial and incremental is dictated by what he recognizes as real limits on man's cognitive capacities. To Oakeshott, this same orientation reflects an affirmation of the basic soundness of the existing order.

27. Ibid., pp. 423–24.

28. Ibid., pp. 429–30.

29. The term "spontaneous social order" is Friedrich Hayek's. See "The Principles of a Liberal Social Order," in *The Essence of Hayek*, eds. Chiaki Nishiyama and Kurt R. Leube (Stanford, Cal.: Hoover Institution Press, 1984), pp. 363–81. See Hayes, *The Limits of Policy Change*, for a fuller review of Hayek's thought.

30. *The Federalist* No. 20 (James Madison).

31. Robert A. Taft, while serving in the Ohio legislature, opposed a bill that would have required public school teachers to read 10 verses of scripture to their classes daily on precisely these grounds. Although such a bill might appeal to contemporary Christians—or at least contemporary evangelicals—it is worth noting that this bill was sponsored by the Ohio Ku Klux Klan. See James T. Patterson, *Mr. Republican: A Biography of Robert A. Taft* (Boston: Houghton Mifflin, 1972), p. 101.

32. For a somewhat different argument in favor of a return to the rule of law, see Hayes, pp. 172–95.

33. Oakeshott, p. 429.

34. Stephen V. Monsma, *Positive Neutrality: Letting Religious Freedom Ring* (Grand Rapids, Mich.: Baker Books, 1993), p. 42. For a similar argument, see Stephen L. Carter, *The Culture of Disbelief* (New York: Basic Books, 1993).

35. Glenn C. Loury, *One by One from the Inside Out: Essays and Reviews on Race and Responsibility in America* (New York: Free Press, 1995), pp. 287–88.

36. Weaver, *Visions of Order*, p. 8.

37. Paul Tillich, *Theology of Culture* (New York: Oxford University Press, 1959), pp. 210–13. Tillich also points out (on page 201) that the purpose of evangelism is not to put the gospel in such a way as to lead people to accept it. Rather, it is to present the gospel in such a way that people can accept it or reject it. There is no expectation in Tillich's work—or in the Bible for that matter—that there will ever be a Christian culture.

38. Paul Tillich, "In Thinking Be Mature," in Paul Tillich, *The Eternal Now* (New York: Charles Scribner's Sons, 1963), p. 161.

39. In recent years, I have been impressed with how often in the gospels evangelism takes the form of bringing people to see Jesus for themselves rather than presenting Christianity as a new theology or alternative religion. Inasmuch as the church is (or ought to be) where Jesus Christ is presented each week, inviting a friend to church is the contemporary equivalent of saying to them: "I think I may have found the Messiah; come and see." It follows that more progress may be made in Christianizing the culture by inviting colleagues to church than by critiquing their worldview.

40. Loury, p. 288. Loury makes this point in a review of Stephen Carter's *Culture of Disbelief*.

41. "Who should Live and Who Should Die? A Debate about the Value of Human Life and the Dignity of the Individual," *Professor Peter Singer v. Rev. Richard J. Neuhaus*, November 16, 2001, Colgate University, Hamilton, N.Y. Sponsored by the Woodford Forum and the Office of the President, Colgate University.

42. Josef L. Altholz, "Lord Acton on the Historian," Acton Institute for the Study of Religion and Liberty *Occasional Paper No. 7* (Grand Rapids, Mich.: Acton Institute, 1997), pp. 1–13.

10. Madison and the Revival of Pure Democracy

John Samples

We live in an age of a revivified direct democracy. The initiative, which allows citizens both to propose and to vote on laws, has been used more and more in the 23 states permitting direct legislation by voters.[1] In California, for example, nine voter initiatives made it to the ballot in the 1960s; 22 made it in the 1970s; 45 in the 1980s; and 62 in the 1990s. In the 1996 general election, Americans voted on more than 90 statewide initiatives, along with an estimated 200 local initiatives and referenda on environmental and land-use issues.[2]

Classical liberalism and direct democracy are not necessarily friends. Classical liberalism affirms the freedom of the individual and argues for just enough government to protect that freedom from enemies abroad and criminals at home. Direct democracy means the rule of a majority of those eligible to vote. If a majority of the people turns out to be thieves, liberalism and democracy fall out and a nation can fall into civil war. James Madison told such a story in *Federalist* No. 10, a story of passionate factions, democratic decline, and civil war. Should those of us who love liberty now as much as Madison did then endorse the renewal of direct democracy?

Madison against Democracy

The work of James Madison belongs to the tradition of classical liberalism and social contract theory. Madison believed that individuals created government as a means to protect rights to property and liberty.[3] Madison did not ruminate much on the priority of liberty among human values. He focused instead on the institutional requirements for the "preservation of liberty." Madison thought private and public coercion both threatened liberty. A constitution

165

had to be strong enough to control criminals and yet not so strong that government endangered the liberties of the people.[4]

In 1789 many thought that popular government itself threatened freedom and property. Madison argued that such worries apply to pure democracy but not all "popular government." In *Federalist* No. 10 Madison defined pure democracy as "a society consisting of a small number of citizens, who assemble and administer the government in person." The direct rule of the people was both passionate and unjust:

> A common passion or interest will, in almost every case, be felt by a majority of the whole; a communication and concert results from the form of Government itself; and there is nothing to check the inducements to sacrifice the weaker party, or an obnoxious individual.

The consequences of pure democracy are stark:

> Democracies have ever been spectacles of turbulence and contention; have ever been found incompatible with personal security, or the rights of property; and have in general been as short in their lives, as they have been violent in their deaths.

Madison believed democracy posed a problem requiring an institutional solution. The Constitution of 1789 was that solution.

Madison believed the new American republic would overcome the majoritarian dangers of democracy through size and delegation. By including more people and interests in the nation, the Constitution made it harder for dangerous majorities to coalesce. Madison also endorsed the representative principle of delegation. He believed that delegating power to legislators would "refine and enlarge" public opinion thereby avoiding majority tyranny and perhaps attaining higher goals: "It may well happen that the public voice pronounced by the representatives of the people, will be more consonant to the public good, than if pronounced by the people themselves convened for the purpose."[5]

Madison's criticisms of pure democracy depended on three assumptions. First, he believed the violent history of "popular government" condemned direct democracy. We have had two more centuries of experience with the American republic and almost a century with the initiative. More experience means more, and perhaps different, lessons learned than those enunciated in *Federalist*

No. 10. Second, Madison argued that passion not reason would dominate direct lawmaking. Studies of the American experience with the initiative might tell us whether Madison was right about the power of passion in direct legislating. Third, Madison believed that only majorities threatened liberty. If minorities in a republic also endanger freedom, classical liberals might wish to revise Madison's conclusions. The starting point for assessing these assumptions of *Federalist* No. 10 should be the recent history of the politics of recovering liberty.

Democracy against Progress

The Populist and Progressive movements overruled Madison and brought America direct legislation. Populists believed that the government should restrain "selfish people" who profit at a cost to the common person and that the "people," not the "money elite," should control government. They advocated the initiative in particular and ongoing direct democracy in general.[6] The Progressives agreed with the Populists that state legislatures of the early 20th century "enact laws for the special advantage of a few and refuse to enact laws for the welfare of the many."[7] They also agreed that direct legislation could bypass corrupt legislatures. These agreements for a time masked larger differences between Populism and Progressivism.

Progressivism differed profoundly from Populism in membership and message. Progressivism was a middle class movement, "moralistic and elitist" in its aspirations and outlook. The Progressives had no great trust in the people as such; like their political descendents, they backed "the people, not the powerful" so long as progressive minds were not powerful. Progressives wished to retain representative democracy. Theodore Roosevelt once said, "I believe in the initiative and referendum, which should be used not to destroy representative government, but to correct it whenever it becomes misrepresentative."[8] Direct legislation would be only a sometime thing, a check on representative government "when it fails to be sufficiently responsive or when it acts in a biased way."[9]

Progressives believed direct legislation would advance their "reform" agenda and expand the ambit of government. In 1915, Benjamin Parke DeWitt wrote that Progressives share "the rapidly growing conviction that the functions of government are too restricted and that they must be increased and extended to relieve

167

social and economic distress."[10] When legislatures still backed limited government for good reasons and bad, Progressives hoped the unfettered will of the people would advance the welfare state.

In the event, direct democracy contributed far less to the growth of the welfare state than did the federal government. The voice of the people could be heard in states and localities only when war, economic crisis, and racial injustices prompted the nationalization of everything. The left has done quite well with the federal government, and the partisans of limited government have had little reason to hope the initiative would be a useful weapon against Leviathan. After all, the party of redistribution and regulation also advocated direct democracy. Supporters of limited government were correct; the initiative seems to have expanded the state in the first half of the 20th century.[11] Lacking friends, direct democracy fell into abeyance during the middle of the 20th century.[12]

In 1978, Proposition 13 in California used direct democracy to restrict the welfare state. Proposition 13 was a state constitutional amendment limiting property taxes, which had been rising 30 percent annually. It limited the assessed value of property, increases in assessed property value, and the tax rate for property. The proposition required a super-majority in the legislature to raise property tax rates. Experts predicted it would cut government revenue by $7 billion in 1978–79, but 69 percent of registered voters voted on Proposition 13 and 65 percent of them voted for it.[13]

Supporters of Proposition 13 argued that the California legislature had defied the people's will about property taxes. They may have been correct. A contemporaneous public opinion poll showed that almost all Californians supported Proposition 13.[14] The legislature had ignored a broad desire for lower property taxes, though it did cut property taxes after Proposition 13 reached the ballot.[15]

Since Proposition 13, citizens of various states have considered 86 anti-tax initiatives, 41 of which passed. Anti-tax initiatives have passed at a much higher rate than initiatives in general and pro-tax initiatives in particular. Moreover, the success rate of anti-tax initiatives in the 1990s appears much higher than in the decade after Proposition 13.[16]

Politics is often less about the morality of procedures than about the distribution of outcomes. Madison thought representative democracy would serve liberty and the public welfare better than direct democracy. Many on the contemporary left believe direct democracy contravenes their favored policy outcomes and have fashioned a neo-Madisonian critique of the initiative. Representative democracy, they say, leads to better laws than a direct vote of the people. Minority rights are in danger when majorities rule absolutely. The people lack the ability and interest to make good laws. The critics also speak a progressive dialect. Direct democracy, they cry, has been hijacked by special interests, especially the rich and big business. Pure democracy, they warn, is undermining both the Madisonian and the progressive republic. The critics' case against the initiative deserves attention but not assent. Democracy has been a good friend of liberty in recent times.

Representative Democracy

The critics of the initiative admire representative institutions. David Broder's recent book *Democracy Derailed: Initiative Campaigns and the Power of Money* begins by praising the republican and representative character of the American Constitution.[17] Similarly, the political scientist John Haskell argues that representative institutions fill the need for informed deliberation, consensus and compromise, all of which lead to government in the public interest.[18]

Those who dislike the initiative invoke traditional arguments for representative democracy. Representative democracy combines specialization and accountability. Most citizens lack the time or interest to delve deeply into public affairs. They can, however, select others to represent their interests and to develop if not expertise at least a working knowledge of public affairs. The voters control government without having to participate in the details of politics.[19] Initiatives remove that accountability and thereby undermine representative democracy.

Critics of the initiative argue that legislatures integrate well the forest and the trees of most policy issues. The legislative committee system, especially budget committees, integrates policies by making trade-offs and compromises. Direct legislation, in contrast, breaks issues into small fragments and loses sight of the whole.[20] For example, critics note, direct democracy addresses only one half of the budgeting equation: taxation.

Critics argue that on most issues legislatures better reflect public opinion than does the initiative. Public opinion is complex about most policy issues. Representative institutions reflect that complexity through deliberation, compromise, and consensus.[21] The initiative, in contrast, offers a simple up or down vote on complex issues.

Skeptics of direct legislation sound like Madison when they point out that representative democracy includes many checks on any proposal before it becomes law. They believe a system with multiple veto points is less likely to produce constitutionally suspect or other flawed legislation. Initiatives bypass all the checks and are more likely to produce bad legislation.[22] As a veteran political operative concluded, "Unlike the governing process debated and accepted by our founders, citizen lawmaking lacks the deliberation, refinement, and real citizen involvement that is essential for enlightened governance."[23]

David Broder believes the initiative both reflects and aggravates citizens' mistrust of politics and government. It implies that representatives cannot be trusted so the people must rule directly. When they do, government becomes ineffective and chaotic, causing more doubt. He worries that such "pervasive distrust" by citizens will subvert the American republic and lead the ship of state into unknown and perhaps hostile waters.[24] Fear of the initiative thus makes the doyen of Washington journalism a Madisonian conservative.

The critics of the initiative overlook the possibility that legislatures can systematically fail. What could failure mean? Economists judge representative democracy by how well it satisfies the preferences of a majority.[25] Classical liberals are concerned that legislatures may fail to protect individual rights and to limit government. Economists and classical liberals can come to blows when efficiency contravenes freedom.[26] Classical liberals should value the initiative because government expands when minorities rather than majorities rule.

Legislatures satisfy majority preferences if one assumes robust political competition, but that assumption need not hold. Representatives can develop a self-interested, careerist outlook that keeps political competition at bay thereby when it benefits their position.[27] Incumbents possess advantages in name recognition and financing that challengers find difficult to overcome, incumbents thus freeing themselves from responsibility to their constituents and voting in the legislature as they please. Restrictions on campaign fundraising enacted by incumbents make the challengers' uphill climbs even more arduous.[28] The long system of checks together with the self-interest of officials precludes reforms that might restore accountability. Citizens end up being ruled more than ruling.[29]

Even when legislatures work well, they can frustrate majority preferences. Consider a hypothetical though realistic example. Imagine a candidate runs for office by taking positions on two issues: for abortion rights and against free trade. The election takes place in a district where supporting both abortion rights and free trade attracts strong majority support. Imagine also that abortion rights are important to most voters but free trade is not. The candidate's stand against free trade will not cost her many votes but may attract some voters who fear free trade. The candidate's position against reform may also attract campaign contributions from entrenched interest groups. That candidate could win her party's nomination and election to office despite holding a minority position on free trade. If this scenario repeats itself, an election could produce a legislative majority that opposed free trade despite the wishes of a majority. In general, legislatures may not follow a majority on an issue that is salient for a minority but not for most voters. If a majority decides whom to vote for on the basis of other issues, a legislature may well adopt a minority position on a particular issue.[30] Trading votes in the legislature may also lead to satisfying the preferences of a minority.[31]

This story of intense minorities and indifferent majorities links liberty and majority preferences. Mancur Olson pointed out that intense minorities have great advantages over apathetic majorities. For example, trade protection offers a small number of businesses or workers huge benefits at a cost spread out over a much larger number of consumers. Organizing to pass or to stop trade protection has costs to interest groups and their members. A union member may expect relatively big gains from protection, gains that outweigh the costs of going to rallies and contacting their member of Congress. Consumers pay a bit more for a protected product, which means they would benefit from free trade; the gain, however, is far less than the costs of opposing protectionism.

Olson's story about the transaction costs of politics suggests that government in general and a legislature in particular would favor interest groups (or particular constituencies) over the electorate and that elections would not lead to policies favoring the general welfare or the preferences of a majority.[32] Olson's analysis implies that public policies may frustrate a median voter; if government is the rule of minorities, we may well end up with more government than a majority would want. Some empirical evidence agrees. The economist John Matsusaka concluded from his empirical study of fiscal policies in the states: "Over the last 30 years the median voter wanted significantly less government expenditure than his representatives delivered."[33]

Madison conjectured that representative government would "refine and enlarge" public opinion by passing majority preferences through the filter of members of Congress. Olson's analysis suggests the opposite. Certain characteristics of collective action lead representatives to serve narrow interests rather than the general welfare. For some issues, at least, Madison now seems too optimistic about representative democracy.

The initiative overcomes the tyranny of minorities. Imagine a different story about abortion and free trade. If policy entrepreneurs propose separate initiatives favoring abortion rights and free trade, a majority could vote for the freedom to have an abortion and for free trade.[34] Most citizens would be more satisfied with the initiative; the initiative would lead to more liberty, less government, and enhanced citizen satisfaction.[35]

The critics of the initiative overrate representative democracy. Modern professional legislatures respond to rent-seeking interest groups whose greed expands the ambit of state power. Initiatives allow a majority to enforce its preferences and to undo exploitation by a minority and thereby to restrain the growth of the state. That will not be enough to convince most followers of *Federalist* No. 10. They will want to know if Madison was right that pure democracy threatens minority rights.

Minority Rights

Contemporary critics also echo, with a twist, Madison's concern for minority rights. Direct legislation may adversely affect minorities when the median voter in the general electorate differs from the median voter in the legislature. In California, the critics note, the general population is much more non-white than the electorate eligible to vote. Legislative districts are based on the general population, not eligible voters, and the Voting Rights Act requires states to create

172

majority-minority districts. For these reasons, minority concerns have a stronger voice in the legislature than in voting on initiatives.[36] Peter Schrag draws dire conclusions for minorities:

> Even at its best, the plebiscitary dynamic . . . has precious little room for spending that immediately benefits someone other than those who must vote on it. It is not prone to generosity and is rarely respectful of minority rights, much less of minority needs. And while it is true that elected legislators often fail to do what their constituents wish (and often do a great deal worse than they deserve), sometimes they also do a little better for those who are underrepresented in the electoral process, something that the initiative process almost never does.[37]

Controls on property taxation, the critics add, reduce the money going to a state's general fund, the source of money for redistribution. The political scientist Elizabeth Gerber suggests that this outcome follows the interests of initiative voters, who are whiter and more conservative than the general population of California.[38]

The critics also believe unrestrained majorities threaten the civil rights of minorities. The attorney Barbara Gamble examined five policy areas—gay rights, AIDS testing, language, school desegregation, housing/public accommodations desegregation—where ballot initiatives involved civil rights. She concluded:

> Our representative government, with its admittedly imperfect filtering mechanisms, seeks to protect the rights of minorities against the will of majorities. Minorities suffer when direct democracy circumvents that system. Not only do they lose at the polls, the very act of putting civil rights to a popular vote increases the divisions that separate us as a people. Instead of fortifying our nation, direct legislation only weakens us.[39]

Schrag's lament about initiatives' resistance to redistribution persuades only those who share his commitment to redistributing wealth. Those who see redistribution as forced labor welcome cuts in spending. Precluding redistribution to favored groups becomes a problem only if the recipients deserve the holdings of others. Initiatives that cut off money to fund minority "needs" go wrong only if such "needs" should be met by taxpayers. Madison, like most classical liberals, favored private property rights and rejected redistribution:

> Government is instituted to protect property of every sort; as well that which lies in the various rights of individuals, as that which the term particularly expresses. This being the end of government, that alone is a *just* government, which *impartially* secures to every man, whatever is his *own*.[40] (emphasis in original)

Madison would not lament initiatives that end redistribution to the favored clients of the welfare state. But what about minority rights?

The critics' worry about minority rights concerns civil rights, "the right of racial, ethnic, and language minorities, gay men and lesbians, and people with AIDS to equal protection of the laws and their right to live free from discrimination in employment, housing, education, and public accommodations."[41]

Should classical liberals worry if majorities reject or preclude laws against discrimination? The answer depends on whether a law regulates public or private choices:

> If private individuals and institutions are to be free and sovereign, they have a perfect right to discriminate in favor of or against other private individuals or institutions—for any reason, good or bad, or for no reason at all. By contrast, public officials and institutions may not discriminate except on grounds that are narrowly tailored to serve the functions for which they were elected, appointed, or created in the first place; for to permit discrimination on other grounds would be to strip a portion of the public of control over, use of, or opportunity with what are, after all, their officials and institutions.[42]

Classical liberals recognize that denying the state the power to punish private discrimination is not the same as approving such discrimination. Once again criticisms of the initiative for endangering minority "rights" seem dependent on accepting the political agenda of the contemporary left.

Even if we accept the left's definition of minority rights, the evidence against the initiative is far from conclusive. Theory indicates no a priori reason to believe initiatives would be better or worse for minority interests than representative democracy.[43] On the empirical side, Barbara Gamble did not randomly select the initiatives included in her study; her conclusions thereby lack all generality.[44] State initiatives involving minority rights are less likely to be approved than the average initiative.[45] In any case, approval of initiatives limiting minority civil rights does not mean that legislatures would do any better.

Classical liberals may still have misgivings about majority rule. What about Madison's concerns about majority rule and private property? Notable in their absence from the annals of successful initiatives are "soak the rich" schemes in which one minority seeks to directly appropriate the wealth of another minority. Scholars say direct democracy does not lead states to adopt more redistributive policies.[46] The traditional classical liberal concern about property rights under direct democracy lacks evidence.

Some risks to freedom may well exist. Recall the election story about abortion and free trade. Imagine the candidate favored abortion rights and opposed restrictions on campaign finance, a constraint on individual freedom. According to polls, a large majority of the public both overwhelmingly supports such restrictions and cares little about campaign finance.[47] In the imagined election, a candidate could be against campaign finance restrictions (and for liberty). On the other hand, an initiative on campaign finance might well lead to restrictions on the freedom of the individual; keeping the issue in the legislature, on the other hand, might preserve the freedom to contribute to campaigns.[48] We should not exaggerate this risk. Not many issues are like campaign finance reform where large American majorities both favor limiting freedom and do not care much about the issue.

Direct democracy in the United States supplements the legislature within a constitutional framework that provides minorities with real protections against abuse by majorities. A successful initiative still must pass the muster of the judiciary. State and federal courts have struck down nearly every state initiative cited by critics as abusive of minorities.[49] The economics of initiatives also protects minorities. Money cannot buy victories in initiative battles. The reverse seems to be the case: any group with enough money can defeat an initiative.[50] That includes a minority willing to defend their freedom.

Special Interests

Skeptics believe the initiative has created a "populist paradox." They recall that the Progressives turned to the initiative in order to

175

free state legislatures from the grip of the Southern Pacific Railroad. Ironically, the critics say, special interests now dominate the proposing and passing of initiatives.[51] The ubiquitous demon of the contemporary left—"Big Money"—manipulates the will of the people:

> Money does not always prevail in initiative fights, but it is almost always a major—even dominant—factor. Like so much else in American politics, the costs of these ballot battles have escalated enormously in the past decade. To a large extent, it is only those individuals and interest groups with access to big dollars who can play in the arena the populists and Progressives created in order to balance the scales against the big-bucks operators.[52]

Big Money means corporate interests who supposedly stop leftist initiatives and preserve the status quo, thereby helping a moneyed elite.[53] The apparent rule of the many cloaks the effective rule of the wealthy few.

Critics also decry the emergence of an initiative "industrial complex" comprising the lawyers who draft the ballot proposals, the firms that collect the necessary names to put a proposal on the ballot, the marketers who design direct mail ads and solicitations, and the campaign consultants who guide the whole effort.[54] Far from forcing citizen demands on government, the initiative now empowers and enriches political professions skilled at manipulating average Americans.[55]

Political scientists Bruce Cain and Kenneth Miller argue initiatives lack accountability in other ways. Voters do not know the true intent of legislation and the interests supporting and opposing it. Voters cannot call to account the experts and policy entrepreneurs who draft initiatives and the subsequent campaigns for and against a measure.[56]

For the critics, direct democracy should embody the rule of all the people. Instead, elites control the electoral agenda and the content of proposed legislation. On election day, a final coup de grace: a small and unrepresentative group votes the initiative up or down.[57]

Classical liberals like Madison support individual freedom under the rule of law. They oppose differential exploitation through government action. Classical liberals in principle should oppose any attempt by a narrow group, including business, to claim benefits (sometimes called corporate welfare) from government. If the critics

176

are right that special interests dominate initiatives, classical liberals should be alarmed.

However, the idea that special interests use the initiative to pass favorable legislation does not wash empirically. Voters are not hapless victims of the powerful; they cast their initiative ballots on the basis of interest and ideology. Moreover, special interests cannot buy victories: "Few special interests will be able to find an ignorant, unanchored electorate and use vast sums of money to sell them a policy that is inconsistent with the voting public's ideas or interests."[58]

This conclusion holds if we define "special interests" as business or economic groups. The political scientist Elizabeth Gerber found that economic groups saw the initiative as too costly and too uncertain. Their proposals almost always lose. She suggests such groups might influence policymaking indirectly by using the initiative process to force legislators to act (when their proposed initiative has enough support to pass) or to signal to legislators their wishes, which then may be acted upon if the group has influence with a legislator.

Gerber finds some evidence that economic interest groups spend much of their money opposing initiatives, with some success:

> The ability of economic interest groups to modify policy through the direct legislation process, either directly or even indirectly is severely limited. Their main effect is to prevent new initiatives from passing. Hence, their influence over policy through the direct legislation process is largely conservative.[59]

Gerber is not alone with that finding. Looking at initiatives comprehensively, Howard Ernst found that organized labor and corporate interests "historically and currently operate at a severe electoral disadvantage in initiative politics."[60]

While critics denounce Big Money, spending on the initiative campaigns actually fosters rational decisions by voters. Bowler and Donovan conclude from their extensive empirical analysis:

> Spending can facilitate broader cognitive reasoning in direct democracy. We suggest that campaign spending and contested campaigns have the potential for enhancing voter competence in direct democracy. If competence is defined as

voting on the basis of a preexisting ideology or party attachment . . . then our results can be interpreted as supporting
the idea that campaign spending in direct democracy—even
one-sided spending—can contribute to the voter's ability to
reason on the basis of party and ideology.[61]

Gerber's work suggests that classical liberals should worry less
about initiatives helping economic special interests and more about
the successes of "public interest" groups in direct legislation.

Aggregate outcomes show that citizen groups are more successful than economic groups at actually passing new laws
by initiative. Initiatives supported by citizens groups pass
at a higher rate than those supported by economic groups,
and the set of successful initiatives reflects citizen group
support and substantive interests.[62]

Such "citizen's groups" are hostile to capitalism and to free markets.
Their victories usually restrict individual freedom.

Voter Failure

Political scientists have long said voters were ignorant, if not
stupid. Early scientific polling found that voters knew little about
politics, politicians, and policy issues.[63] The first major book about
the new era of direct legislation echoed this dim view of citizen
competence:

The majority of ballot measures are decided by voters who
cannot comprehend the printed description, who have only
heard about the measure from a single source, and who are
ignorant about the measure except at the highly emotional
level of television advertising, the most prevalent source of
information for those who have heard of the proposition
before voting.[64]

Some scholars believe most citizens cannot vote in line with their
underlying preferences or political ideology.[65] They note that legislature elections offer cues to voters like party affiliation. Absent such
guidance, these skeptics say voting on initiatives becomes a random
game of electoral roulette with unpredictable outcomes and
consequences.[66]

Classical liberals believe that most people are capable of leading their own lives free of the paternal concern of government bureaucrats. Should this faith in humanity apply to politics? Madison thought passion would lead voters astray. Students of public choice say voters may be rationally ignorant of the arguments surrounding an initiative.[67] If so, the classical liberal faith in the individual need not transfer to public activity. Doubts about voter competence in the initiative, however, seem exaggerated.

Ballot propositions may be quite complex. Gaining enough information to understand and assess that complexity is costly, and few people will make the effort. Voters may nonetheless find shortcuts to cast a reasonably well-informed vote by following signals from more well-informed political participants.[68] Votes on initiatives also reflect consistent, underlying attitudes toward politics and policy. Initiative voters would not select incompatible policies even if voting on a number of ballot initiatives.[69]

Voters do reasonably well given the difficulty of the task and the rationality of remaining ignorant: "The voter is not necessarily the weak link in the process of direct democracy. By employing a fairly conservative voting strategy and by voting on the basis of limited but readily available information, voters sort through the choices presented by direct democracy."[70] Voters are rational enough given their ideology and political preferences. The real question is whether the ideologies and political preferences Americans harbor make initiatives risky for freedom, a question addressed later.

Beyond Madison

Madison offered republican cures for political ills. He recommended a fragmentation of authority supported by a division of powers itself protected by a confluence of interest and constitutional office. Scholars of American collective choice understand well the republican ills of our time: rent seeking and minority rule. Direct democracy provides a democratic remedy for these republican maladies.

Outsider Politics

Madison believed the new American republic would be responsive to, and endangered by, majorities. He doubted a minority could exploit a majority: "If a faction consists of less than a majority, relief is supplied by the republican principle, which enables the majority

179

to defeat its sinister views by regular vote."[71] A minority could not long resist the true power in a republic, a majority of the people. Madison underestimated the ingenuity and advantages of political insiders.

The political class has no reason to limit government or to protect individual freedom. The power of members of Congress grows alongside the ambit of the federal government. More regulation creates more problems for constituents, problems assuaged by congressional staff.[72] More regulation means more job opportunities for retired members of Congress who lobby the industries they once regulated. Redistribution and pork barrel spending attract (and corrupt) voters. Liberty finds few friends among political insiders.

Normal elections offer little hope of disciplining political insiders. Incumbents have great advantages over challengers including name recognition and the expectation of remaining in office. Few incumbents seeking reelection to Congress lose, short of being indicted or dying.[73] "Normal" democracy seems fated to Mancur Olson's legislative status quo: rent-seeking and burgeoning government.

Initiatives impose the preferences of a majority on political insiders.[74] Tax and expenditure limitations constrain the ambition and avarice of state legislators. Term limits go further and limit incumbency and thereby the growth of a permanent political class. No legislature would contradict the interests of its members and either limit terms or constrain their taxing and spending powers.[75] Initiatives offer outsiders an opportunity to resist political insiders. In contemporary American politics, classical liberals remain outsiders.

Initiatives Reduce the Size of Government

Empirical evidence indicates the initiative restricts government spending. John Matsusaka, an economist at the University of Southern California, looked at government spending from 1960 to 1990 in the 23 states that have the initiative and in the 27 states with elected legislatures. States with the initiative had less government spending than the ones relying solely on legislatures, about 4 percent less per person per year. He also discovered that initiative states skew spending more toward the local level. Initiative states also rely more on user charges (and not taxes) to pay for government.[76] Overall, Matsusaka believes the initiative by itself means less spending and less redistribution.[77]

180

The political scientist Michael New has recently studied the effectiveness of tax and expenditure limitations passed by initiative and those passed by state legislatures. He finds legislative limits are associated with higher state spending. The limits passed by the initiative, in contrast, are associated with lower per capita government spending. New argues that the most effective measures limit government spending to the rate of inflation plus population growth and mandate immediate rebates of government surpluses.[78]

Classical liberals should not conclude that the initiative always and everywhere reduces the size of government. Matsusaka studied the fiscal effects of the initiative in the first half of the 20th century. States with the initiative then spent *more* than non-initiative states. If legislators want to spend more money than the average taxpayer, the initiative offers a way to restrain outlays. If legislators want to spend less than the average voter, direct legislation leads to more government.[79]

Virtue among Us

Speaking at the Virginia convention to ratify the Constitution, Madison asked, "Is there no virtue among us?" If not, he continued, "we are in a wretched situation." Any form of government, he noted, requires virtue among its people to secure liberty and happiness.[80] Matsusaka's evidence from the first half of the 20th century poses a similar question for Americans today. Do Americans now want more government and less freedom? Is there virtue among us, the inheritors of Madison's legacy?

Many libertarians think Americans want bigger government. If Americans widely support limited government, they ask, why do we have such a huge state and why so little demand for less coercion? The question assumes that the government we have reflects the popular will. But that may be wrong. Mancur Olson's story of exploiting minorities and exploited majorities explains both why we have big government and why so little can be done to change the status quo. The mere fact that big government exists does not mean socialist views are widely held by Americans.

The question of how public preferences might affect initiative outcomes is really three questions. Do public preferences increase liberty under the status quo where 23 states have direct democracy? Would public preferences increase liberty if some or all of the other

Table 10.1
ALTERNATIVES FOR THE INITIATIVE

Alternatives	Size of Electorate	Effect on Liberty
Status quo	Eligible voters in 23 states and the District of Columbia	Positive overall
Additional state initiatives	Eligible voters in 23 states, D.C., and up to 27 other states	Unknown
National initiative	All eligible voters in the United States	Unknown

27 states adopted the initiative? Would public preferences increase liberty if the entire nation adopted the initiative? These alternatives are summarized in Table 10.1.

On the whole, the evidence presented here suggests the initiative has increased liberty under the status quo. Since Americans have no experience with the other two alternatives (more states adopting the initiative and a national initiative), we can only speculate about their effects on liberty.

Should advocates for classical liberal ideals struggle to extend the initiative to any or all of the 26 states without direct democracy? The answer to that question depends on the state in question. Direct democracy in New York might well reduce the sum total of individual freedom. But perhaps not. If New Yorkers used the initiative to collectivize everything, they would—among others things—attract leftists to the state and repel non-leftists. New Yorkers with the initiative might create both a more left-wing New York and more non-left states elsewhere. The losses of freedom in New York would not necessarily be higher than the gains for freedom elsewhere.[81]

Some data can inform speculation about the spread of the initiative. Presidential election returns are a rough general indication of ideological preferences in a state. In the last four presidential elections combined, 14 of the 26 states with the initiative voted for Democratic presidential candidates three or more times; 7 of those states voted for the Democrat in all four elections. Nine of the 26 states voted for the Republican candidate three or more times; 6 of those states voted for the Republican in all four elections.[82] If the initiative were extended to the 26 states without it, more voters in more heavily Democratic states would be making legislation directly. Partisan affiliation does not perfectly correspond to support for individual freedom; some Republicans propose limiting individual freedom on some issues. Nonetheless, it seems unlikely that having the initiative in every state would expand the liberty of the individual, especially in economic affairs. However, if the initiative extended only to the six strongly Republican states that do not now have it, it is probably that the sum total of liberty, especially as measured by the taxation level, would increase.

A national initiative presents even more uncertainty. A national initiative might go some way toward replacing representative democracy with national direct democracy. *Federalist* No. 10 would be directly relevant. The results of a national initiative might well be similar to presidential outcomes assuming voting turnout was similar. On the whole, we might expect that liberty would do less well in national initiative than it has done under the status quo. The electorate for a national initiative would comprise both the electorates of the 26 states without the initiative and the 24 with the initiative. Inevitably the electorate for a national initiative would be less committed to liberty than the status quo is; the 26 non-initiative electorates are markedly more Democratic than the electorates that now have the initiative. Absent other considerations, a national initiative seems unlikely to advance the cause of freedom.

Classical liberals should not be too pessimistic about the United States as a whole. Some evidence suggests Americans lack a moral foundation for the welfare state. The welfare state thrives when citizens believe that inequalities deserve collective remediation. A remarkable new study by the political scientist Alberto Alesina and his colleagues indicates that only rich, leftwing Americans condemn inequality, a definite contrast to Europe. Most Americans, including the poor, see social mobility in civil society as the way to a better life.[83] Most Americans, especially the less affluent, do not see politics and government as the natural locus of success. They are not likely to vote for more government in a national initiative.

Historians and political scientists have also suggested that Americans and American political culture tend toward classical liberalism.[84] The expansion of the state ran against the ancient current of

183

the American river: "distrust of government came over on some of the first ships from England" and persists down to our day.[85] For five decades now professors have condemned (and occasionally lauded) the persistence of a liberal political culture in the United States. Their complaints bespeak the health of the republic.

Conclusion

Should classical liberals praise or deplore the return of direct democracy? Critics of the initiative often assume that American values are at odds with individual freedom and limited government. Much of their ostensibly Madisonian criticism should have no standing with classical liberals. The strong empirical evidence that the initiative leads to lower state spending should encourage libertarians because it saddens the progeny of Progressivism.

Classical liberals should qualify their assent to the rule of the people. The initiative might lead to less freedom on issues like campaign finance regulation. The success of "public interest" groups with the initiative might grow into a real danger for liberty. Majorities might use initiatives to restrict the freedom of the same minorities studied by Barbara Gamble. Extending the initiative to all the states or to the nation as a whole also seems questionable.

What might happen is different from what has happened, but on the whole, the initiative as it has existed has advanced the cause of individual freedom. The initiative is not without risks for liberty, but neither is a political status quo rotten with rent-seeking and blundering toward Leviathan. The people are likely to be a better friend of liberty than the political class.

This conclusion qualifies but does not refute James Madison's criticisms of direct democracy. His concerns may apply to a national initiative; we do not have enough evidence to decide that question. His criticisms seem incorrect when measured by the results of state initiatives. Madison's defense of representative democracy did not foresee how republics could be prey to minorities bent on redistribution and regulation. A half-century of experience with the initiative suggests direct legislating can complement representative government and offer a democratic and libertarian cure to republican ills. Classical liberals should offer two cheers for direct democracy.

Notes

1. David S. Broder, *Democracy Derailed: Initiative Campaigns and the Power of Money* (New York: Harcourt, 2000), p. 7. The direct initiative allows citizens to both propose

and decide the fate of laws. The indirect initiative requires that proposed laws first be submitted to a legislature; if that body rejects or amends the proposal in unacceptable ways, citizens may then vote directly on the law. Legislatures may also propose laws for the people's approval or rejection through referendums; 49 states allow for referendums. See "What Is Initiative and Referendum?" at www.iandrinstitute.org/, the website of the Initiative and Referendum Institute.

2. Howard R. Ernst, "The Historical Role of Narrow-Material Interests in Initiative Politics" in *Dangerous Democracy? The Battle over Ballot Initiatives in America*, eds. Larry J. Sabato, Howard R. Ernst, and Bruce A. Larson (Lanham, Md.: Rowman and Littlefield, 2001) provides a comprehensive study of the usage and success of initiatives. See also Peter Schrag, "Rule by Referendum" *The American Prospect*, July 17, 2000, p. 38.

3. Gary Rosen, *American Compact: James Madison and the Problem of Founding* (Lawrence, Kans.: University of Kansas Press, 1999).

4. *The Federalist* No. 51 (James Madison).

5. Ibid. Alexander Hamilton at the Constitutional Convention: "It has been observed, by an honorable gentleman, that a pure democracy, if it were practicable, would be the most perfect government. Experience has proved that no position in politics is more false than this. The ancient democracies, in which the people themselves deliberated, never possessed one feature of good government. Their very character was tyranny; their figure, deformity. When they assembled, the field of debate presented an ungovernable mob, not only incapable of deliberation, but prepared for every enormity." In *The Debates in the Several State Conventions, on the Adoption of the Federal Constitution*, ed. Jonathan Elliot, vol. 2 (Washington: privately printed, 1836), p. 253.

6. Bruce E. Cain and Kenneth P. Miller, "The Populist Legacy: Initiatives and the Undermining of Representative Government" in *Dangerous Democracy?*, p. 35.

7. David Magleby, *Direct Legislation: Voting on Ballot Propositions in the United States* (Baltimore: Johns Hopkins University Press, 1984), pp. 22–23.

8. Stephanie R. Milton, "Who's Paying for Democracy? Subsidizing the Intitiative Process to Influence Public Policy," Paper presented at the annual meeting of the Midwest Political Science Association, April 2001, p. 1.

9. Cain and Miller, p. 38.

10. John M. Allswang, *The Initiative and Referendum in California, 1898–1998* (Stanford: Stanford University Press, 2000), pp. 8, 30. Dewitt was a leading Progressive writer. His book *The Progressive Movement* reduced Progressivism to an attack on political corruption, the redesign of government institutions, and a concern for social and economic justice. See Benjamin Parke Dewitt, *The Progressive Movement* (Seattle: University of Washington Press, 1968, orig. 1915).

11. John M. Matsusaka, "Fiscal Effects of the Voter Initiative in the First Half of the Twentieth Century," *Journal of Law & Economics* 43 (October 2000) p. 641.

12. For evidence of the decline of direct legislation, see Todd Donovan and Shaun Bowler, "Overview of Direct Democracy" in *Citizens as Legislators: Direct Democracy in the United States*, ed. Shaun Bowler, Todd Donovan, and Caroline J. Tolbert (Columbus: Ohio State University Press, 1998), p. 10.

13. Allswang, pp. 105–7.

14. The exceptions were African Americans and "strong liberals."

15. Allswang, 108–9.

16. See "A Brief Analysis of Voter Behavior Regarding Tax Initiatives, from 1978 to 1999" at www.iandrinstitute.org/. Forty-three percent of all anti-tax initiatives passed from 1978 to 1989 while 53 percent passed from 1990 to 1999.

17. Broder, pp. 15–16.

18. John Haskell, *Direct Democracy or Representative Government? Dispelling the Populist Myth* (Boulder, Colo.: Westview, 2001), p. 11.

19. Ibid. p. 163.

20. Ibid. p. 119.

21. Ibid. p. 155.

22. Cain and Miller, p. 42.

23. Sue Tupper, "Challenging Initiatives: More than Just Special-Interest Money, An Issue of Civility" in *Dangerous Democracy?*, p. 29.

24. Broder, p. 20

25. For justifications of majority rule, see Dennis Mueller, *Public Choice II* (New York: Cambridge University Press, 1989), pp. 96–111.

26. This may only be true when economics consists of establishing an objective standard (such as Pareto's optimality) to judge exchanges among individuals. The general welfare economist sees "market failure" when free exchanges fails to meet that criterion and proposes reforms like Pigouvian taxes or direct regulations. The "subjectivist-contractarian" tradition of economists precludes conflicts between freedom and efficiency. See Ludwig Van den Hauwe, "Constitutional Economics," *The Elgar Companion to Law and Economics*, Jurgen G. Backhaus, ed. (Northhampton, Mass.: Edward Elgar, 1999), pp. 100–114.

27. Robert Cooter Jr., *The Strategic Constitution* (Princeton: Princeton University Press, 2000), p. 145: "Indirect democracy, however, can create a political cartel whose members conspire to blunt electoral competition."

28. See Thad Kousser and Ray LaRaja, "The Effect of Campaign Finance Laws on Electoral Competition," Cato Policy Analysis no. 426 (Washington: Cato Institute, 2002).

29. Cain and Miller, p. 49.

30. Timothy Besley and Stephen Coate, "Issue Unbundling via Citizens' Initiatives," NBER Working Paper 8036 (National Bureau of Economic Research: Cambridge, December 2000), p. 21.

31. Ibid., pp. 2–4. See also Gordon Tullock, Arthur Seldon, and Gordon L. Brady, *Government: Whose Obedient Servant? A Primer on Public Choice* (London: Institute of Economic Affairs, 2000), chapter 3.

32. Mancur Olson, *The Rise and Decline of Nations: Economic Growth, Stagflation and Social Rigidities* (New Haven: Yale University Press, 1982).

33. John G. Matsusaka, "Fiscal Effects of the Voter Initiative: Evidence from the Last 30 Years," *Journal of Political Economy* 103 (1995): 618. Only one study concludes that initiatives do not lead to policies that do not better reflect public preferences: see Edward L. Lascher Jr., Michael G. Hagen, and Steven A. Rochlin, "Gun behind the Door? Ballot Initiatives, State Policies and Public Opinion," *The Journal of Politics* 58, 3 (August 1996): 760–75.

34. Cooter, pp. 145–6.

35. Some scholars argue that initiatives limiting taxation may force state governments to depart from public preferences over the long run. Tax and expenditure limitations can change the "rules of the game" in important ways and may restrict spending and taxing long after the initiative has passed. If the voters want more

spending later, the initiative would frustrate the will of a majority. See Todd Donovan and Shaun Bowler, "Responsive or Responsible Government?" in *Citizens as Legislators: Direct Democracy in the United States,* eds. Shaun Bowler, Todd Donovan, and Caroline J. Tolbert (Columbus: Ohio State University Press, 1998), p. 256. This criticism seems misplaced. Unless prior tax-cutting initiatives preclude future initiatives raising taxes, the majority that wants more spending later could simply raise taxes through an initiative. (I owe this latter point to Peter VanDoren.)

36. Cain and Miller, 51. For a similar argument see Haskell, p. 111.

37. Peter Schrag, *Paradise Lost: California's Experience, America's Future* (New York: The New Press, 1998), pp. 224–25.

38. Elisabeth R. Gerber, *The Populist Paradox: Interest Group Influence and the Promise of Direct Legislation* (Princeton: Princeton University Press, 1999), p. 143.

39. Barbara S. Gamble, "Putting Civil Rights to a Popular Vote," *American Journal of Political Science* 41 (January 1997): 245–69.

40. James Madison, National Gazette, March 17, 1792, in *The Papers of James Madison,* vol. 14, ed. R. A. Rutland (Chicago: University of Chicago Press, 1976), p. 266.

41. Gamble, p. 252.

42. Roger Pilon, "Discrimination, Affirmative Action, and Freedom: Sorting Out the Issues," *American University Law Review* 45 (February 1996): 775–90.

43. Lynn Baker, "Direct Democracy and Discrimination: A Public Choice Perspective," *Chicago-Kent Law Review* 167 (1991): 707.

44. Donovan and Bowler, "Responsive," p. 267.

45. Ibid., pp. 267–8. Donovan and Bowler do argue that local, homogenous communities do represent a threat to minority civil rights. If so, the case for protecting minority civil rights would require limiting initiatives to statewide votes, rather than localities. The case would not preclude the initiative across the board.

46. Donovan and Bowler, "Responsive," pp. 264.

47. Campaign finance in fact has little salience with the public; see William G. Mayer, "Public Attitudes on Campaign Finance" in *A User's Guide to Campaign Finance Reform,* ed. Gerald C. Lubenow (Lanham, Md.: Rowman and Littlefield, 2001), pp. 61–2. The public approves many restrictions on campaign finance that are clearly unconstitutional. They also support amending the Constitution to allow restricting campaign finance.

48. The Maine legislature refused to pass public financing of campaigns. Public financing later came through initiative. See Patrick Basham, "Public Financing in Maine," policy analysis forthcoming from the Cato Institute.

49. Donovan and Bowler, "Overview," p. 17.

50. Allswang, p. 249. Donovan and Bowler, "Overview," p. 19.

51. Gerber, *The Populist Paradox,* p. 5. Gerber tests rather than endorses the idea.

52. Broder, p. 163.

53. Daniel A. Smith, "Campaign Financing of Ballot Initiatives in the American States" in *Dangerous Democracy?,* pp. 71–90. See also Magleby, p. 29.

54. Donovan and Bowler, "Overview," p. 12, and Todd Donovan, Shaun Bowler, and David S. McCuan, "Political Consultants and Initiative Industrial Complex," in *Dangerous Democracy?,* pp. 101–2.

55. David B. Magleby and Kelly D. Patterson, "Consultants and Direct Democracy," *PS: Political Science and Politics* 31 (1998): 160–69.

56. Cain and Miller also say democracy demands fairness, which means consulting with the opposition and allowing time for the expression of dissenting opinions as well as known voting rules. Cain and Miller, pp. 45–48. See also Haskell, p. 165.

57. Allswang, p. 249.

58. Donovan and Bowler, "Responsive," p. 259.

59. Gerber, *The Populist Paradox*, pp. 137–40.

60. Ernst, p. 26.

61. Shaun Bowler and Todd Donovan, *Demanding Choices: Opinion, Voting and Direct Democracy* (Ann Arbor: University of Michigan Press, 1998), p. 163.

62. Gerber, *The Populist Paradox*, p. 140.

63. Michael X. Delli Carpini and Scott Keeter, *What Americans Know about Politics and Why It Matters* (New Haven: Yale University Press, 1996), pp. 41–42.

64. Magleby, p. 198.

65. Donovan and Bowler, "Overview," p. 12.

66. Magleby, p. 198.

67. The term came to prominence in the work of Anthony Downs, who drew on Joseph Schumpeter. See Mueller, p. 205.

68. Arthur Lupia,"Shortcuts versus Encyclopedias: Information and Voting Behavior in California Insurance Reform Elections" *American Political Science Review* 88 (1994): 63–76. See also Bowler and Donovan, *Demanding Choices*, pp. 58–65. A broader treatment of the same issue can be found in Arthur Lupia and Mathew D. McCubbins, *The Democratic Dilemma: Can Citizens Learn What They Need to Know?* (New York: Cambridge University Press, 1998).

69. Susan A. Banducci, "Searching for Ideological Consistency" in *Citizens as Legislators*, p. 147.

70. Ibid., p. xiii.

71. *The Federalist* No. 10 (James Madison).

72. Morris P. Fiorina, *Congress: Keystone of the Washington Establishment*, 2d ed. (New Haven: Yale University Press, 1989), pp. 40–43.

73. For reelection rates in the House, see Norman J. Ornstein, Thomas E. Mann, and Michael J. Malbin, *Vital Statistics on Congress 1999–2000* (Washington: AEI Press, 2000), p. 57.

74. Insiders do fight back. Most Americans assume that when an initiative passes, it changes policy in a state. That need not be the case. Initiatives often depend on government actors to be implemented or enforced. Legislatures often must appropriate funds to implement an initiative or bureaucrats must create and follow instructions for carrying out the initiative. When making these decisions, these officials often reinterpret and sometimes reverse the election results on the initiative. Elisabeth R. Gerber, Arthur Lupia, Mathew D. McCubbins, and D. Roderick Kiewiet, *Stealing the Initiative: How State Government Responds to Direct Democracy* (Upper Saddle River, N.J.: Prentice Hall, 2001), pp. 4–5.

75. Some state legislatures have passed tax and expenditure limitations. Such limits are far less effective than limits passed by initiative.

76. Matsusaka, "The Last 30 Years," p. 590.

77. Ibid., p. 620.

78. Michael J. New, "Limiting Government through Direct Democracy," Cato Institute Policy Analysis no. 420, December 2001.

79. Matsusaka, "First Half of the Twentieth Century," p. 641.

80. James Madison, "Speech in the Virginia Ratyifying Convention," June 20, 1788.

81. This scenario assumes New York would not be allowed to impose the costs of socialism on other states through redistribution by the federal government. If that assumption does not hold, socialism in New York might reduce the sum total of

188

human freedom. Note, however, that the reason for that reduction would be the federal government's redistribution and not the existence of direct democracy in New York.

82. Author's calculations based on presidential election data available at www.uselectionatlas.org.

83. Alberto Alesina, Rafael Di Tella, and Robert MacCulloch, "Inequality and Happiness: Are Europeans and Americans Different?" National Bureau of Economic Research Working Paper 8198, April 2001. The paper can be found at www.nber.org/papers/8198.

84. Louis Hartz, *The Liberal Tradition in America* (New York: Harcourt Brace, 1955); Theodore J. Lowi, *The End of the Republican Era* (Norman: University of Oklahoma Press, 1995); Seymour Martin Lipset and Gary Marks, *It Didn't Happen Here: Why Socialism Failed in the United States* (New York: Norton, 2000).

85. H. W. Brands, *The Strange Death of American Liberalism* (New Haven: Yale University Press, 2001), p. 1.

11. The Rule of Law and Freedom in Emerging Democracies: A Madisonian Perspective

James A. Dorn

> That is not a just government, nor is property secure under
> it, where the property which a man has in his personal safety
> and personal liberty, is violated by arbitrary seizures of one
> class of citizens for the service of the rest.
>
> —James Madison[1]

The collapse of communism in Eastern bloc countries in 1989–90 and in the Soviet Union at the end of 1991 paved the way for the emergence of a host of new democratic states. This latest wave of democratization continues a trend that began slowly in the first part of the 20th century, with the fall of empires and the rise of electoral democracies, and gained momentum during the second half of the century.

In 1900, there were no fully democratic governments, in the sense of sanctioning universal suffrage; in 1950, there were 22 democratic states that were home to 31 percent of the world's population; and by the end of the century, there were 120 democracies accounting for 58.2 percent of the global population (Figure 11.1).[2]

The problem is that universal suffrage does not guarantee a free society in which government is limited, human rights are protected, and the rule of law is upheld. Indeed, Freedom House finds that, of the 120 electoral democracies, only 85 (representing 38 percent of the world's population) can be classified as "free."[3] The real measure of progress will be the success of emerging democratic nations at cultivating freedom by limiting the powers of government and safeguarding persons and property, thereby stemming the growth of the welfare state.

The challenge is to foster the growth of liberal democracies in the Madisonian sense, not simply to promote the rise of majoritarianism.

Figure 11.1
Number of Electoral Democracies in the World, 1900–2000

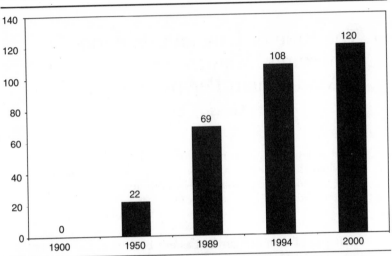

Source: Freedom House, *Freedom in the World* (various years).
Note: Electoral democracies are those in which universal suffrage prevails.

If people are to secure "the blessings of liberty," they must learn to think about the long-run gains from constitutional rules that constrain the power of government and not be lured by the promise of short-run benefits from clever redistributive schemes engineered by roving majorities. James Madison sought to reconcile liberty and democracy within a constitutional order. It is fitting, therefore, that on the 250th anniversary of the birth of James Madison (1751–1836), the "chief architect" of the U.S. Constitution, we reconsider his views on the principles of a liberal constitutional order and derive lessons for emerging democracies.

Principles of a Liberal Constitutional Order

For Madison, "the essence of government is power; and power, lodged as it must be in human hands, will ever be liable to abuse."[4] The problem is to institute a government of limited powers while protecting individual rights, so that order and liberty can coexist and people can pursue their happiness while promoting the common good.

The genius of Madison was to draw from his predecessors the key elements of a liberal constitution and to apply those ideas to the American experiment. To understand the importance of Madison's contributions to what F. A. Hayek called "the constitution of liberty," one needs to examine Madison's ideas on constitutional political economy, especially his vision of law, liberty, and justice; his view of democracy; his emphasis on the spontaneous order of the free market and its dependence on private property and the rule of law; and his constitutional ethics as the basis for a free society.[5]

Law, Liberty, and Justice

Madison's primary interest was law, not legislation. He sought to craft a constitution that incorporated the ideals of the American Revolution and that provided a framework for protecting fundamental rights within a republican form of government. The U.S. Constitution, as the law of the land, was meant to narrowly limit the power of government in order to ensure liberty and justice for all Americans.[6]

Law, liberty, and justice are inseparable for Madison. When the law of the land is used to limit government to its legitimate functions of safeguarding persons and property, people will be free to pursue their own happiness without violating the rights of others, and justice will prevail. "In a just and free government," wrote Madison, "the rights both of property and of persons ought to be effectually guarded."[7]

Madison regarded it as self-evident "that persons and property are the two great subjects on which governments are to act; and that the rights of persons, and the rights of property, are the objects, for the protection of which government was instituted."[8] He viewed justice not as the use of government power to achieve some particular outcome or distribution of income but, rather, as the protection of an individual's natural rights to life, liberty, and property. "That alone is a *just* government," wrote Madison, "which *impartially* secures to every man, whatever is his *own*."[9]

Madison was no friend of the redistributive state.[10] The Constitution as "a charter of freedom" was meant to prevent "arbitrary seizures of one class of citizens for the service of the rest."[11] There is no evidence that he ever thought the General Welfare Clause (Article I, Section 8) granted the federal government enough power to provide a foundation for the modern welfare state. Rather, he saw limited government, not a paternalistic state, as the surest way to "promote the general welfare." In a passage written some three decades after the ratification of the Constitution, Madison stated:

> With respect to the words "general welfare," I have always regarded them as qualified by the detail of powers connected with them. To take them in a literal and unlimited sense would be a metamorphosis of the Constitution into a character which there is a host of proofs was not contemplated by its creators.[12]

Unlike modern advocates of "welfare rights," Madison adhered to the notion that justice requires the protection of property, not its seizure to enrich others. No one has a right to other people's property, even for compassionate purposes. Charity is a private not a public good. That is why Adam Smith and his contemporaries made a sharp distinction between rights that are consistent with liberty, which they called "perfect rights," and those that are not. Perfect rights do not violate the principle of "commutative justice" or consent, whereas "imperfect rights" do because they are associated with "distributive justice" and cannot be exercised without violating someone's property rights. To say that a person has a "right" to welfare, for example, is to use the word "right" in "a metaphorical sense," according to Smith, and thus to abuse its proper meaning.[13]

Madison's liberal constitutional republic would have much room for *private* charity and compassion but little space for government largess. Indeed, as William Niskanen pointed out: "The U.S. Constitution ... provides no explicit authority for federal welfare programs. Article 1, Section 8 describes 18 specific powers of the federal government, without a hint that these powers authorize the redistribution of income."[14]

Freedom and Democracy

The overriding principle of Madison's liberal constitutional order is freedom under the rule of law. Without law, there would be no freedom.[15] The difficulty was in determining the proper extent of the law and hence of government. Madison's moral philosophy, which was strongly influenced by John Locke, guided him in that endeavor. He held that (1) individuals have natural rights that precede government, (2) government exists to secure those rights and obtains its power from the "consent of the governed," and (3) majorities cannot attenuate those rights without violating the principle of justice.

Madison made liberty paramount—for reasons of both morality and utility. He envisioned a liberal republic in which freedom trumps democracy "in the small," that is, crude majoritarianism.[16] However, if one views democracy "in the large," that is, as a regime consistent with the rule of law and limited government, then liberty and democracy are fully compatible.

In a truly liberal democracy, people would be free to choose and to follow their own interests provided no one's legitimate rights were violated.[17] People would be allowed to do good, but only at their own choice and expense. Minority rights would be protected and majority interests would be limited by the first principles of Madison's liberal constitutional order and by the federalist structure of the Union. As Madison wrote in 1829, "The only effectual safeguard to the rights of the minority must be laid in such a basis and structure of the government itself as may afford, in a certain degree, directly or indirectly, a defensive authority in behalf of a minority having right on its side."[18]

The federalist system was to offer a means of controlling government, both by placing substantive limits on governmental powers and by introducing competition into government. A decentralized power structure and a distribution of powers among the executive, legislative, and judicial branches of government were intended to check the Leviathan's appetite for ever-greater power and to safeguard a liberal social order. "The preservation of liberty," Madison contended, "requires that the three great departments of power should be separate and distinct."[19]

The Rule of Law and Spontaneous Order

Although Madison looked to freedom under the law to morally justify his vision of limited government, he knew the beneficial effects his constitution of liberty would have through creating economic harmony and wealth. Like Adam Smith, Madison recognized the overriding importance of private property, freedom of contract, and voluntary exchange in promoting a spontaneous market order and in increasing the wealth of a nation. He regarded property as a fundamental human right and its protection as a necessary requirement for economic development: "Property as well as personal rights is an essential object of the laws, which encourage industry by securing the enjoyment of its fruits."[20]

Madison favored free trade and opposed government intervention. He called himself a "friend to a very free system of commerce" and regarded as self-evident the notion "that commercial shackles are generally unjust, oppressive, and impolitic." He recognized that "all are benefited by exchange, and the less this exchange is cramped by Government, the greater are the proportions of benefit to each."[21]

At the core of Madison's constitutional order is what Hayek called the "central concept of liberalism"—namely, the idea of "spontaneous order":

> Under the enforcement of universal rules of just conduct, protecting a recognizable private domain of individuals, a spontaneous order of human activities of much greater complexity will form itself than could ever be produced by deliberate arrangement, and that in consequence the coercive activities of government should be limited to the enforcement of such rules.[22]

Madison adhered to laissez faire as a general principle. He contended that, in the absence of government intervention, labor and capital would be allocated "in a more certain and direct manner than the wisdom of the most enlightened Legislature could point out."[23]

One of the chief reasons for a federal constitution was to end the protectionist practices of the individual states under the Articles of Confederation and to prevent the debasement of money and the impairment of contracts. Madison sought to institute a constitution that would establish free trade among the states and end rent seeking, in order to "give a regular course to the business of society."[24] Thus, he fully supported the economic clauses in the Constitution that gave Congress the authority "to regulate Commerce with foreign Nations, and among the several States" and "to coin Money" and "regulate the Value thereof" (Article I, Section 8). His liberal stand on property rights and freedom of contract was reflected in the Fifth Amendment, which he authored, and in the Contracts Clause (Article I, Section 10).

For Madison, economic and civil liberties were equally important—freedom was a single cloth that could not be divided into separate components without lessening the strength of the whole.

His conviction that economic liberties and personal freedoms cannot be separated made him recognize the importance of constitutional prohibitions against bills of attainder and ex post facto laws, as well as against laws designed to impair the obligation of contracts. In *Federalist* No. 44, he stated, "Bills of attainder, ex post facto laws, and laws impairing the obligation of contracts, are contrary to the first principles of the social compact and to every principle of sound legislation."

By instituting general rules designed to limit the power of government and protect economic liberties, Madison helped to create the basis for a vibrant free-market system in the United States. Unfortunately, the gradual erosion of the economic constitution of liberty has led to the demise of the minimal state and the rise of the redistributive state. That change has caused a corresponding weakening of "the spirit of a free people" that Madison so cherished as the ultimate protection against overbearing government.[25]

Constitutional Ethics

The survival and strength of a liberal democratic republic ultimately depend on widespread respect for property and the rule of law. If citizens are unwilling to take a long-run view and to limit the activities of government to the defense of persons and property, universal suffrage will operate to undermine the constitution of liberty. Madison clearly recognized the dangers of majority rule in an unlimited democracy in which people put their short-run parochial interests ahead of the safeguarding of individual rights. If voters know that their vote will not be decisive under majority rule, that redistributive schemes are permissible, and that the costs of voting for such programs will be borne by a small group of high-income taxpayers, then there will be a strong incentive to expand government beyond the minimal state envisioned by Madison.

To maintain his constitutional republic, Madison emphasized the importance of virtue and reason: "I go on this great republican principle, that the people will have virtue and intelligence to select men of virtue and wisdom. . . . To suppose that any form of government will secure liberty or happiness without any virtue in the people, is a chimerical idea."[26] It appears that Madison regarded virtue as a public good because it would dispose individuals toward conduct supporting a liberal constitutional order and discourage them from wanting a redistributive or welfare state.

With the growth of government during the 20th century, and the crowding out of private charity by public welfare, many people have lost sight of the first principles that Madison sought to embody in the heart of the Constitution. Since those principles are meta-legal principles that ultimately find their foundation in the hearts and minds of the people, there is no way to preserve the Constitution as a charter of freedom if the people themselves prefer the false security of the welfare state to the freedom and responsibility of the liberal market order. When the ethos of economic liberty fades, the economic constitution of liberty becomes a mere parchment.

Institutions that secure property rights and just laws matter in shaping economic incentives and behavior, but culture matters too. A drift away from a culture of individual responsibility toward one of collective responsibility will chip away at the fabric of freedom. That is why in 1792, in his essay "Charters," Madison wrote, "Liberty and order will never be *perfectly* safe, until a trespass on the constitutional provisions for either, shall be felt with the same keenness that resents an invasion of the dearest rights; until every citizen shall be an Argus to espy."[27] For Madison, each citizen in a constitutional republic has a duty to serve as a check on government. That sense of responsibility, however, has been eroded today as many people have come to view government, not as a necessary evil but as an instrument for doing good.

In classical mythology, Argus is a giant with 100 eyes who acts as a guardian, and in Madison's case, as a guardian of our liberties. In a free society, citizens must be vigilant and be able "to espy"— that is, to see at a distance—and use reason to discern the long-run implications of alternative policies. For, unless people learn to judge policy from a constitutional or long-run viewpoint, and not just consider policy in the post-constitutional setting of majority rule, they will lose their freedom. If they take a long-run view, individuals are more likely to agree to constitutional limits that insulate economic life from politics and prevent rent-seeking behavior that redistributes wealth rather than creates it. As Buchanan so eloquently stated:

> The vision of constitutional order that informed the thinking
> of James Madison and his peers among the Founders was
> carried forward for more than a century of our national
> history. This vision embodies both an understanding of the

principles of constitutional order and recognition that the individual, as citizen, must accept the ethical responsibility of full and informed participation in a continuing constitutional convention.

The Madisonian vision, with its embodied ethic of constitutional citizenship, is difficult to recapture once it is lost from the public consciousness. The simple, yet subtle, distinction between strategic choices within rules and constitutional choices among sets of rules ... must inform all thinking about policy alternatives. The individual, as citizen, cannot restrict his or her attention to policy options within rules. ... Constitutional citizenship requires that the individual also seek to determine the possible consistency between a preferred policy option and a preferred constitutional structure.[28]

The challenge is to recapture the Madisonian vision of a liberal constitutional order and to reawaken in the people a constitutional ethic that binds all branches of government to upholding the constitution of liberty. That will be no easy task in the United States; it will be even more difficult in emerging democracies—especially ex-communist countries—crippled by corruption and rent seeking.

Lessons for Emerging Democracies

There are several important lessons that emerging democracies can learn from Madison's liberal constitutional vision:

- For true democracy to prevail, government must be limited and must be just; the security of persons and property must take precedence over electoral politics.
- To prevent rent seeking and corruption, economic freedom must prevail; people must accept a rule of law that treats people equally and safeguards private property rights and freedom of contract.
- A spontaneous market-liberal order will arise to coordinate economic activity and create wealth, provided the government minimizes its role in the economy and lets people be free to choose.
- A free society cannot coexist with a redistributive state—there is no "third way"; people must be ever watchful to ensure that majorities are prevented from attenuating the rights of minorities in the name of distributive justice.

How fast those lessons are learned in countries making the transition to democracy will depend crucially on the size and scope of government in the old regime and the duration of the old regime. In countries that had all-powerful long-entrenched governments and central planning, the transition to a liberal democratic state with the rule of law and free markets will go slower than in countries with smaller governments, some experience of markets, and a memory of freedom.

Among ex-communist countries, those with a pre–World War II history of liberalism—such as Hungary, Poland, the Czech Republic, Slovenia, and the Baltic States—are making more rapid progress toward democratic capitalism. Progress has been slower in countries such as Russia and Ukraine that had very strong government control of all aspects of life for many years and no space for cultivating the free market or civil society.

Table 11.1 shows the Freedom House rankings for democratization and economic liberalization in ex-communist countries as of June 1999.[29] Nearly all of the post-Soviet states, or newly independent states (NIS), lag significantly behind Eastern and Central European countries that had previous experience with a liberal political and economic order. Poland has the highest relative ranking for both democratization and economic liberalization (1.44 and 1.67, respectively, with a score of 1 being the highest and 7 the lowest). Russia, on the other hand, ranks relatively low with a score of 4.25 for democratization and 4.33 for economic liberalization.

Similar results hold for Freedom House's rankings for adherence to the rule of law and for the extent of corruption (again based on a scale of 1 to 7). Ex-communist countries that had experienced the rule of law prior to World War II and respected property rights— such as Hungary, Poland, and Slovenia—have made faster progress toward establishing the rule of law and reducing corruption during the transition to democratic capitalism than have countries such as Russia and Ukraine (Table 11.2).

Russia's slow progress should not be surprising; it takes time to change one's thinking after so many years under totalitarian rule. As Alexander Tsypko, a professor of philosophy at Moscow State University, wrote just prior to the collapse of the Soviet Union, "It is hard—very hard—to admit that your life and your work are being senselessly wasted and that you are living in an unnatural, false

Table 11.1
FREEDOM HOUSE RANKINGS FOR DEMOCRATIZATION AND ECONOMIC LIBERALIZATION IN EX-COMMUNIST COUNTRIES AS OF JUNE 1999

Country	Democratization Score (1 = highest)	Country	Economic Liberalization Score (1 = highest)
Poland	1.44	Poland	1.67
Czech Rep.	1.75	Hungary	1.75
Hungary	1.75	Czech Rep.	1.92
Slovenia	1.94	Estonia	1.92
Lithuania	2.00	Slovenia	2.08
Estonia	2.06	Latvia	2.50
Latvia	2.06	Lithuania	2.83
Slovakia	2.50	Slovakia	3.25
Mongolia	3.13	Armenia	3.58
Romania	3.19	Croatia	3.67
Bulgaria	3.31	Georgia	3.67
Macedonia	3.44	Bulgaria	3.75
Moldova	3.88	Kyrgyz Rep.	3.83
Georgia	4.00	Mongolia	3.92
Croatia	4.19	Moldova	4.00
Russia	4.25	Romania	4.17
Ukraine	4.31	Russia	4.33
Albania	4.38	Albania	4.50
Armenia	4.50	Kazakhstan	4.50
Kyrgyz Rep.	4.88	Macedonia	4.58
Bosnia	5.13	Ukraine	4.58
Kazakhstan	5.38	Azerbaijan	5.00
Azerbaijan	5.50	Yugoslavia	5.33
Yugoslavia	5.50	Bosnia	5.58
Tajikistan	5.69	Tajikistan	6.00
Belarus	6.44	Belarus	6.25
Uzbekistan	6.44	Uzbekistan	6.25
Turkmenistan	6.94	Turkmenistan	6.42

SOURCE: Adrian Karatnycky, Alexander Motyl, and Aili Piano, eds., *Nations in Transit, 1999–2000* (New Brunswick, N.J.: Transactions Publishers, 2001), p. 19.

Table 11.2
FREEDOM HOUSE RANKINGS FOR ADHERENCE TO THE RULE OF LAW AND EXTENT OF CORRUPTION IN EX-COMMUNIST COUNTRIES AS OF JUNE 1999

Country	Rule of Law Score (1 = highest)	Country	Corruption Score (1 = lowest level of corruption)
Slovenia	1.75	Slovenia	2.00
Poland	1.88	Poland	2.25
Hungary	2.13	Hungary	2.50
Estonia	2.63	Czech Rep.	3.25
Czech Rep.	2.75	Estonia	3.25
Latvia	2.75	Latvia	3.50
Lithuania	2.88	Lithuania	3.75
Slovakia	3.13	Slovakia	3.75
Mongolia	3.75	Mongolia	4.00
Bulgaria	4.13	Romania	4.25
Romania	4.25	Bulgaria	4.75
Georgia	4.50	Georgia	5.00
Macedonia	4.63	Macedonia	5.00
Croatia	5.00	Belarus	5.25
Moldova	5.00	Croatia	5.25
Russia	5.25	Armenia	5.75
Ukraine	5.25	Albania	6.00
Armenia	5.38	Azerbaijan	6.00
Albania	5.50	Bosnia	6.00
Kyrgyz Rep.	5.50	Kazakhstan	6.00
Azerbaijan	5.75	Kyrgyz Rep.	6.00
Kazakhstan	5.75	Moldova	6.00
Belarus	5.88	Tajikistan	6.00
Tajikistan	5.88	Turkmenistan	6.00
Bosnia	6.00	Ukraine	6.00
Yugoslavia	6.00	Uzbekistan	6.00
Uzbekistan	6.25	Russia	6.25
Turkmenistan	6.38	Yugoslavia	6.25

SOURCE: Karatnycky, Motyl, and Piano, p. 25.

society, headed with your country for the dead end of history."[30] He recognized that half measures would not solve the problems of communism:

> There is no third way between modern civilization and socialism as it is. The market cannot be combined with a government monopoly on the organization of labor or with public ownership of the means of production. A return to the market is impossible . . . without broad-based privatization. It is impossible to have the rule of law without a multiparty system, without renouncing the communist monopoly on power. It is impossible to adopt moral values and to earn the right to return to civilization, to the European home, without rejecting the idea . . . of the forcible transformation of society.[31]

Madison could not have said it better. When force rather than consent is the governing principle of society, justice and civility lose ground and individuals become pawns of the state. The longer totalitarian regimes remain in power, the more corrupt they become and the longer it will take to restore or to create the principles of a liberal constitutional order.

The fact that communism has failed does not mean that leftist sentiments have disappeared.[32] Many people in ex-communist countries as well as in advanced democracies still want the government to bring about "social justice" by attenuating property rights and redistributing income.[33] Thus, the dangers that Madison warned about—"arbitrary seizures of one class of citizens for the service of the rest," "arbitrary restrictions, exemptions, and monopolies," and "unequal taxes" that "oppress one species of property and reward another species"—are still present.[34]

Electoral democracy is neither necessary nor sufficient to generate long-run economic growth. Initially the transition to a democratic regime may boost economic growth if the new regime increases political freedom and stability and better protects property rights. However, if electoral democracy is not bound by an effective constitution that limits the power of government and safeguards both civil and economic liberties, rent seeking will increase and wealth creation will be replaced by redistributive activities that will impede real income growth. As Robert Barro explained, "In places that have already achieved a moderate amount of democracy, a further increase impairs growth because the dominant effect comes from the intensified concern with social programs that redistribute resources."[35]

To avoid that pitfall, emerging democracies must pay more attention to limiting the power of government, which means they must pay more attention to the proper place of government in a free society. They should do this not just to maintain a strong economy but also to protect fundamental human rights. When government fails to safeguard private property and interferes with free trade, the rule of law is weakened and basic human rights are violated as surely as when freedom of speech and other civil liberties are attenuated. In this regard, Milton Friedman noted, "While economic freedom facilitates political freedom, political freedom, once established, has a tendency to destroy economic freedom."[36] Madison would surely agree.

The evidence from ex-communist countries shows that the countries that have experienced the greatest economic liberalization have also experienced the most democratization (Figure 11.2). That those two variables move together suggests that they may reinforce each other, at least up to a point. But, once again, that point depends on the size and scope of government. If electoral democracy is constrained by a constitutional ethos of liberty, then universal suffrage will present no threat to either political or economic freedom.

The reality is that, under communism and central planning, economic liberalization eventually requires political reform. As Czech president Vaclav Havel put it, "The state should be less and less visible."[37] Private free markets are a threat to the Communist party's monopoly on political power. At some point, constitutional and political reform is inevitable if economic reform is to continue. At that juncture, Madison's constitutional vision becomes indispensable. The multiparty elections that now characterize the former Soviet Union are a welcome addition to freedom. Thus far, however, many of the NIS have not been able to limit the discretionary power of government. Special interests continue to dominate the political process and to use the force of legislation to plunder the national wealth at the expense of the vast majority of citizens.

The Future of Democracy

Newly emerging democracies, whether in the former Soviet bloc or elsewhere, need sound written constitutions based on market-liberal

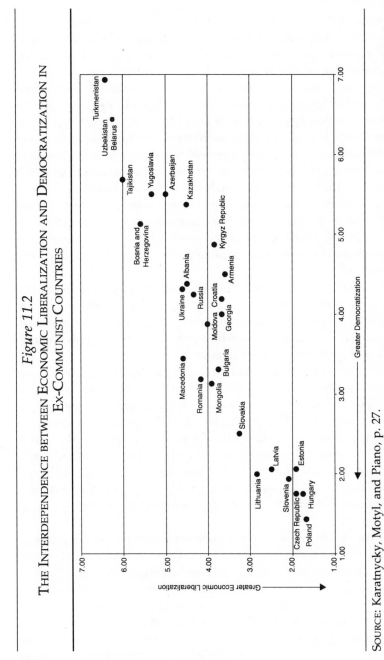

Figure 11.2

THE INTERDEPENDENCE BETWEEN ECONOMIC LIBERALIZATION AND DEMOCRATIZATION IN
EX-COMMUNIST COUNTRIES

SOURCE: Karatnycky, Motyl, and Piano, p. 27.

NOTE: Rankings for economic liberalization and democratization are based on a scale of 1 to 7, with 1 being the highest score. The rankings were calculated by Freedom House and reflect the period through June 1999.

principles if democracy is not to degenerate into tyranny.[38] There must be widespread acceptance of the principles of a liberal order and a general understanding of justice under the law of liberty, ideas that Madison so clearly laid out in his writings.

Mounting evidence shows that the rule of law and economic freedom are key ingredients in the recipe for economic development.[39] In the information age, countries that fail to create market-supporting institutions, including a transparent legal system, do so at their own peril. Private property makes people responsible for their decisions about the use of scarce resources and thus gives people an incentive to search for the most profitable uses of their labor and capital. Under the rule of law and limited government, people are better able (and more inclined) to focus on the long-run consequences of their actions. When government overreaches, on the other hand, investment decisions will become politicized and resources will be wasted.

In a study of 150 countries, Lee Hoskins and Ana Eiras found that those countries in which private property rights are secure and transparent have created more wealth (as measured by real GDP per capita) than countries in which private property rights are insecure and corruption is high (Figure 11.3).[40]

Gwartney, Holcombe, and Lawson, in a study of 60 countries over the period 1980–95, found that "a 10 percentage point increase in the size of government [measured by total government spending as a percentage of GDP] at the beginning of the period was associated with approximately a six-tenths of a percentage point reduction in growth during the entire 15-year period."[41] They also found that if government were limited to its "core functions," it would spend about 15 percent of gross domestic product. Any greater government spending would lead to "a negative impact on the wealth of nations."[42]

Those empirical results point to the importance of private property rights and limited government, not only for creating a just society in the Madisonian sense, but also for alleviating poverty. To limit government, however, requires stemming the growth of the redistributive state, which means cultivating an ethos of individual freedom and responsibility. If nations want to create and preserve a spontaneous market-liberal order, which Madison considered the system most consistent with a free people, they need to cultivate

Figure 11.3
STRONGER PROPERTY RIGHTS EQUAL GREATER WEALTH

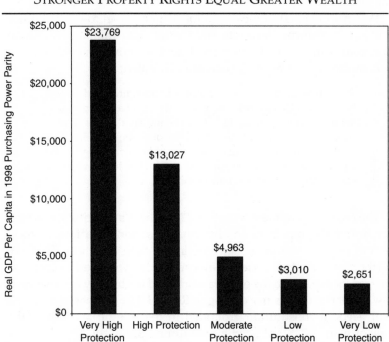

Protection of Property Rights

SOURCE: Lee Hoskins and Ana I. Eiras, "Property Rights: The Key to Economic Growth," in Gerald P. O'Driscoll Jr., Kim R. Holmes, and Mary Anastasia O'Grady, eds., *2002 Index of Economic Freedom* (Washington and New York: The Heritage Foundation and *Wall Street Journal*), p. 40.

"democracy in the large," not simply "democracy in the small." The emerging democracies, as seen in ex-communist countries, are beset by corrupt elites, rent seeking, and the danger of abandoning democratic rule. The challenge is to help people see the benefits of limited government and to recognize the costs of unlimited democracy.

Emerging democracies need to learn the lessons Madison has to offer about the morality and practicality of limited government and free markets. Following some third way, in which government tries to plan the market and equalize outcomes rather than to enforce "rules of just conduct" that protect persons and property, is a recipe for failure.

Perhaps the greatest challenge for democracy in the 21st century will be to transform China into a free nation with limited government and competitive private markets. Doing so, however, will require constitutional reform. As Jixuan Hu has stated:

> By setting up a minimum group of constraints and letting human creativity work freely, we can create a better society without having to design it in detail. That is not a new idea, it is the idea of law, the idea of a constitution. Real constitutional government is a possible alternative to the dream of a perfectly designed society. . . . The idea is to apply the principle of self-organization.[43]

The recent amendment to Article 11 of China's constitution, which recognizes the importance of the nonstate sector and affords protection to private enterprise, is a step in the right direction. To move further toward a free society, however, China will need to continue to open its markets to the outside world and to abide by international law. In particular, as my colleague Roger Pilon emphasized, China will need "a constitution grounded in the rule of law, not in the rule of man; . . . it will need a constitution of liberty."[44]

The problem of moving from a nondemocratic regime to a constitutional democracy that protects "life, liberty and property" is largely one of credibility: How can a credible commitment be made to real constitutional change when there is a long history of abuse of individual rights and no rule of law?[45] That problem deserves more careful study if the liberal order that Madison so desired is to prevail in the future.

Notes

1. Quoted from Madison's 1792 essay "Property," in Gaillard Hunt, ed., *The Writings of James Madison,* vol. 6, 1790–1802 (New York: G. P. Putnam's Sons, 1906), p. 102.

2. Adrian Karatnycky et al., eds. *Freedom in the World: The Annual Survey of Political Rights & Civil Liberties, 1999–2000* (New York: Freedom House, 2000), pp. 590–92.

3. Ibid, p. 592.

4. James Madison, "Speech in the Virginia State Convention of 1829–30, on the Question of the Ratio of Representation in the Two Branches of the Legislature," December 2, 1829, in Madison, *Letters and Other Writings of James Madison,* vol. 4, 1829–1836 (Philadelphia: J. B. Lippincott, 1865), p. 51.

5. For a detailed discussion of Madison's constitutional political economy, see James A. Dorn, "Madison's Constitutional Political Economy: Principles for a Liberal Order," *Constitutional Political Economy* 2 (1991): 163–86.

6. The fact that the universal principles enshrined in the Constitution were not universally applied at the time of the framing does not mean that the principles themselves are invalid. Madison never tried to justify slavery from a moral standpoint; he knew it was wrong and hoped that it would eventually be abolished. See Edward McNall Burns, *James Madison: Philosopher of the Constitution* (New York: Octagon Books, 1968), pp. 76–78.

7. Madison, "Notes on Suffrage" (1829), in *Letters and Other Writings*, p. 22. Madison defined "property" in a broad Blackstonian sense as "every thing to which a man may attach a value and have a right; and which leaves to everyone else the like advantage." He did not separate economic rights from other rights; thus, an individual "has property . . . in the safety and liberty of his person" and "an equal property in the free use of his faculties and free choice of the objects on which to employ them." In brief, "as a man is said to have a right to his property, he may also be equally said to have a property in his rights." Madison in Hunt, p. 101.

8. Madison, "Speech in the Virginia State Convention," p. 51.

9. Madison in Hunt, p. 102.

10. In his biography of Madison, Burns writes (p. 49), "Madison did not consider it desirable that government should intervene directly in the interest of the less fortunate members of society. Compassion is due them, he graciously conceded, but not direct beneficence."

11. Madison in Hunt, p. 102.

12. Madison, "[Letter] to James Robertson," April 20, 1831, in *Letters and Other Writings*, pp. 171–72.

13. Adam Smith, "Of Jurisprudence" (1762), in R. L. Meek, D. D. Raphael, and P. G. Stein, eds., *Lectures on Jurisprudence* (Indianapolis: Liberty Classics, 1982), p. 9. See also Dorn, "Equality: A Constitutional Perspective," in Thomas R. Dye, ed., *The Political Legitimacy of Markets and Governments* (Greenwich, Conn.: JAI Press, 1990), pp. 94–95.

14. William A. Niskanen, "A Constitutional Approach to Taxes and Transfers," *Cato Journal* 6 (1986): 352.

15. According to F. A. Hayek, Montesquieu and other liberals (who preceded Madison) stood steadfast behind the idea that "government of law" is "the essence of liberty." Hayek, *The Constitution of Liberty* (Chicago: University of Chicago Press, 1960), p. 194.

16. See Roger Pilon, "On the First Principles of Constitutionalism: Liberty, then Democracy," *American University Journal of International Law and Policy* 8 (Winter/Spring 1992/93): 531–49. According to Ralph Ketcham, "A great gulf . . . separates the thought of Madison (and other Founding Fathers) from that of believers in such later concepts as Benthamite utilitarianism and simple majoritarian democracy, who denied that principles of justice and virtue can be identified and made the foundation of government, and therefore have a higher sanction than the will of the majority." Ketcham, *James Madison: A Biography* (Charlottesville: University Press of Virginia, 1990), p. 43.

17. In 1837, John O'Sullivan, political editor of *The United States Magazine and Democratic Review*, defined "the fundamental principle of the philosophy of democracy," not as the popular right to vote, but as the moral obligation "to furnish a

system of the administration of justice, and then leave all the business and interests of society to themselves, to free competition and association; in a word, to the *voluntary principle*." In J. L. Blau, ed., *Social Theories of Jacksonian Democracy: Representative Writings of the Period 1825–1850* (New York: Liberal Arts Press, 1954), p. 28. Madison viewed democracy in this classical-liberal sense. See Burns, chap. 3.

18. Madison, "Speech in the Virginia State Convention," p. 52.

19. *The Federalist* No. 47 (James Madison). ,

20. Madison, "Notes on Suffrage," in *Letters and Writings*, p. 22.

21. Madison, "Speech in First Congress," April 9, 1789, in Saul K. Padover, ed., *The Complete Madison: His Basic Writings* (New York: Harper and Bros., 1953), pp. 269–70.

22. F. A. Hayek, "The Principles of a Liberal Social Order," in Hayek, *Studies in Philosophy, Politics, and Economics* (Chicago: University of Chicago Press, 1967), p. 162. James M. Buchanan, a pioneer in the fields of public choice and constitutional political economy, has argued that "the most important central principle in economics" is the "principle of spontaneous order." Buchanan, *What Should Economists Do?* (Indianapolis: Liberty Press, 1979), pp. 81–82.

23. Madison, "Speech in First Congress," in Padover, p. 269.

24. *The Federalist* No. 44 (James Madison).

25. Madison, "Letter to Thomas Cooper," March 22, 1824, in Padover, p. 273.

26. Madison, "Speech in Virginia Convention," June 20, 1788, in Padover, pp. 48–49.

27. Madison,"Charters," in Robert A. Rutland et al., eds., *The Papers of James Madison*, vol. 14, April 6, 1791–March 6, 1793 (Charlottesville: University Press of Virginia, 1983), p. 192.

28. Buchanan, "Socialism Is Dead but Leviathan Lives On," in Buchanan, *The Logical Foundations of Constitutional Liberty*, vol. 1 of *The Collected Works of James M. Buchanan* (Indianapolis: Liberty Fund, 1999), p. 372.

29. Democratization refers to the degree of electoral and political freedom while economic liberalization reflects the freedom of the market and the security of private property rights. For an explanation of the ratings methodology, see Aili Piano, "Explanatory Notes," in Adrian Karatnycky, Alexander Motyl, and Aili Piano, eds., *Nations in Transit, 1999–2000* (New Brunswick, N.J.: Transaction Publishers, 2001), p. 42.

30. Alexander Tsypko, "Revitalization of Socialism or Restoration of Capitalism?" *Cato Journal* 11 (1991): 289.

31. Ibid.

32. See Buchanan, "The Ethics of Constitutional Order," in *The Logical Foundations of Constitutional Liberty*, pp. 368–73.

33. See Hayek, *The Mirage of Social Justice*, vol. 2 of *Law, Legislation, and Liberty* (Chicago: University of Chicago Press, 1976).

34. Madison in Hunt, pp. 102–3.

35. Robert J. Barro, "Determinants of Democracy," paper presented at the general meeting of the Mont Pelerin Society, Vienna, Austria, September 10, 1996, p. 1. See also Barro, "Democracy and Growth," *Journal of Economic Growth* 1 (March 1996): 1–27.

36. Milton Friedman, "Economic Freedom, Human Freedom, Political Freedom," The Smith Center for Private Enterprise Studies, Inaugural Lecture, November 1, 1991 (Hayward, Calif.: The Smith Center for Private Enterprise Studies, 1992), p. 7.

37. Vaclav Havel, *Summer Meditations* (London: Faber and Faber, 1992), p. 78.

38. For a study of the future of democracy in East Asia, see Dorn, "Economic Liberty and Democracy in East Asia," *Orbis* 37 (Fall 1993): 599–619.

39. See, for example, Barro, *Determinants of Economic Growth* (Cambridge, Mass.: MIT Press, 1997), and James Gwartney, Randall Holcombe, and Robert Lawson, "The Scope of Government and the Wealth of Nations," *Cato Journal* 18 (1998): 163–90.

40. Lee Hoskins and Ana I. Eiras, "Property Rights: The Key to Economic Growth," in Gerald P. O'Driscoll Jr., Kim R. Holmes, and Mary Anastasia O'Grady, eds., *2002 Index of Economic Freedom* (Washington and New York: The Heritage Foundation and the *Wall Street Journal*, 2002), pp. 37–48.

41. Gwartney, Holcombe, and Lawson, p. 182.

42. Ibid., p. 188. According to the authors (p. 167), the "core functions" of government include the safeguarding of persons and property, the provision of national defense, education, highways, sewage, sanitation, and environmental protection, and the creation of a central bank. Madison's list would have been shorter; it certainly would not have included a central bank.

43. Jixuan Hu, "The Nondesignability of Living Systems: A Lesson from the Failed Experiments in Socialist Countries," *Cato Journal* 11 (1991), p. 44.

44. Roger Pilon, "A Constitution of Liberty for China," in Jim Dorn, ed., *China in the New Millennium: Market Reforms and Social Development* (Washington: Cato Institute, 1998), p. 352.

45. On the credibility problem for constitutions and how commitment to a set of rules limiting the power of government and safeguarding property rights can create wealth, see Douglass North and Barry Weingast, "Constitutions and Commitment," *Journal of Economic History* 49 (1989): 803–32. For a survey of the literature on credible commitment, see Gary J. Miller, "The Impact of Economics on Contemporary Political Science," *Journal of Economic Literature* 35 (September 1997): 1173–1204.

12. Governance beyond the Nation State: James Madison on Foreign Policy and "Universal Peace"

John Tomasi

I begin my essay with the admission that I am not a Madison scholar. I am not an American historian or even a constitutional theorist. My background is in political philosophy. So I was delighted to hear that contributors to this volume are invited to consider Madison not only as an historical figure but also as "a fount of ideas for the future." I am going to take that invitation seriously.

I shall examine Madison's protectionist foreign policy and, especially, his essay "Universal Peace." But I shall conduct those examinations not to learn about the American founding moment, or even to see what lessons Madison might have for those of us living in America today. Rather, I wish to consider what Madison may have to tell us about the future. In particular, I wish to consider what Madison might have to tell us about the future not just for America, but also for the world as a political whole.

We celebrate the 250th anniversary of James Madison's birth at a time when great changes shape our world. Interconnectivity—technological, economic, cultural, and political—is the emblem that historians in the future will likely affix to our age. Of course, interconnectivity has been a steady feature of the human social experience.[1] The movement toward connectedness in our world today is neither unique nor unidirectional—the period of Taliban rule in Afghanistan stands merely as the most vibrant marker of an urge to retreat felt by many in our world.

Nonetheless, there seems to be something fundamentally different about the processes of interconnection the world is experiencing today. Historically familiar processes of human interconnection have widened in scope, with many dimensions of connection becoming genuinely global for the first time. The connective processes have intensified as the changes that come with contact occur more quickly than ever before.[2] The changes in scope and intensity of interconnectivity dramatically affect global capital markets. This "electronic herd," as Thomas Friedman has called it, is more muscular, faster moving, and more disruptive of inherited political forms—Westphalian conceptions of state sovereignty in particular—than any economic force seen in the world before.[3]

I wish to consider what James Madison might say about the political implications of the complex phenomenon we call globalization. What lessons might Madison have for us today about the proper relations between nations in our increasingly interconnected world? How might studying Madison open our minds today to unexpected possibilities for political relations on our planet tomorrow?

Protectionism and Republicanism

One approach to this question would be to study Madison's own views of foreign policy—especially his approach to international political economy—and then apply them to problems of international political economy in our world. Thus, as Americans, we might seek to uncover the principles that Madison thought should govern the fledgling American nation in its relations to other nations in his day. We might then examine those same principles as potential guides to relations between the United States and other nations today.

This approach would require that we attempt to enter into the very different world in which Madison and his political cohort were operating. To take this path, we would need to reconstruct, as best we could, the political and cultural background against which Madison's own views of foreign relations developed. The colonists were a diverse lot—from Puritans in New England and Quakers in Pennsylvania to the "new aristocrats" of the South. The American colonies lacked any common outlook on foreign policy before 1776. Despite their diversity, however, the colonists had all participated in a core curriculum that later made a coordinated foreign policy outlook possible. All the colonists—albeit from diverse perspectives—had been schooled by witnessing the struggles of 18th-century England, their Mother Country, in her dealings with other European states. Washington's Farewell Address powerfully expressed the master lesson taken by the Americans from that curriculum: a nation that wishes to prosper by way of trade must keep itself away from the political entanglements of the Continent.[4]

This approach to studying Madison—by which one studies Madison's own views of foreign policy for guiding insights about American foreign policy today—might start from that broad background and then pick out the distinctively Madisonian foreign policy twists. The most infamous of such twists, of course, is the policy of commercial discrimination that Madison advocated as a member of Congress beginning in the early 1790s and through to his presidency. While Alexander Hamilton emphasized the importance of good relations with Great Britain as a condition of America's internal economic development, Madison took a more confrontational view. Madison's notion of economic independence was intimately conditioned by his own agrarian version of republicanism. It was his republicanism that led Madison to distrust British financiers and made him wary of the development of large-scale manufacturing on the British model in the United States. Most important, Madison objected to the old system of British mercantilism and sought to liberate his new republican nation from that system's economic hold.

Since the peace of 1783, Great Britain had refused to enter into commercial treaties on conditions of equality with its erstwhile colonies. As a vocal member of the First Congress and later as President, Madison vehemently objected to this. He saw British mercantilism as an assault on America's commercial independence, an attempt by outsiders to disrupt what Madison saw as the "natural" course of America's economic development. Madison advocated a form of retaliatory commercial legislation—a scheme of higher tariffs that would be applied to nations not in mutually agreed upon commercial treaties with the United States—aimed at pressuring the British to lift their "orders of council," which required every ship trading with Europe to stop first in Great Britain and pay taxes.[5]

Famously, Madison's strategy failed. His argument for commercial discrimination was premised on the idea that the British were more economically dependent upon the Americans than the Americans were on them. On Madison's account, the British would never risk a full-blown commercial war with the United States because the Americans exported to Great Britain "necessities"—raw materials and foodstuffs—while importing from them only "superfluities"—clothing and manufacturing hardware. Madison's critics found that claim ludicrous and, most importantly, so did the British. The Americans, squeezed between British and Napoleonic demands, eventually were forced to back down.

No doubt there are some anti-protectionist lessons that might be gleaned by Americans today from a study of Madison's ill-fated program of commercial discrimination. I suspect, however, that any serious examination of that issue would generate results that are more nuanced and mixed. Madison's views about international political economy were intimately linked to his republican conception of domestic economic development. Because he was a republican, questions about domestic virtue and not just raw economic output were central to Madison's conceptions of foreign policy success or failure. These questions about the precise role of Madison's agrarian republicanism as a shaper of the protectionist foreign policies he advocated are fascinating, unjustly neglected, and fully deserving of a paper of their own. But such a project is not my ambition here.

The Late 18th Century and the Early 21st

There is another less historical and more philosophical way of using Madison to illuminate problems of international relations in our world today. To take us forward to the very different use of Madison, I begin by going back not to the Founding period but to 1948.

In 1948, Carl Van Doren, a historian, published an important book called *The Great Rehearsal*, a magisterial account of the making and the ratifying of the U.S. Constitution. Van Doren was a starry-eyed citizen of the world. An intellectual stepchild of H. G. Wells and the other architects of the League of Nations, Van Doren advocated a literal form of cosmopolitan citizenship.[6] Especially after witnessing World War II, with the alarming advent and first use of nuclear weapons, Van Doren called for a dramatic reform and extension of the United Nations. Perhaps partaking in some of the fatal conceit characteristic of his day, Van Doren advocated the establishment of something like a federal world government.

The Great Rehearsal begins with a brief introduction in which Van Doren presents a grand analogy. The relationship between the states in early America, he suggested, is very like the relationship between nation-states or countries in his own mid-20th-century world. Van

Doren argued that the great problem facing Americans in 1787 was to learn how to think nationally, not locally, about the United States.

Similarly, Van Doren suggested, the problem facing people in 1948, the great problem of his time, was to learn to think globally. "It is obvious that no difficulty in the way of world government can match the danger of a world without it," he wrote. Accordingly, Van Doren called his book about the American Constitutional Convention *The Great Rehearsal*. The uniting of the states in early America, Van Doren believed, presaged—and should be a model for—the political unification of the states of the whole world.

In *Hamlet*, Shakespeare makes Polonius say "Brevity is the very soul of wit." Even Polonius would be satisfied with Van Doren on this score: the introduction in which Van Doren suggests his grand analogy is barely three pages, and Van Doren does not return again to the analogy or to his conception of cosmopolitan citizenship. But it is an arresting idea. In light of the processes of global interconnectivity, the analogy of the relation of nations in the world to that of the several states in early America may have even more salience in *our* time than in Van Doren's.

At the time of the Founding, there were separate states, each with a discrete system of governmental institutions, linked to a geographically defined territory. The political leaders of each state claimed to exercise a coercive monopoly on power within that domain, with claims of sovereignty—both internal and external— very much in play. So too today we have nation states, with a territorial connection, and the same coercive, sovereignty-based claims being made. The states at the time of the American Founding were diverse. They were diverse religiously, culturally, and even politically to some degree. The states were diverse even regarding basic moral matters, for example, regarding the question of slavery. These same dimensions of diversity are apparent in the system of nation-states in our world today. Then, the states were organized only loosely under the Articles of Confederation, a document predicated upon an explicit recognition of exclusive unit sovereignty. The political structure made possible by the Articles, the central government as it were, had no power to tax, no standing army, and indeed no effective power to enforce its edicts at all. Rather than being a government, pre-Constitutional America was a mere diplomatic assembly of states. Today we have the United Nations Charter, predicated on much the same notion of unit sovereignty. As a government, the United Nations has similar limitations as the confederation of American states, and others besides.

In both historical periods, however, in early American and in our world today, we see parallel changes under way. Both periods are marked by a massive increase in interconnectivity between politically sovereign units. In both cases, the underlying forces generating those new systems of connection seem to have a life of their own, as though the changes were being worked out according to a logic from a deeper level than that of the prevailing political structures. Time, trade, and technology bring people into contact. There was a sense at the time of the Founding, as now, that the problems of governance increasingly escaped the reach of the existing political systems, formally based, as each system was, on a rigid notion of unit sovereignty. In early America, there were fast-expanding communication networks, a more elaborate system of roads, better riverboats, and new navigational technologies. So too in the world today we have the Internet and soon, perhaps, the evernet. Between the diverse states then as between diverse nation-states now, we see a rapidly growing network of law and morality not just between the units but also between their members as individuals, a set of transitions in both cases tied to increasing flows of trade. There was a sense that the scale of identity, in both cases, was changing and growing. The colonies had a nascent sense of themselves as one. So too, according to a growing number of contemporary cosmopolitans, there is an inchoate but building sense of oneness among the people of the world today.

Further, the arguments made then about how or whether to supersede the existing political arrangements are similar to the arguments that are increasingly being heard today. In 1787 some thought that the existing system of separate states should be maintained. Existing political boundaries were said to be important for protecting cultural and religious differences and should if anything be strengthened. Others thought that the state walls should be made more porous, especially so as to extend the benefits of free trade. Similar arguments are made now regarding national boundaries.

Opponents of the proposed United States of America argued that this new entity would simply be too vast. This proposed new political creature was a behemoth: fully 10 times larger than any federation that had been tried in previous history. Ten times larger! Anti-federalists argued that such an entity could never be held together by a single constitution. Supporters of the Constitution replied that a large federation has advantages, since it would become harder for any one faction to dominate the rest. In early America, some argued that proponents of the Constitution misunderstood the nature of the interconnectivity around them, that a series of regional federations would be a sufficient political response to the new world they were entering. So too today—with the European Union, the Free Trade Area of the Americas, and the like—some argue that we are experiencing regionalization rather than globalization and that forces of interconnectivity will never be strong enough to require any greater political realignment than we have already seen.

Opponents of the Constitution argued that the United States would amount to a kind of superstate, distant, arrogant and powerful, a Leviathan that would destroy the liberties of individual citizens. Better to limit power to the governments of individual states, which, being closer to the people, would better serve as guarantors of individual liberty. Supporters of the Constitution replied that conflicting sovereignties are the greatest cause of war. Through war, not only are lives lost, but liberties are eroded as government increases in size and scope. Similar arguments are being made today by those who favor something like a world government and those who fear that outcome above all else.

Madison the Internationalist

I think it fascinating to look at Madison's ideas from this perspective, from the perspective of Van Doren's grand analogy applied to our world today. Madison offered a Virginia plan for America. Might those same ideas, Madison's ideas, bear within them something like an American plan for the world? Robert McDonald, another contributor to this volume, describes America as a state of mind. It is worth asking: What is that state of mind? What might it mean to expand that state of mind and offer to share it, politically, with other people everywhere in the world?

The approach to political thinking that I wish to scrutinize—where one looks to previous federations to propose new bigger ones—is precisely the sort of thinking that Madison himself engaged in. In 1786, before the Annapolis convention, Madison wrote to his friend

Thomas Jefferson who was living in Paris and asked him to comb the bookstores and send him everything he could find about previously existing federations. Those studies greatly deepened Madison's understanding of the dangers and opportunities of political construction along federalist lines. Madison used the old to illuminate the new, with his crucial adjustments for scale and size.

Would Madison approve of thinking about political arrangements on a supranational scale, as he had himself advocated new political arrangements on a suprastate scale? There are clues in his essay "Universal Peace," published in the *National Gazette* on February 2, 1792. "Among the reforms which have been offered to the world, the projects for universal peace have done the greatest honor to the hearts, though they seem to have done very little to the heads of their authors."[7] Madison chides Rousseau in particular for his proposal for a supranational council of deputies, presiding over a great confederation of sovereign states. Rousseau thought such a council might be empowered to resolve disputes between states and to put down revolutions within them. Such a plan, Madison objected, could never be put into effect. The causes of war are so numerous and intractable that the resolution of international conflict simply through discussion and adjudication would be impossible. Any supranational political council that was strong enough to settle disputes between states would have to take onto itself extraordinary powers. Madison claimed that a supranational council such as Rousseau's would become a despotic superstate, its very formation cutting off the last hope of the oppressed. Thus, "A universal peace, it is to be feared, is in the catalogue of events, which will never exist but in the imaginations of visionary philosophers, or in the breasts of benevolent enthusiasts."[8]

A closer look at the essay "Universal Peace" reveals, however, that Madison was not a simple anti-federalist when it comes to supranational governance. After voicing his skepticism of Rousseau's proposed council, Madison continues: "It is still however true, that war contains so much folly, as well as wickedness, that much is to be hoped from the progress of reason; and if any thing is be hoped, every thing ought to be tried."

Madison then divides wars into two classes: those that flow only from the will of the government, and those that arise from the will of the people. Madison saw the former class of war—where war benefits the rulers at the expense of their own people—as by far the more common. This most customary sort of war depends "on those whose ambition, whose revenge, whose avidity, or whose caprice may contradict the sentiment of the community." According to Madison, wars of this kind are conducted by those who spend the public money rather than those who supply it, by those who direct the public forces rather than support them, by those who gain more control and power by the war rather than by those who are to be made more subservient and powerless by it.

On Madison's analysis of the nature of war, it was obvious why wars between nations could not be stopped by the institution of some powerful external agency, such as Rousseau's supranational council. In modern economic terms, the incentives were structured so that war was the preferred outcome of domestic leaders on an ongoing basis. Warfare could be prevented only by a radical restructuring of those domestic incentives. In Madison's view, this required a regeneration of governments themselves. Governmental decisions, especially ones regarding prospective warfare, must be made subordinate to, indeed be made one with, the will of the people. The blunder made here by the great republican Rousseau was ironic. Instead of proposing a supranational council as a means to peace and then advocating republican self-governance for states within that confederation, Rousseau should have *begun* with a republican remedy. Regarding the great problem of universal peace between nations, domestic, republican solutions must be the first step rather than any external, despotic one. Self-governing countries have reasons to avoid going to war that non–self-governing countries lack.

If all the nations of the world became democratic, the greatest and most common class of war would thus be eliminated. But there would remain that other class of war, where war is conducted not simply according to the will of the government but according to the will of the people themselves. Madison saw this class of war as less easily remedied but not beyond any imaginable antidote. "As wars of the first class were to be prevented by subjecting the will of the government to the will of society, those of the second class can only be controuled [sic] by subjecting the will of the society to the reason of the society." So Madison recommended some pacific remedies in the form of "permanent and constitutional maxims of conduct."

These pacific remedies must be constitutionally fixed in order to prevail over passions and other "inconsiderate pursuits" that stir even democratic peoples on the brink of national wars. Again in economic terms, the constitution should be arranged so that the costs of war-making cannot be externalized to others, excluding especially the externalization of those costs to fellow nationals in future generations. Madison argued that long-term schemes of national indebtedness for war should therefore be constitutionally prohibited: "Each generation should be made to bear the burden of its own wars, instead of carrying them on, at the expense of other generations."[9]

If the nations of the world became more and more democratic, and if an ever greater number of them adopted pacific constitutional amendments about war debts like those Madison described, would Madison think that a sufficient condition for the attainment of universal peace? Did Madison think Rousseau got it completely wrong by recommending the supranational form of governance embodied in his proposed council, or did Madison think Rousseau got it wrong simply by advocating the external council before the widespread achievement of self-governance as a domestic matter?

Madison does not answer those questions, if indeed they even occurred to him as worth asking. At one point Madison does exhibit some "benevolent enthusiasm" regarding the possibilities of universal peace in an increasingly democratic world. Regarding Rousseau, who proposed his supranational council well before the republican revolutions in America or France, Madison opines toward the end of "Universal Peace": "Had Rousseau lived to see the rapid progress of reason and reformation, which the present day exhibits, the philanthropy which dictated his project would find rich enjoyment in the scene before him." Perhaps Madison's enthusiasm sprang simply from the spread of democracy, along with the prospect of pacific constitutional amendments. Perhaps his enthusiasm would be undeterred by the massive military-industrial-political complexes that have so prominent a place in the economies of contemporary democracies (as well as in the psyches of citizens in democracies today). However that may be, there is nothing deeply anti-Madisonian about proposals for the free unification of sovereign, self-governing political units. Indeed, this whole approach to inter-unit relations—where one seeks to combine with one's political brethren rather than conquer or ignore other states—is basic not only to Madison's thought but to that of the early American federalists as a whole. Contemporary international relations theorists have aptly labeled this combinationist attitude—whether taken toward other states or toward other nations—the "Philadelphian approach."[10]

Free Trade, Free Migration, and Peace

So we are back to Van Doren's analogy again. Might Madison's ideas throw light on contemporary proposals for confederal arrangements between sovereign nations—even though Madison did not advocate supranational governing structures in his day?

Of course, Van Doren's grand analogy has obvious limitations. There are salient differences that might be brought out to balance every point of analogy. Indeed, whether one decides in the end that the two periods are eerily similar, utterly dissimilar, or somewhere in between may reveal as much about one's own intellectual disposition as about the alleged analogy itself.[11]

We must also be gentle with the historical Madison, especially when asking what, if anything, he might have to teach us about something so utterly foreign to his experience as the problem of individual freedom in the complexly interconnected world of nation-states in which we heirs of Madison's Constitution find ourselves today. Madison was above all an agrarian republican. Agrarianism was a crucial element of his proposed confederacy of republics. It is not obvious how Madison's agrarian vision could accommodate industrialism, much less how it could accommodate the post-industrial economies of today's advanced democratic states. Questions of political economy and their impact on the virtue or decadence of the citizenry were central to Madison's ideal for America, and he routinely invoked a conception of the disinterestedness of public leaders that few of us can take seriously today. My colleague Gordon Wood remarked to me recently that James Madison would be appalled at our world. I think that is true, and it is a warning worth remembering.

Nonetheless, I think that Madison's project throws interesting light on the supranational political projects that many people are beginning to talk about again in our day.

Thought about this way, Madison offers a distinctive approach to the perils and promise of many nascent schemes of supranational political order. In the early American case, Madison sought to find a balance between the centrifugal forces of confederation and the centripetal forces of consolidation. His idea was to use the supposed problem of size as a means to strike this balance. So Madison saw himself as attempting to remodel the traditional republican house to fit on the new, much more vast geographic foundation that the proposed United States represented. Madison's solution, of course, was that of a compound republic with a system of dual sovereignty. The Articles of Confederation could be thought of as an attempt to overlay a scheme of partial national sovereignty atop the system of complete sovereignty of the States. On this score, Madison called the Articles "imbecilic." The Constitution as he imagined it was to be neither national nor federal but a combination of both: rather than being a mere overlay, the Constitution was itself to embody the formula for a compound republic.

Underlying all Madison's well-known design features is an extremely important idea, Madison's most admirable, indeed sterling, ambition. For Madison was motivated not merely by a concern for the stability of a political form, but by a concern for the lives of individual people throughout America. Madison's deep ambition in drafting the U.S. Constitution was to secure for every citizen "life and liberty, with a right of acquiring and using property, and generally of pursuing and obtaining happiness and safety." A Madison today might plausibly have that ambition still: to offer to self-governing peoples a form of political union in which each individual might enjoy the benefits of life and liberty, with the right of acquiring and using property, and generally of obtaining happiness and safety. And such a Madison might plausibly have that ambition, not just for inhabitants of the United States, but for individual humans living anywhere in the world.

At the outset of this essay I admitted that I was not an historian but rather a normative philosopher. I should say now, though, that even though I am a philosopher, I am not completely naïve. I am aware, for example, that I am writing this essay for a volume to be published by the Cato Institute. So I am aware that the use of Madison I am suggesting may fall strangely on the eyes of some readers of this volume. In considering Madison this way, you may be hearing me call for something like a new founding moment dedicated to the construction of a planetary superstate, complete with a massive standing army—gently referred to as the "domestic police." Some of you may even think that I've switched genres yet again, not history or philosophy or even science fiction, but something more like the genre of Stephen King—horror!

I am sympathetic to that concern. Like many others, though, who are thinking about the political consequences of global interconnectivity, I am genuinely unsure what path is best for those of us who care most about individual freedom. A concern for freedom should take the form of a concern for the freedom of all people, no matter behind what political boundary or beneath what national label we were taught to think of them while growing up. Indeed, it would be the greatest political irony if libertarians allowed themselves to think only locally, and not globally, about liberty simply because they inherited a world crisscrossed by the collectivist assumptions of the Westphalian paradigm.

If we allow ourselves to think globally and not just nationally about individual freedom, what political direction should our thoughts take? One alternative to the system of sovereign states is anarcho-capitalist. This would be a system where states are abolished (or their significance greatly weakened) and power is devolved to emergent, functional units. On this model, systems of authority may lose any rigid territorial connection. Such authority structures would be defined functionally instead of spatially, and they would tend to be polycentrically rather than hierarchically ordered with respect to one another.

Some epochs within the Middle Ages in Europe have been claimed to fit this description, with complex overlapping authority structures (familial, geographic, trade-based, secular, religious) doing the work of social coordination that later came to be claimed for themselves by the rulers of geographically defined states.[12]

Bruno Frey has proposed a similar system as global alternative to today's remaining Westphalian order—with dynamic systems of functional, overlapping, competing jurisdictions of authority (familial, geographic, economic, religious, etc.) taking the place of the very state system by which the medieval system was itself once displaced.[13]

Frey's model is in many ways an attractive one for the future. But nothing is simple when we commit ourselves to conceiving of the imperatives of individual freedom on a global scale. Indeed, in a post-Westphalian world, a basic division may well arise between libertarians and classical liberals on what a commitment to freedom requires. This division becomes discernable only when each of those views—libertarian and classical liberal—is projected onto a screen of a size that planetary thinking requires. For even on the most extreme reading of Madison's relevance to global politics today—where Madison's combinatory impulses are used to call for something like a world state—it is not immediately clear what people committed to individual liberty should think.

When I was in high school, I remember vividly pulling up behind an old truck at a red light. The truck had a peeling bumper sticker that read: "Free Trade, Free Migration, and Peace." It struck me as a strange combination. But when I put those ideas together in my mind, a light turned green for me. Part of what I have always found attractive about that ideal—free trade, free migration, and peace—is that it is cosmopolitan in its essence. That slogan, which has been a beacon to me ever since, implies a normative commitment to reach out across inherited boundaries and to recognize other people everywhere as politically equal to one another. But it has occurred to me recently that this beacon, my beacon—free trade, free migration, and peace—is a pretty apt description of the *internal* conditions of a nation-state of a certain kind. Within the boundaries of a well-functioning classical liberal society, one founded along the lines that James Madison had in mind when writing the U.S. Constitution, citizens are to be guaranteed the benefits of free trade, free migration, and peace—at least between one another. So maybe, just maybe, people who care most about liberty in our world today should be not only for the minimal state, but also for the biggest state of all.[14] Maybe, just maybe, they should be for something like a global federal constitution, along the original American lines. James Madison may be a fount of ideas for that possible future.[15]

Notes

1. By some measures, for example, the flow of capital or the level of international migration, the world of the 19th century was more interconnected than it is today. A particularly clear exposition of this point is Stephen Krasner, *Sovereignty: Organized Hypocrisy* (Princeton: Princeton University Press 1999), pp. 220–28.

2. A helpful account of what is distinctive about the contemporary processes of globalization is David Held, *Democracy and the Global Order: From the Modern State to Cosmopolitan Governance* (Stanford: Stanford University Press, 1995), pp. 16–23 and 101–35.

3. Thomas L. Friedman, *The Lexus and the Olive Tree: Understanding Globalization* (New York: Anchor Books, 1999).

4. A masterful account of the development of a common foreign policy in early America is Felix Gilbert, *To the Farewell Address: Ideas of Early American Foreign Policy* (Princeton: Princeton University Press, 1961).

5. I am indebted to Drew McCoy's argument that Madison's support of retaliatory duties is intimately connected to his republicanism. See his "Republicanism and American Foreign Policy: James Madison and the Political Economy of Commercial Discrimination, 1789 to 1794," *William and Mary Quarterly* 31, no. 4 (October 1974). I also thank Jon Bassett for emphasizing for me the irony within this connection: Madison's anti-British trade policy encouraged capital, especially in New England, to be invested in cotton mills rather than international trade, spurring precisely the urban industrialization that Madison feared (e-mail correspondence of 6 June 2001).

6. The popular blueprint for the League was "The Idea of a League of Nations" by H. G. Wells et al., *The Atlantic Monthly* 123 (January 1919): 106–26.

7. All quotations are from "Universal Peace" in Gaillard Hunt, ed., *James Madison: Writings* 6 (New York: Putnam Press, 1907), pp. 88–91.

8. I note that it is unclear how well Madison understood Rousseau. A helpful account of Rousseau's position can be found in Stanley Hoffman and David Fidler, *Rousseau on International Relations* (New York: Oxford University Press, 1991) especially at 20–22.

9. Madison writes: "Were a nation to impose such restraints on itself, avarice would be sure to calculate the expenses of ambition; in the equipoise of these passions, reason would be free to decide for the public good; and an ample reward would accrue to the state, first, from the avoidance of all its wars of folly, secondly, from the vigor of its unwasted resources for wars of necessity and defense. Were all nations to follow the example, the reward would be doubled to each; and the temple of Janus might be shut, never to be opened more." ("Universal Peace," p. 91).

10. See the pathbreaking article by Daniel Duedney, "Binding Sovereigns: Authorities, Structures, and Geopolitics in Philadelphian Systems," in *State Sovereignty as Social Construct*, Thomas Biersteker and Cynthia Weber, eds. (New York: Cambridge University Press, 1996).

11. I develop this analogy, and provide a detailed analysis of its strengths and weaknesses, in "Commerce, Sovereignty and Cosmopolitanism: Lessons from Early America for the Future of the World," *Social Philosophy & Policy*, Special Issue: After Socialism (forthcoming January 2003).

12. See Alexander Murphy, "The State System as Political-Territorial Ideal: Historical and Contemporary Considerations," in *State Sovereignty as Social Construct*.

13. See "A Utopia? Government without Territorial Monopoly," Institute for Empirical Research in Economics, University of Zurich, Working Paper No. 47, June 2000.

14. An example of the kind of classical liberal positions I have in mind can be found in Friedrich Hayek, *The Road to Serfdom* (Chicago: University of Chicago Press, 1944), especially Chapter 15, "The Prospects of International Order," pp. 220–239.

15. This essay is based on a lecture I delivered at the Cato Institute in March of 2001, at a conference celebrating the 250th anniversary of the birth of James Madison. I am grateful to the audience on that occasion for their energetic and stimulating

response. For conversation and e-mail exchanges on these ideas in the months since, I am indebted to Walter Grinder, John Majewski, and Jonathan Bassett. I am pleased to record my special debt to John Samples, who provided substantive comments, and editorial advice, on the essay.

List of Contributors

James M. Buchanan won the 1986 Nobel Prize in Economic Science. Professor Buchanan got his start with a B.A. from Middle Tennessee State College in 1940, followed by an M.S. from the University of Tennessee in 1941. After graduating from the University of Chicago with a Ph.D. in 1948, he held teaching positions at the University of Virginia, the University of California at Los Angeles, and the Virginia Polytechnic Institute. Among the many influential books he has written are *The Calculus of Consent: Logical Foundations of Constitutional Democracy* (1962) with Gordon Tullock; *Cost and Choice* (1969); *The Limits of Liberty* (1975); and *Liberty, Market, and State* (1985); and his autobiography, *Better than Plowing and Other Personal Essays* (1992). Most recently he published with Roger Congleton *Politics by Principle, Not Interest*.

Judge Alex Kozinski is circuit judge of the United States Court of Appeals for the Ninth Circuit. He received his B.A. and J.D. from the University of California at Los Angeles. He served in the Office of Counsel to the President (1981) and at the Merit Systems Protection Board (1981–82). He also was a judge in the United States Claims Court from 1982 to 1985.

Steven A. Engel is law clerk to Judge Kozinski. Mr. Engle has a J.D. from Yale University awarded in 2000.

Roger Pilon is the founder and director of the Cato Institute's Center for Constitutional Studies. Pilon's writings have appeared in the *New York Times, Washington Post, Wall Street Journal, Los Angeles Times, Legal Times, National Law Journal, Harvard Journal of Law & Public Policy, Notre Dame Law Review, Stanford Law & Policy Review, Texas Review of Law & Politics*, and elsewhere. He has appeared, among other places, on ABC's "Nightline," CBS's "60 Minutes II," National Public Radio, Fox News Channel, CNN, MSNBC, and

229

CNBC. He lectures and debates at universities and law schools across the country and testifies often before Congress. Prior to joining Cato, Pilon held five senior posts in the Reagan administration, including posts at State and Justice. Pilon holds a B.A. from Columbia University, an M.A. and a Ph.D. from the University of Chicago, and a J.D. from the George Washington University School of Law.

Joyce Lee Malcolm, a professor of history at Bentley College and a senior fellow in the MIT Security Studies Program, is the author of *To Keep and Bear Arms: The Origins of an Anglo-American Right.* She holds a bachelor's degree from Barnard College and a doctoral degree from Brandeis University, and is a Fellow of the Royal Historical Society. Professor Malcolm's first book, *Caesar's Due: Loyalty and King Charles,* was published by the Royal Historical Society and Humanities press.

Robert M. S. McDonald is assistant professor of history at the United States Military Academy. A graduate of the University of Virginia and Oxford University, he received his Ph.D. from the University of North Carolina at Chapel Hill. He has published several book chapters and articles in *The Journal of the Early Republic, Southern Cultures,* and *The Historian.* He is working on a book to be titled *Confounding Father: Thomas Jefferson and the Politics of Personality* and editing for publication a collection of essays, *Thomas Jefferson's Military Academy: Founding West Point.*

Tom G. Palmer is senior fellow at the Cato Institute and director of Cato University. He was very active in the late 1980s and the early 1990s in the propagation of classical liberal ideas in the Soviet bloc states and their successors. Before joining Cato he was an H. B. Earhart Fellow at Hertford College, Oxford University, and a vice president of the Institute for Humane Studies at George Mason University. He has published reviews and articles on politics and morality in scholarly journals such as the *Harvard Journal of Law and Public Policy, Ethics, Critical Review,* and *Constitutional Political Economy.* He received his B.A. in liberal arts from St. John's College in Annapolis, Maryland; his M.A. in philosophy from The Catholic University of America, Washington, D.C.; and his D.Phil. in politics from Oxford University.

Jacob T. Levy is assistant professor of political science at the University of Chicago, and is the author of *The Multiculturalism of Fear* and a number of articles and chapters on multiculturalism, nationalism, and the rights of indigenous peoples. He received a Ph.D. in politics from Princeton University.

Walter Berns is Resident Scholar at the American Enterprise Institute. He is the author of seven books including his recent work, *Making Patriots*. His earlier books include *Taking the Constitution Seriously* and *In Defense of Liberal Democracy*. He held senior faculty appointments at Georgetown University, Louisiana State University, Yale University, Cornell University, Colgate University, and the University of Toronto. He has served as a member of the Judicial Fellows Commission, the National Council on the Humanities, and the Council of Scholars in the Library of Congress. He also was the United States delegate to the UN Commission on Human Rights.

Michael Hayes is professor of political science at Colgate University. He is the author of *The Limits of Policy Change, Incrementalism and Public Policy*, and *Lobbyists and Legislators*. He holds a B.A. from the University of Kansas and a Ph.D. from Indiana University.

John Samples directs Cato's Center for Representative Government, which studies how the state encroaches on civil society and the positive contribution of limited constitutional government to liberty. He also teaches at Georgetown University and the Johns Hopkins University. Prior to joining Cato, Samples served eight years as director of Georgetown University Press and before that, as vice president of the Twentieth Century Fund. He received his B.A. in political science from Eastern Kentucky University and his Ph.D. in political theory from Rutgers University. He has published scholarly articles in *Society, History of Political Thought*, and *Telos*.

James Dorn is vice president for academic affairs at the Cato Institute, editor of the *Cato Journal*, and director of Cato's annual monetary conference. He directed Cato's Project on Civil Society from 1993 to 1995. From 1984 to 1990, he served on the White House Commission on Presidential Scholars. He has edited ten books, and his articles have appeared in numerous publications. He has lectured in Estonia, Germany, Hong Kong, Russia, and Switzerland and has directed international conferences in London, Shanghai, Moscow, and Mexico City. He has been a visiting scholar at the Central European University in Prague and at Fudan University in Shanghai, and is currently professor of economics at Towson University in Maryland. Dorn holds an M.A. and a Ph.D. in economics from the University of Virginia.

John Tomasi is the author of *Liberalism beyond Justice: Citizens, Society, and the Boundaries of Political Theory*. Tomasi earned a B. Phil. and D. Phil. in philosophy from Oxford and has held teaching and research positions at Princeton, Stanford, and Harvard Universities. He is currently an associate professor of political science at Brown University.

Index

Marshall, John, 52, 53, 105, 122, 128, 135, 138
Marxism, 80
materialism, 153
Matsusaka, John, 180, 181
McDonald, Michael, 99
McDonald, Robert M. S., 3, 59–70, 219, 230
McGuffey's *Readers*, 141–42
McLoughlin, William, 127
Meigs, Return, 127
meliorative liberals, 150, 151
Memorial and Remonstrance against Religious Assessments (Madison), 5, 136, 143
Mennonites, 139
Meyer, Frank S., 151
Middle Ages, 225
Middle East, comparisons with, 84–85, 97, 128
military
  civilian control over, failures of, 128
  conscientious objection, 139–40
  standing institutions, creation of, 63, 224
Miller, Keith, 176
minority factions, protection of, 54–55, 75, 78, 88–89, 124, 131, 167, 169, *see* group representation and group rights; Indians; multiculturalism
minority preferences and representative democracy, 171–72
minority veto, 80–81
Missouri Crisis of 1819-1821, 66–67
mobility, freedom of/restrictions on, 95, 96, 100–103, 226
Monroe, James, 124, 126, 128
Monsma, Stephen, 157–58
Montesquieu, Charles-Louis de Secondat, 49, 50, 51, 71–72, 103, 140
Monticello, 65, 66
Montpelier, 65
Moore, R. I., 97–98
morality, *see* virtue, morality, and ethics
Morrison decision, 18
Morse, Jedediah, 125
multiculturalism, 4–6, 51, 54–55, 71–119
  African Americans, 79–81
  authenticity of group representation, 79–81, 93

bipolar conflict, permanent minority in, 78–79
black Americans, 79–81
Calhoun, group representation theories of, 82–85
common good, 4, 71–77
conservatism, Christianity, and separation of church and state, 157–61
Constitutional allowance for common good and general welfare, 74–75
equality, 73, 77–78, 85–89
equality as form of oppression, 85–89
exemptions to laws for minority groups and religions, 96, 138–39
factionalism, 3–5, 72, 121–22, 131
general welfare clause of Constitution, 74
group representation and group rights, *see* group representation and group rights
Indians, *see* Indians
Madison's embrace of, 71–77, 107–8, 121–22, 130–31
pathological forms of, 147, 153, 154, 158, 161
pure/direct democracy, minorities, and majorities, 167, 169, 171–78, 179–80
redistribution of wealth, 74
religion and, 4, 5, 72, 147
reparations, 5, 89–94
representative democracy and, 171–72
special interests, *see* group representation and group rights
"tyrannizing core" of central culture, 153–56, 157, 160–61
Muslims, 96, 136

National Conference of Social Work, 33
National Socialism, 80, 89
nationalists, 13, 20, 99, 140
Native Americans, *see* Indians
natural rights concept, 27, 32, 137
"necessary and proper" clause, 65–66, 100
Neuhaus, Richard J., 159, 160
New Deal, 2, 20, 26, 31, 33, 36
new government, right of people to institute, 2–3
New, Michael, 181
New York, Lochner v., 33

241

Cato Institute

Founded in 1977, the Cato Institute is a public policy research foundation dedicated to broadening the parameters of policy debate to allow consideration of more options that are consistent with the traditional American principles of limited government, individual liberty, and peace. To that end, the Institute strives to achieve greater involvement of the intelligent, concerned lay public in questions of policy and the proper role of government.

The Institute is named for *Cato's Letters*, libertarian pamphlets that were widely read in the American Colonies in the early 18th century and played a major role in laying the philosophical foundation for the American Revolution.

Despite the achievement of the nation's Founders, today virtually no aspect of life is free from government encroachment. A pervasive intolerance for individual rights is shown by government's arbitrary intrusions into private economic transactions and its disregard for civil liberties.

To counter that trend, the Cato Institute undertakes an extensive publications program that addresses the complete spectrum of policy issues. Books, monographs, and shorter studies are commissioned to examine the federal budget, Social Security, regulation, military spending, international trade, and myriad other issues. Major policy conferences are held throughout the year, from which papers are published thrice yearly in the *Cato Journal*. The Institute also publishes the quarterly magazine *Regulation*.

In order to maintain its independence, the Cato Institute accepts no government funding. Contributions are received from foundations, corporations, and individuals, and other revenue is generated from the sale of publications. The Institute is a nonprofit, tax-exempt, educational foundation under Section 501(c)3 of the Internal Revenue Code.

CATO INSTITUTE
1000 Massachusetts Ave., N.W.
Washington, D.C. 20001